THE CAPITALIST MANIFESTO

THE CAPITALIST MANIFESTO

by Louis O. Kelso

and Mortimer J. Adler

GREENWOOD PRESS, PUBLISHERS
WESTPORT, CONNECTICUT

Library of Congress Cataloging in Publication Data

Kelso, Louis O
   The capitalist manifesto.

   Reprint of the ed. published by Random House,
New York.
   1. Capitalism. 2. United States--Economic
policy. I. Adler, Mortimer Jerome, 1902-
joint author. II. Title.
[HB501.K43 1975]   330.12'2   75-14280
ISBN 0-8371-8210-7

Burgess
HB
501
.K43
1975

c. 2

Originally published in 1958 by Random House, New York

Reprinted with the permission of Louis O. Kelso

Reprinted in 1975 by Greenwood Press
A division of Congressional Information Service, Inc.
88 Post Road West, Westport, Connecticut 06881
Library of Congress catalog card number 75-14280
ISBN 0-8371-8210-7

Printed in the United States of America

10 9 8 7 6

CONTENTS

PART TWO : THE PROGRAM OF THE CAPITALIST REVOLUTION

PREFACE

While signing my name to THE CAPITALIST MANIFESTO as coauthor with Louis Kelso, I wish to disclaim any credit for the original and basic theory of capitalism on which this Manifesto is based. That theory is entirely Mr. Kelso's. It is the product of many years of inquiry and thought on his part. The full statement of it will soon be published in *Capitalism,* of which Mr. Kelso is sole author.

I would also like to explain how I came to appreciate the critical importance of the theory of capitalism; and why I felt that its revolutionary insights and program should be briefly summarized in the form of a manifesto addressed to all Americans who are concerned with the future of a democratic society, with the achievement of the fullest freedom and justice for all men, and, above all, with a twentieth-century reinterpretation of everyone's right to life, liberty, and the pursuit of happiness.

In the twenty years or more in which I have been developing a theory of democracy as the only perfectly just form of government, I slowly came to realize that political democracy cannot flourish under all economic conditions. Democracy requires an economic system which supports the political ideals of liberty and equality for all. Men cannot exercise freedom in the political sphere when they are deprived of it in the economic sphere.

John Adams and Alexander Hamilton observed that a man who is dependent for his subsistence on the arbitrary will of another man is not economically free and so should not be admitted to citizenship because he cannot use the political liberty which belongs to that status. If they had stated this point as a prediction, it would have been confirmed by later historic facts. The progressive political enfranchisement of the working classes has followed their progressive economic emancipation from slavery and serfdom, or from abject dependence on their employers.

As I first saw the problem, it came to this: What is the economic counterpart of political democracy? What type of economic organization is needed to support the institutions of a politically free society? The answer suggests itself at once, at least verbally: "economic democracy." But we do not really have an answer unless we can give concrete meaning to those words.

We begin to form some notion of the economic counterpart of political democracy, or of the economic substructure needed to support free political institutions, when we recognize that it must involve two things: (1) *economic liberty, i.e.,* the abolition of all economic slavery, servitude, or dependence; and (2) *economic equality, i.e.,* the enjoyment by all men of the same economic status and, therewith, of the same opportunities to live well.

But what do we mean by the abolition of all forms of economic servitude or dependence? Certainly, that no man should work as a slave. But that by itself would hardly seem to be enough. In the whole of the pre-industrial past, economic freedom was thought to depend

on the possession of sufficient property to enable a man to obtain subsistence for himself and his family without recourse to grinding toil.

In the oligarchical republics or feudal aristocracies of the past, the
few who enjoyed the political freedom of citizenship or noble rank
were always men of relatively independent means. The principle of
universal suffrage in our democratic republic now confers the political freedom of citizenship on all. If that is effective only when it is
accompanied by economic freedom, are we called on to envisage
a society in which all men will have the same kind of economic independence and security that only the few enjoyed in the past?

The question of what is meant by *economic equality* is even more
difficult. We can be sure of only one thing. Economic equality cannot
mean *equality of possessions* any more than political equality means
equality of functions. Yet if we proceed by analogy with the ideal of
political democracy, which we conceive as a politically classless society with a rotating aristocracy of leaders, we can at least surmise
that an economic democracy must somehow be conceived as an economically classless society, and that, too, with a rotating aristocracy
of managers.

Until very recently, as I thought about these questions, I had grave
doubts that what has come to be called "capitalism" could establish
the kind of economic democracy which political democracy required
as its counterpart. I now understand the reasons for my doubts. They
were based on an understanding of "capitalism" which was colored by
the sound criticisms that had been leveled against its injustices and
inequities, not only by Marx and Engels, and by socialists generally,
but also by Popes Leo XIII and Pius XI, and by social philosophers
or reformers as diverse as Alexis de Tocqueville, Horace Mann,
Henry George, Theodore Roosevelt, Woodrow Wilson, Hilaire Belloc,
Jacques Maritain, Amintore Fanfani, and Karl Polanyi. Of these, only
Marx, Engels and their followers proposed communism as the remedy.

What all these men were criticizing was *nineteenth-century capitalism as it existed in England and the United States,* the two countries

in the world most advanced industrially. That nineteenth-century capitalism was unjust, no one can question. But there is a question as to whether nineteenth-century capitalism conforms to the idea or ideal of capitalism; and with this goes the question whether the historic injustices committed by the capitalism of the nineteenth century are historic accidents or are intrinsic to the very idea of capitalism itself.

Ten years ago, at a time when I did not understand the idea or ideal of capitalism as something quite different from what existed under that name in the nineteenth century, I naturally tended to suppose that the economic injustices perpetrated in the nineteenth century were intrinsic to capitalism. If that were so, then they could not be remedied without giving up capitalism itself, and finding some alternative to it— socialism, a co-operative system, a corporative order, or something else.

In that state of mind, I was also bothered by the fact that the very expression I had been forced to use in order to give some meaning to economic democracy—the expression "classless society"—was the slogan and banner of the communists. The *Communist Manifesto* called for the overthrow of the class-structured bourgeois society, divided into owners and workers, oppressors and oppressed, and set before men's minds the ideal of a classless society, achieved through the dictatorship of the proletariat, in which the state itself would be the sole owner of the means of production, and all men would be "equally liable to labor."

I could not help agreeing with those who pointed out the fatal flaws in the communists' revolutionary program. If men are dependent for their subsistence upon the arbitrary will of the state, or on that of its bureaucrats who manage the state-owned means of production, they are as unfree economically as when they are dependent upon the arbitrary will of private owners. Furthermore, "the equal liability of all to labor," which is a basic principle in the communist program, impedes rather than promotes economic freedom. The communist classless society is, therefore, hardly the economic democracy we are looking for as the counterpart of political democracy.

But while proponents of capitalism have argued against communism as the foe of political liberty and equality, they have not offered a positive program for establishing an economically classless society. They have not countered the call for a communist revolution by proposing a capitalist revolution which, by carrying out the true principles of capitalism, would produce the economic democracy we need as the basis for political democracy.

One other fact obscured my understanding of the problem, or at least led me to consider a wrong solution of it. That was the extraordinary change which had taken place in the American economy during my lifetime. Beginning with Theodore Roosevelt and Woodrow Wilson, and running through all the administrations of Franklin Roosevelt and his successors, Republican as well as Democratic, capitalism in twentieth-century America has undergone a remarkable transformation which puzzles many European observers who cannot understand precisely how America has managed to remain a capitalist country, and yet has succeeded in avoiding the Marxist prediction that capitalism would be destroyed by its own imbalance between production and consumption. Or, to put it another way, they wonder whether capitalism in twentieth-century America is still *capitalism in essence.* They suspect that it is really one of the "many paths to socialism."

This suspicion is not unfamiliar to Americans. Many of them, especially the most outspoken opponents of the New Deal, have voiced it themselves. They have deplored, again and again, the "creeping socialism" which has been eroding, if not overthrowing, the institutions and principles of capitalism. If the charge of creeping socialism is correct, then it can be argued that America has produced an economy which supports political democracy only by gradually, and perhaps self-deceptively, substituting socialist for capitalist principles. What is true of America is also true of England, with a little less self-deception in the latter case.

To understand the charge of "creeping socialism," one need only make a check-list out of the ten-point program which Marx and Engels proposed in 1848 and which they described as a way of making progressive "inroads on the rights of property, and on the conditions of bourgeois production." The measures they proposed for "socializing" the economy by wresting "all capital from the bourgeoisie" and centralizing "all instruments of production in the hands of the State," are as follows:

1. Abolition of property in land and application of all rents of land to public purposes.
2. A heavy progressive or graduated income tax.
3. Abolition of all right of inheritance.
4. Confiscation of the property of all emigrants and rebels.
5. Centralization of credit in the hands of the State, by means of a national bank with State capital and an exclusive monopoly.
6. Centralization of the means of communication and transport in the hands of the State.
7. Extension of factories and instruments of production owned by the State; the bringing into cultivation of waste lands, and the improvement of the soil generally in accordance with a common plan.
8. Equal liability of all to labor. Establishment of industrial armies, especially for agriculture.
9. Combination of agriculture with manufacturing industries; gradual abolition of the distinction between town and country, by a more equable distribution of population over the country.
10. Free education for all children in public schools. Abolition of children's factory labor in its present form. Combination of education with industrial production, etc., etc.

In his recent book, *Contemporary Capitalism,* John Strachey, the leading English Marxist, refers to the industrial economy of the mid-nineteenth century as "early stage capitalism." That was capitalism prior to political democracy, prior to the technological advances which accelerated capitalization, and prior to the enactment, in whole or in

part, of the revolutionary measures proposed by Marx and Engels.
Strachey refers to contemporary capitalism—the capitalism of England and the United States in the middle of the twentieth century—as "latest stage capitalism." That is not only a technologically advanced economy with ever increasing accumulations of capital. It is not only a capitalistic system that is being operated by a democratic society. It is also, in Strachey's judgment, a partly socialized capitalism which has been brought into being by the legislative enactment of much of the Marxist program and without the violent revolution Marx thought would be necessary. But in his view it is a revolution nonetheless—a revolution still in process, the ultimate goal of which, according to his projection, is "last stage capitalism," or the completely socialized industrial economy in which the State is the only capitalist.

Strachey's account of what has happened in the last hundred years is not far from the truth. The radical differences he points out between "early stage" and "latest stage" capitalism are unquestionable. His description of the present economy of England and the United States as partly socialized capitalism is accurate. But his notion that the process of socialization must be completed to remove the inherent conflicts between capitalism and democracy is as wrong as it can be.

The socialization of the economy can be completed, according to Strachey, only when the abolition of private property in the means of production replaces the present highly attenuated private ownership of capital. But when that happens, all capital property must be vested in the State; and then, as Milovan Djilas has pointed out, you have a new class of "owners"—the bureaucrats who form the managerial class in a totalitarian State. Djilas's book, *The New Class*, offers irrefutable evidence that a completely socialized economy, far from creating a free and classless society, creates one in which there is sharp class division between the rulers who are, in effect, the owners and the workers who are economically as well as politically enslaved. In the light of it, we can see clearly that it is socialism, not capitalism, which is essentially incompatible with democracy.

For many years I was prone to some of the errors and fallacies which blind socialists to the truth about capitalism and democracy. They are shared by many Americans, including our leading economists, who, while they would not go as far as Strachey, nevertheless think that the progressive socialization of the economy during the last fifty years has been an advance toward the ideal of the democratic society. It was precisely these errors in my own thinking which made me doubt that capitalism as such (*i.e.,* not creeping socialism disguised as capitalism) could create the economic democracy—the economically free and classless society—which would provide the very soil and atmosphere in which political democracy can prosper.

These errors remained with me until I became acquainted with the thought of Louis Kelso. According to Mr. Kelso's theory, capitalism perfected in the line of its own principles, and without any admixture of socialism, can create the economically free and classless society which will support political democracy and which, above all, will help us to preserve the institutions of a free society. In what we have become accustomed to call "the world-wide struggle for men's minds," this conception of capitalism offers the only real alternative to communism, for our partly socialized capitalism is an unstable mixture of conflicting principles, a halfway house from which we must go forward in one direction or the other.

No one with any sense of justice or devotion to democracy would wish to go back to capitalism in its original or primitive form. No one with any sense of the scientific-industrial revolution that is just beginning, and which will transform our society in the next hundred years, would regard our present partly capitalistic and partly socialistic arrangements as constituting a system that is capable of maintaining itself statically in spite of its obviously unstable equilibrium between two opposing forces.

One is the tendency toward socialization and the attenuation of property rights in capital. The other is the effort to retain the vestiges of private property in capital. In one direction lies the goal of the socialist or communist revolution. In the other, by means of giving full strength to the rights of private property in capital while at the same time harmonizing those rights with the applicable principles of economic justice, lies the goal of the capitalist revolution.

The latter is clearly the better of the two revolutions, even if both, by virtue of technological advances administered for the welfare of all men, were able to achieve the same high standard of living for all. A high standard of living is at its best a plentiful subsistence, consisting of the comforts and conveniences of life. It does not by itself ensure freedom or the good life. It is compatible with slavery to a totalitarian State, and with subservience to the wrong ends.

There is all the difference in the world between a good living and living well. The goal of the capitalist revolution, as Mr. Kelso sees it, is not economic welfare as an end in itself, but rather the good human life for all. In achieving this end, the capitalist revolution will not sacrifice freedom for welfare. It will secure liberty as well as equality for all men. It will subordinate economic to political activity—the management of things to the government of men.

Mr. Kelso gave me the opportunity to read the manuscript of a book about capitalism which he first drafted some ten years ago. In the last two years, I have had many conversations with him while he has been in the process of rewriting that book, which is now completed. In the course of these conversations, we have both come to see the broad philosophical and historical significance of the fundamental tenets of a sound theory of capitalism. It was with these discoveries in mind that I persuaded Louis Kelso to engage with me in the writing of THE CAPITALIST MANIFESTO.

The first part of this Manifesto explains the philosophical and historical ideas that are involved in a sound understanding of the principles of capitalism and of the revolution to which those principles lead.

The second part sets forth a practical program which we believe is a feasible way of accomplishing the capitalist revolution in the United States within the next fifty years. By making our society a pilot model of democratic capitalism we can also make the United States the world's leader in the march toward freedom and justice for men everywhere.

Mortimer J. Adler

San Francisco, February, 1958

PART ONE

THE IDEA
OF THE
CAPITALIST
REVOLUTION

1 WHY A CAPITALIST MANIFESTO?

THEN AND NOW

In 1848, a world-shaking document, now known as the *Communist Manifesto,* sounded the call to overthrow primitive capitalism —a term we will define later. Actually, the title was *Manifesto of the Communist Party.* This fact is significant for the comparison we wish to draw between that manifesto and this one, which we hope will replace it as a call to action.

Ours is not the manifesto of a revolutionary party dedicated to overthrowing the established order. It is instead a revolutionary manifesto which calls upon the American people as a whole to find in the established order the reasons for its renovation and the seeds of the better society we can develop. The end, at last in view, is that ideal society to which America has always been dedicated and toward which it has made great progress since its beginning.

THE CAPITALIST MANIFESTO is intended to replace the *Communist*

Manifesto as a call to action, first of all in our own country, and then, with our country's leadership, everywhere else in the world. It is our industrial power and capital wealth, together with our institutions of political liberty and justice, that make America the place where the capitalist revolution must first take place to establish economic liberty and justice for all.

But while we intend this Manifesto *for* capitalism, to replace the earlier one *against* it, and while we have every reason to hope that the principles and program of this Manifesto can win the minds of thinking men, we cannot deceive ourselves that it will ever have the blind emotional appeal that made the earlier Manifesto so powerful a revolutionary force.

Perhaps a word should be said about our use of the words "capitalism" and "capitalist." These words have different connotations for different people, as do "communism" and "communist."

The unfortunate connotations of "capitalism" come from the widely prevalent habit of applying it to the kind of industrial economy which flourished in England and the United States in the middle of the nineteenth century, and which persisted with only minor modifications until the first decades of the twentieth. Almost everyone agrees today that that economy needed to be reformed; and in consequence, many who approve of some or all of the economic reforms that have occurred in America in the last thirty years are apt to be sensitive to certain overtones that the word "capitalism" has in general usage.

Nevertheless, we feel that "capitalism" is the right word to use as the name for the ideally just organization of an industrial economy. In later chapters we shall identify and name forms of capitalism which are far from being embodiments of economic justice, among them not only nineteenth-century capitalism but also the kind of capitalism that exists at present in England and the United States, on the one hand, and the kind that exists in Soviet Russia, on the other.

It would be a mistake to relinquish the word "democracy" because that word was used in the past for a form of government that was far from being just, as in the case of the slave societies of antiquity in which only a small portion of the population was admitted to citizenship and granted the political rights to which all men are entitled as a matter of justice. We think it would be a mistake of the same sort to relinquish the word "capitalism." As we employ the name "democracy" for the just polity that has only recently begun to exist, so we should employ the name "capitalism" for the just economy that can be brought into existence. To bring that about is the objective of the capitalist revolution.

THE PREVAILING SENSE OF WELL-BEING

We are initially addressing ourselves to Americans—to men who feel well-off—and not to the starving, downtrodden victims of injustice and oppression. We cannot exhort them to engage in violence, and to do so without fear because they have nothing to lose but their chains. We must persuade them, in much calmer tones than that, to act rationally, with insight and prudence, because they do have something to lose—their freedom—which an abundance of creature comforts may have lulled them into forgetting.

Men who *think* they already nave all the liberty and justice they can expect, in addition to plenty of material goods, cannot be emotionally exhorted to take radical measures for the improvement of their society. They can only be asked to *think again.*

We might properly begin THE CAPITALIST MANIFESTO with the statement that the specter of communism is still haunting Europe and the world. Such a declaration should strike terror in the hearts of Americans. But most Americans have been rendered impervious to it by the pervasive feeling that it cannot happen here. Most of us do not realize that something approaching it has already happened here, and that if we continue along the paths we have taken in the last thirty years, we can go even further in the wrong direction. Again, it is our general sense of well-being that prevents us from realizing what has happened to us and what threatens to happen.

When the *Communist Manifesto* first announced that the specter of communism was haunting Europe, that society as a whole was split into two great hostile camps—the owners of capital and the employers of labor, on the one hand; and the propertyless workers, or proletariat, on the other. Marx and Engels admired the power of capital. "The bourgeoisie," they asserted, "during its rule of scarce one hundred years, has created more massive and more colossal productive forces than have all preceding generations together." But they deplored the consequences of the power wielded by the owners of capital.

Capital property was owned by less than one-tenth of the population, under whose tyrannical will the remaining nine-tenths lived like slaves. Hence the authors of the *Communist Manifesto* called for the transfer of all private property in capital instruments to the State, where it would be administered—they claimed—for the benefit of all men.

Let us now consider the situation in America today and the condition of those to whom THE CAPITALIST MANIFESTO is addressed. This manifesto is written in an atmosphere that is not merely free from the starvation and degradation of the masses, but in which almost the whole of society is enjoying the highest standard of material well-being ever known to a nation or to any significant number of individuals. Not only do we have high wages and full employment, but so great an opportunity for employment that a proportion of wives and mothers higher than ever before can find jobs in commerce and industry, in many cases to raise even higher an already high family standard of living. Largely through the efforts of labor unions, heavily fortified by legislation born during the Great Depression of the nineteen-thirties, the general hours ot employment have been reduced again and again, until today few people regularly work more than forty hours a week. Some industries are already stabilized at thirty-six hours a week, and the leaders of the great union, the AFL-CIO, are already talking seriously about the thirty-hour week, the regular month-long vacation, the periodic three-month vacation and more holidays.

The general talk about "American Capitalism," "Modern Capitalism," or "People's Capitalism" pictures something that looks like the very opposite of nineteenth-century capitalism as described by Marx and Engels. On all sides we hear that this current brand of capitalism is something entirely new in the last three decades, and that it fulfills the promise of a high standard of living for all, a high degree of freedom from toil for all, and the most generous measure of personal freedom for all. The secret formula of this happy state of affairs we attribute in large measure to the intellect of John Maynard Keynes. The principal parts of the formula can be stated as follows:

1. Mass consumption is necessary if all members of a society are to have a high standard of living. What is more significant, mass consumption is necessary to support mass production in an industrial economy.
2. But mass consumption cannot exist or continue unless there is a mass distribution of purchasing power.
3. The proper method of creating a mass distribution of purchasing power is mass employment: *i.e.,* "full employment" or the employment of every person who would like to be employed.
4. Since prosperity and well-being depend upon the successful distribution of purchasing power, this can be achieved through progressively raising, by union pressure and legislation, wages, social security payments, unemployment compensation, agricultural and other prices; and through the free use of income taxing power and other powers of government to promote full employment.

By the Employment Act of 1946, we have adopted a national policy of maximum employment.

At last we seem almost on the verge of feeling that we can cope with that nightmare of an industrial economy—*the depression.*

In short, capitalism, once denounced as exploiting and oppressing the worker, seems to have evolved into a system which provides the benefits once claimed for socialism, but without—it is believed—the loss of freedom that inheres in socialism.

The good life for the worker seems to have been discovered in America. Justice seems to have reformed and made decent the once pitiless primitive capitalistic economy.

OUR MACHINE-PRODUCED HAPPINESS

The cause of this felicitous state of affairs, we are told, is the ever increasing use of ever more efficient capital instruments. These tend constantly and endlessly to raise the "productivity of labor," and thus account for an ever increasing output of goods and services per worker employed. The principal guide to management and labor in negotiating these perpetually increasing wages is that "wage increases and benefits should be consistent with productivity prospects and with the maintenance of a stable dollar."[1]

Labor leaders are in full agreement with this principle. They openly and frankly support technological advances which in turn raise the "productivity of labor," which in turn calls for increases in wages to provide the mass purchasing power to support the mass production, etc.[2]

The net result of all this, and of the general progress of scientific development in and for industry, is that the rate of technological advance is accelerating. Instead of finding ourselves confronted with a point of diminishing returns, we find that this happy state of affairs promises to get happier as we make more and more technological progress, to which there is no end in sight.

[1] Economic Report of the President, 1957, p. 3.
[2] See Philip Murray, *Annual Report, 14th Constitutional Convention,* C.I.O., 1952 (reprinted in Supplement to *The People Shall Judge,* Chicago, 1956). See also hearings before the Subcommittee on Economic Stabilization of the Joint Economic Committee on *Automation and Technological Change,* 1955: pp. 120, 220, 234, 287, 337, 419, 455, 463.

No specter can threaten us while we are under the care of our guardian angel—our modern capitalistic economy!

OUR FEELING ABOUT SOCIALISM

In addition to the general sense of well-being that we all share and attribute to our form of capitalism, we are united in our feeling about socialism. As a people, we dislike it and rule it out as an acceptable alternative to capitalism.

It is all but universally agreed in the United States that socialism is the antithesis of the American way, that it infringes on human freedom, and that it should be avoided at all costs.

It is recognized—sometimes articulately, sometimes only intuitively —that the combination of economic power and political power in the hands of government officials is the very opposite of the American principle of the separation of powers and of our system of checks and balances. It is widely felt that such fusion of political and economic power, which inevitably results when the same bureaucracy not only runs the political machinery of the state but also wields the economic power that is inherent in the state's ownership of industry, leads to the destruction of individual liberties. It is generally thought that individual freedom and private property are inseparably connected.

Our sense of the undesirability of socialism and our rejection of it as the antithesis of the American way of life adds to our satisfaction with the new capitalistic economy we have developed. By creating purchasing power to provide full employment, a satisfactory standard of living for all households, and high incomes for city dwellers as well as for farmers, we seem to have accomplished all that could be desired and, once and for all, to have discredited socialism as a remedy for the ills and instability of the modern industrial economy.

THE AMBUSH

With this economic paradise at hand, why would anyone have the audacity, the ingratitude, or the effrontery to call for the renovation of our society by a capitalist revolution?

A memorial to the new capitalism? Yes. A guidebook to explain its inner secrets to the uninitiated? Yes. But why a revolutionary manifesto?

Our answer is: To point out that while no specter is haunting America, socialism in a variety of ways is coming in by the back door; to explain that capitalism—"pure capitalism" or capitalism unmixed with socialism—is the only economic system compatible with political democracy; and to show not only that we are a long way from having such an economic system, but also that we have not yet become clear about the principles of such a system.

The picture of accomplished politico-economic perfection is an illusion. What has been acclaimed as *American Capitalism, Modern Capitalism,* or *People's Capitalism* is a mixture of capitalism and socialism. If the process of socialization is carried forward with the tremendous technological advances now impending, we will be brought closer and closer to complete socialism; *i.e.,* State capitalism. Nothing can stop this process except the capitalist revolution.

What appears to be the increasing productiveness of labor is *not* the increasing productiveness of labor but the increasing productiveness of capital.

What appears to be the preservation of private property in the means of production, particularly in the capital wealth of corporations, is characterized by only a fraction of the rights that would justify its being called private property.

What appears to be justice in the distribution of incomes is in fact gross injustice.

What promises to free men from unnecessary toil is of such a nature that it must unavoidably saddle them with unnecessary toil.

What seems at first glance to be an economic order consistent with the American system of separated and balanced powers, as the most dependable safeguard of human freedom, is in fact creating a centralization of power that would have brought our ancestors to arms.

Though it is fashionable today to believe that we are advancing toward a sound capitalism, an understanding of the principles of capitalism will disclose that we are retreating from it and, instead, advancing toward a socialist state.

Never before has a society marched more joyously into ambush by the very forces it implacably opposes but does not recognize. We are faced with the spectacle of a nation sincerely seeking democracy and economic justice through means which it fails to recognize as destructive of both.

That is why we think a capitalist manifesto is in order. It is to clear up this case of mistaken identity that we wish to re-examine the nature of economic freedom, private property, justice in distribution, industrial production, and economic democracy. And, to supplement this, we will propose a series of wholly feasible changes, which we believe should be brought about to set our society on the course toward the fully developed capitalism that is the counterpart of political democracy.

AN APPEAL TO REASON

We have called this brief statement of theory and this outline of practical proposals a Manifesto because we think the occasion calls for a public declaration of the principles of "pure capitalism" and of a program which is calculated to achieve it.

The principles of capitalism have heretofore been seen only fragmentarily and in a confused manner. In their simplicity, they are applicable only to a mature industrial economy. Only in an economy which produces the preponderant portion of its goods and services by capital instruments, and which is well enough equipped with such capital instruments to produce and enjoy a high standard of living, can the truth, as well as the feasibility, of a capitalistic economy be readily seen.

To grasp the truth of these principles, and to understand their consequences, requires careful, sustained, rational thought. The only appeal this Manifesto makes is an appeal for such thought about the problems we face.

2 ECONOMIC FREEDOM:
PROPERTY AND LEISURE

THE THREE ELEMENTS OF ECONOMIC FREEDOM

In all the slave societies of the past, human beings were divided into two classes. On the one hand, there were the owners of property—in land, animals, slaves, raw material and tools. They were the masters and as such they were economically free men. On the other hand, there were the toilers who had no property of the aforementioned sort. They were the slaves, men without any economic freedom.

Aristotle distinguished between two types of slavery: (1) the chattel slavery of those who were the *property of other men* and so were totally deprived of property, even of property in their own labor power; and (2) what he called the "special and separate slavery" [1] of the meaner sort of artisan or mechanic who had no property beyond his own labor power and so was forced to lead a servile life.

What is true of the chattel slaves and servile artisans of ancient

[1] *Politics,* Book I, Ch. 13, 1260b1–2.

Greece and Rome is essentially true of the serfs in the agrarian economies of feudal Europe, and of the wage slaves who formed the industrial proletariat in the middle of the nineteenth century. At no time in the past were the working masses economically free men. Nor, until the power of organized labor gave them some measure of the economic independence which property in capital always bestowed on the leisure class, were they admitted to suffrage and the political freedom of a voice in their own government.

Before the rise of industrial production and organized labor, the members of the ruling class were for the most part identical with the members of the leisure class. This is true of colonial America and of the first decades of our republic as well as of the republics of ancient Greece and Rome. The men of property were economically free men. Because they had through property a freedom which they wished to protect, they strove to safeguard it with the rights and privileges of political status and power. Their economic freedom was the basis of their claim to political liberty.

But their economic freedom was also the basis of their opportunity to lead a human as opposed to a subhuman life. In all the pre-industrial societies of the past, this opportunity was open only to those who could engage in the liberal activities of leisure because they obtained all they needed for subsistence and comfort from income-bearing property other than their own labor power.

To understand this, let us contrast the condition of the slave with that of the economically free man. We shall see that there are three elements in economic freedom, the most significant of which is freedom from toil or freedom for leisure. This is indispensable to leading a free, as opposed to a servile, life. The slave not only lacked such freedom, but also the economic independence and security without which political liberty cannot be effectively employed or enjoyed.

In the following threefold contrast between the conditions of economic slavery and freedom, the word "slave" is used in the broadest sense to cover not only men who belong to other men as their private chattels, but also all who are forced by lack of property to lead servile or subhuman lives.

1. The slave was a man who worked for the good or profit of another man, and worked as an instrument or tool of that other man as well as in his interests. He was exploited in the sense that the fruits of his labor were alienated from his good to that of another. In contrast, the economically free man engaged in no activity in which he served as the instrument of another man, and did nothing which served any good except his own or the common good of his society.

2. The slave was a man who was dependent for his subsistence on the arbitrary will of another man, his master. In this condition, he was always threatened with economic destitution—starvation or worse. He had no economic security or freedom from want. In contrast, the master as an owner of property was an economically independent man. This is not to say that any man is ever wholly secure from misfortune. Since wealth is among the goods of fortune, it is always subject to accidents. But allowing for accidents, the economically free man is one who has enough property to be free from want without greater dependence on other men than they have upon him, and to be relatively secure against the threat of destitution.

3. The slave was a man who spent most of his time and energy in toil. Toil for him began in childhood and ended with his death, usually an early one; and it occupied almost all of his waking life, seven days a week. What time was left he needed for sleep and other basic biological functions in order to keep alive. In contrast, the man who obtained all the subsistence he needed, or much more than that, from the use of his property, including the labor of his slaves, had economic freedom in the most important sense of this term: freedom from toil. Only when such freedom is added to freedom from want, insecurity, or destitution—and to freedom from exploitation by another and from dependence on the arbitrary will of another—do we approach the ideal of liberty in the economic sphere of human life.

These three contrasts between the condition of masters and the condition of slaves, as men who are and are not economically free, can be summarized by the antithesis Aristotle draws between the servile and the free life. Some men, according to Aristotle, merely subsist; others are able, beyond subsistence, to live well, *i.e.,* to engage in leisure activities.[2] The servile life consists in nothing but toil in order to subsist. Men who have the misfortune of being chattels or of being propertyless are forced to lead a servile life—a life of toil, insecurity, and dependence.

Of course, some men who are fortunate enough to have sufficient property to live well actually degrade themselves to the level of the servile life by using all their time and energy in accumulating wealth and even by engaging in toil to do so. While men without property cannot live well, not all men with property do live well, but only those who, understanding the difference between labor and leisure, direct their activities to the goals of the free life.[3]

LABOR, LEISURE AND FREEDOM

The distinction between labor and leisure is generally misunderstood in twentieth-century America. Leisure is misconceived as idleness, vacationing (which involves "vacancy"), play, recreation, relaxation, diversion, amusement and so on. If leisure were that, it would never

[2] Aristotle describes the occupation of virtuous men of property in the following manner: "Those who are in a position which places them above toil have stewards who attend to their households while they occupy themselves with philosophy and politics" (*Politics,* Book I, Ch. 7, 1225b35–38). In this passage, the words "philosophy" and "politics" are shorthand for all the activities of leisure—engagement in the liberal arts and sciences and occupation with the institutions and processes of society.

[3] Distinguishing between two kinds of wealth getting, Aristotle says that "accumulation is the end in the one case, but there is a further end in the other. Hence some persons are led to believe that getting wealth is the object of household management, and the whole idea of their lives is that they ought either to increase their money, or at any rate not to lose it. The origin of this disposition in men," he declares, "is that they are intent upon living only, and not upon living well" (*Politics,* Book I, Ch. 9, 1257b35–1258a2).

have been regarded by anyone except a child or a childish adult as something morally better than socially useful work.

The misconception of leisure arises from the fact that it involves free time—time that is free from the biological necessity of sleep, and of labor to obtain the means of subsistence. Such time can, of course, be filled in various ways: with amusements and diversions of all sorts, or with the intrinsically virtuous activities by which men pursue happiness and serve the common good of their society. Leisure, properly conceived as the main content of a free, as opposed to a servile, life, consists in activities which are neither toil nor play, but are rather the expressions of moral and intellectual virtue—the things a good man does because they are intrinsically good for him and for his society, making him better as a man and advancing the civilization in which he lives.

In all the pre-industrial societies of the past, when only a few were exempt from grinding toil, the activities of leisure were as sharply distinguished from indulgence in amusements or recreations as they were from the drudgery of toil. Husbandmen, craftsmen, and laborers of all sorts provided society with its means of subsistence and its material comforts. They had little or no time free for leisure or for play. Ample free time belonged only to those who obtained their subsistence from the property they owned and the labor of others. If these men had frittered away their free time in frivolity and play, the civilization to which we are the heirs would never have been produced; for civilization, as opposed to subsistence, is produced by those who have free time and use it creatively—to develop the liberal arts and sciences and all the institutions of the state and of religion.

Play, like sleep, washes away the fatigues and tensions that result from the serious occupations of life, all the forms of labor which produce the goods of subsistence and all the leisure activities which produce the goods of civilization. Play and sleep, as Aristotle pointed out, are for the sake of these serious and socially useful occupations. Since the activities of leisure can be as exacting and tiring as the activities of toil, some form of relaxation, whether sleep or play or both, is required by those who work productively.[4]

As play is for the sake of work, so subsistence work is for the sake of leisure activity. To confuse leisure either with idleness or amusement is to invert the order of goods which gave moral significance to the class divisions in all the pre-industrial societies of the past. Those among our ancestors who were men of virtue as well as men of property would find it difficult to understand how any self-respecting man could regard indulgence in amusements as the goal of life. They looked upon the labor of slaves and artisans as the means which provided them with the opportunity to engage in leisure, not in play. To expect the masses to labor from dawn to dusk and throughout life so that a small class of men could waste their free time in idleness, amusement, or sport would express, in their view, a degree of childishness or immorality that could be found only in the most depraved or vicious members of their class.[5]

Since the confusion of leisure with idleness or amusement is rampant in our industrial society, when, for the first time in history, it has become possible for all men to have enough free time to engage in

[4] See Aristotle's *Politics*, Book VII, Chs. 9, 14 and 15; Book VIII, Ch. 3.
[5] When, in 1825, the journeymen carpenters of Boston struck for higher wages and shorter hours, the master carpenters, their employers, replied that "the measures proposed [were] calculated to exert a very unhappy influence on our apprentices—by seducing them from that course of industry and economy of time to which we are anxious to inure them." They also maintained "that it will expose the journeymen themselves to many temptations and improvident practises from which they are happily secure," adding "that we consider idleness as the most deadly bane to useful and honorable living." They were supported in this by the "gentlemen engaged in building," who did not regard their own free time as an occasion for vice. Two years later when a strike of journeyman carpenters in Philadelphia led to a city-wide federation of labor unions, the Preamble of the Mechanics' Union of Trade Associations declared that they were placed "in a situation of such unceasing exertion and servility as must necessarily, in time, render the benefits of our liberal institutions to us inaccessible and useless." They looked to the progressive shortening of the working day as the means whereby all the useful members of the community would gradually come to possess "a due and full proportion of that invaluable promoter of happiness, leisure" (reprinted in *The People Shall Judge*, Chicago, 1953: Vol. I, pp. 580–583).

leisure, it may be difficult for our contemporaries to understand that labor and leisure are the two main forms of human *work,* and that the first is for the sake of the second. Unless they do understand this, however, they will not see the ultimate moral significance of the capitalist revolution. It may increase human freedom and strengthen the institutions of a free society, but freedom itself is only a means. Freedom can be squandered and perverted as well as put to good use.

Only if freedom from labor becomes freedom for leisure will the capitalist revolution produce a better civilization than any so far achieved, and one in the production of which all men will participate. Only if men thus use their opportunity for leisure will the capitalist revolution result in an improvement of human life itself, and not merely in its external conditions or institutions. As labor is for the sake of leisure, so freedom and justice for all are the institutional means whereby the good life that was enjoyed by the few alone in the pre-industrial aristocracies of the past will be open to all men in the capitalistic democracies of the future.[6]

The current misuse of the word "leisure" requires us to find other words for expressing the basic distinction which is so essential to the understanding of the capitalist revolution. We may not always be able to avoid using that word, but at least we can try to correct misunderstanding by the employment of other words or phrases for expressing its meaning.

It may be helpful to observe that where Aristotle drew a sharp line between labor and leisure, Adam Smith made the same distinction in human activities by drawing an equally sharp line between what he

---

[6] Sleep, play, toil, and leisure represent diverse goods in human life. But they do not have the same moral value. As contrasted with idleness, indolence, or the wanton waste of human time and energy, sleep and play contribute to human well-being. But they contribute less than productive toil and leisure. All the goods that contribute positively to human well-being must be sought in the pursuit of happiness, but they must be sought in the right order and proportion. A man defeats himself in the pursuit of happiness if he places the goods of the body above the goods of the soul, or if he plays so much in his free time that he has little time left for leisure.

called "productive labor" and "non-productive labor." His use of the word "labor" shows that he had socially useful work in mind in both cases, and not idleness or play. By "non-productive labor," he meant the activities of the clergy, statesmen, philosophers, scientists, artists, teachers, physicians and lawyers. He called these activities "labor" because, like the forms of work that are productive of wealth, they are not playful but serious, and serve a socially useful purpose. And he called such labor "non-productive" because, unlike other forms of work, the socially useful purpose they serve is not the production of wealth or the goods of bodily subsistence, but the production of civilization, or the goods of the human spirit.

We think it is better to use the term "work" for both forms of activity. We shall speak of "subsistence work" when we mean the activities that are productive of wealth (*i.e.*, the necessities, comforts and conveniences of life); and we shall speak of "liberal work" or "leisure work" when we mean the activities that are productive of the goods of civilization (*i.e.*, the liberal arts and sciences, the institutions of the state and of religion).

Whenever we revert to the use of the words "labor" and "leisure" without qualification, we hope it will be understood that labor is identical with subsistence work and leisure with liberal work. The fact that leisure is equated with one of the two principal forms of human work should help to prevent anyone from confusing it with play or idleness. The fact that the goods which it produces are so different from the goods produced by subsistence work should also help to preserve the distinction between labor and leisure, which is so necessary for all that follows.

THE FORM AND CHARACTER OF HUMAN WORK

So far we have distinguished two main forms of human work solely by reference to what they produce, or the ends they serve: on the one hand, the goods of the body, the biological goods of subsistence, the necessities, comforts and conveniences of life; on the other hand, the goods of the soul, the goods of civilization or of the human spirit, such things as the arts and sciences, the institutions of the state and of religion.

Work can be differentiated by reference to its human quality as well as by reference to its end or purpose.

Certain forms of work are mechanical in quality. They involve repetitive, routine operations which call for little or no creative intelligence upon the part of the worker. They also involve bodily exertion, or at least some manual dexterity; but it is the mechanical character of the task to be performed, not the physical character of the performance, which makes such work stultifying.

The materials on which the worker operates, but not his own nature, are improved by his efforts. After he has acquired the minimum skill required for doing it, he learns nothing more. He may increase the store of useful goods in the world, but he does not himself grow in stature as a man.

The Greek word *banausia* expressed the degrading quality of the mechanical work done by slaves—the dullness of the repetitive which is most intense in the kind of toil we call "drudgery." Because of its repetitiveness, the person who is engaged in it does not grow mentally, morally, or spiritually. On the contrary, drudgery stunts growth.

Because it is intrinsically unrewarding, such work must be extrinsically compensated. It is done under compulsion—the need for subsistence. Anyone who could secure his subsistence from other sources would try to avoid it, or do as little of it as possible. Hence such work is normally done for extrinsic compensation of some sort, whether in the shape of immediately consumable goods, or wages, or the meager subsistence meted out to a slave.

At the opposite extreme from work that is mechanical in quality as well as done to produce and obtain subsistence, there is work that is creative in quality as well as liberal in the end at which it aims. All leisure activities constitute work of this sort. The creative aspect of such work is signified by the Greek word for leisure, which was *scholé*. Like our English word "school," it connotes learning—mental, moral, or spiritual growth.

Such work is, therefore, intrinsically rewarding. It is something which every man *should,* and any virtuous man *would,* do for its own sake. If he has sufficient property to secure for himself and his family a sufficiency of the means of subsistence, the virtuous man gladly engages in liberal work without extrinsic compensation. Like virtue itself, such work is its own reward.

We have just seen that the forms of human work can be differentiated by reference to their human quality, or the effect they have on the worker, as well as differentiated by reference to the goods they produce for society as a whole. We must now observe that these distinctions can be compounded.

At one extreme in the scale of human work, certain socially useful activities combine having the production of wealth as their aim with being mechanical in quality. At the opposite extreme are the highest activities of leisure, which combine being creative in quality with having as their aim the production of the goods of civilization and of the human spirit. In between these extremes, there are the mixed forms of work: on the one hand, subsistence work which, while it aims at the production of wealth, is creative rather than mechanical in quality; on the other hand, work which, while mechanical in quality, nevertheless serves a purpose which is identical with the aim of liberal work.

This fourfold division of the kinds of work is of critical significance when we come subsequently to consider the variety of tasks to be performed in our modern industrial society. For the present, we shall use it in order to call attention to a widely prevalent misunderstanding about the dignity of human work.

In the ancient world—in fact, in all the pre-industrial societies of the past—no one made the mistake of supposing that equal dignity attaches to all human activity. Human dignity was thought to reside primarily in those activities which are specifically or characteristically human, *i.e.,* activities which have no counterpart whatsoever in the life of brute animals or in the operations of machines.

Brutes as well as men struggle for subsistence. Though the subsistence activities of brutes are largely instinctive, while those of men usually involve some employment of intelligence or reason, the goal or end of such activities is the same in both cases. Human life has its distinctive worth or dignity only insofar as it rises above biological activities and involves activities which are not performed by brutes, or at least not performed in the same way.

Man's special dignity lies in goods which no other animal shares with him at all, as other animals share with him the goods of food, shelter, and even those of sleep and play. Hence man has no special dignity as a producer of subsistence or wealth, but only as a user of wealth for the sake of specifically liberal activities productive of the goods of the spirit and of civilization.

It follows, therefore, that the only dignity there is in working to produce subsistence comes from such creative use of intelligence or reason as may be involved in the performance of tasks that are nonmechanical in quality. Even so, they have less dignity than nonmechanical or creative work which is liberal in its aim. Work which is not only mechanical in quality but also has the production of subsistence as its only aim is lowest in the scale. Such dignity as attaches to any work productive of subsistence, whether mechanical or creative, derives from the fact that the production of wealth, rightly understood, serves to support the leisure activities that constitute the dignity of human life.

It may be thought that St. Paul preaches a Christian message to the contrary when he says of those who do not work, neither shall they eat. But it should be remembered, in the first place, that the toil by which man eats in the sweat of his face is a punishment for sin, not an honor or a blessing. And, in the second place, it should be observed that the word St. Paul uses, in making this remark, means any form of socially useful activity, and not labor in the narrow sense of toil for the sake of subsistence.[7] What he is saying, in short, is that all men are under a moral obligation not just to work for a living, but to work in order to deserve a living. In the Christian sense, those who, having the means of subsistence, do not try to live well by doing liberal work enjoy a living they do not deserve.

THE IMAGE OF AN ECONOMICALLY FREE SOCIETY

So far we have seen how the life of a master in a slave society contains all the elements of economic freedom, and therewith the opportunities for leading a good life, which he will use well only if he is a man of virtue.

The possession of sufficient productive capital property enables a man to be economically free, but by itself it cannot make him lead a free and liberal life rather than a life devoted to the production or consumption of subsistence. He may engage in toil or trade even if he does not have to, because he does not have the virtue to rise above it; or, worse than that, he may squander his time and energies in indolence, or in pastimes which, no matter how innocuous, corrupt him precisely because he has elevated them to the level of ends. It should be added that pastimes seldom remain innocuous when they have to fill most of a man's waking time.

In the pre-industrial aristocracies of the past, only the fortunate few possessed all the elements of economic freedom; and of these, fewer still—those who were virtuous as well as fortunate—employed that freedom to do the work of leisure to the benefit of themselves and their society. These advantages were bought at the terrible price of slavery and misery for the masses who toiled not merely for their own meager subsistence, but to provide the wealth that supported the

[7] See Jacques Maritain, *Freedom in the Modern World,* New York, 1936: p. 59.

pursuit of happiness and the development of civilization by those who had economic freedom and used it well.

Freedom built upon slavery, the leisure of a privileged class supported by the unremitting toil of the masses, the opportunity for the few to lead a decent human life as the flower of a civilization whose roots lay in the submerged and subhuman lives of the toiling masses —this was the accepted order in all the class-divided societies of the pre-industrial past.

We now know what our ancestors did not know: that, under conditions of industrial production, and with the promise of capitalism fulfilled, it is possible for a whole society to be economically free and for all men to have the opportunity to live like human beings.

From the Egyptians, the Chaldeans, the Jews, and the Greeks down to the middle of the nineteenth century, or even to the end of it, it was generally supposed that slavery, or the equivalent of it in grinding toil and drudgery, was the necessary price that mankind had to pay for the advancement of civilization itself, as contrasted with the static and rudimentary culture of primitive life. If all men had to work for a living, that is, if every one had to spend most of his time in subsistence work in order to support himself and his family, no one would be left free for leisure or nonsubsistence work—the liberal work of civilization itself.

Prior to the industrial revolution, it was almost impossible to conceive a practicable division of labor which, while securing enough wealth to provide the means of liberal work as well as subsistence for a whole society, would also permit all members of the society to engage in liberal activities as well as in subsistence work. The only practical solution seemed to be slavery or slave labor in one form or another. The enslavement of the many, in lives occupied almost entirely with toil, emancipated the few for the pursuits of civilization. Prior to this century, the achievements of Western civilization—all its fine arts, pure sciences, all its political and religious institutions—were the product of the liberal work done by the virtuous members of its leisure class, just as obviously as all its economic crafts and goods were the product of the subsistence work done by its toiling masses.

We said a moment ago that no one prior to our own time could conceive of any practical solution other than one which involved slavery, or at least a life for the masses devoted to the mechanical work of producing subsistence, upon which all men might live and some might, in addition, live well. This amounts to saying that no one could conceive an *economically free society, i.e.,* an economically classless society in which all men, not just a few, would be economically free and would live like human beings if they were virtuous enough to use their economic freedom well. The statement is literally true if by "conceive" we mean thinking out in detail a practicable plan for the economic organization of a society that would make all its members economically free.

But one man, more than 2,300 years ago, was able to imagine, even if he could not practically conceive, an economically free society. His was the kind of fantasy that it takes a genius to dream. Though it was only a dream for him, the image he conjured up is no dream for us. It is the quite practicable ideal of a classless society of economically free men, with slavery or its equivalents abolished, and with the mechanical work of producing subsistence reduced to a minimum for all.

Though Aristotle did not and could not dream up the capitalist revolution in concrete practical terms, he did, in a single sentence, imagine a possibility that capitalism, and capitalism alone, can realize. He said:

If every instrument could accomplish its own work, obeying or antici-pating the will of others. . . if the shuttle could weave and the plectrum touch the lyre without a hand to guide them, chief workmen would not want servants, nor masters slaves.[8]

[8] *Politics*, Book I, Ch. 4, 1253^{b}34–1254^{a}1. This passage occurs in the context of a statement to the effect that "instruments are of various sorts; some are living, others lifeless; in the rudder, the pilot of a ship has a lifeless, in the look-out man, a living instrument; for in the arts the servant is a kind of instru-

Since we are dealing with a dream, let us indulge ourselves in one more moment of dreaming. In that single sentence, Aristotle projected in his imagination a society which has gone beyond the industrial revolution to a state of *complete* automation: a thorough substitution of automatic machines for slaves, *i.e.,* for human beings doing subsistence work of a purely mechanical sort.

It is important to realize that machines can be substituted for men *only* where men perform tasks that are mechanical in quality; *i.e.,* repetitive tasks performed by rote or rule, and without any involvement at all of creative thought. What men do mechanically, machines can do as well, and usually much better. The task (for example, extended calculation) may be mechanical, even though the end for which it is performed is liberal.

With this clearly in mind, we can see that the dream of *complete* automation envisages all work that is mechanical in quality (whether or not its end is subsistence) being done by automatic machines, including the production of the machines themselves. The invention or improvement of these machines and the management of the productive processes in which they are engaged is work that aims at the production of subsistence, but it is liberal in character. Though its end is subsistence, it is creative; being nonmechanical, it cannot be done by machines. In our dream of complete automation, we must, therefore, be careful to exclude the *technical* work involved in the invention or improvement of machines, and the *managerial* work involved in the organization and administration of the productive process as a whole.

Even with these two significant exclusions in the sphere of subsistence work, we know that *complete* automation is impossible, but we also know that within the next hundred years progressively increasing automation will achieve a remarkable approximation of the dream. Hence, by analyzing the dream as if it were real, we can learn some-

ment . . . [An economic] possession is an instrument for maintaining life. And so, in the arrangement of the family, a slave is a living possession, and property a number of such instruments; and the servant is himself an instrument which takes precedence over all other instruments" (*ibid.,* 1253b27–33).

thing about an ideal that it will be practicable for us to realize approximately.

Let us, then, for one more moment of projection, imagine a society in which machines do all or most of the mechanical work that must be done to provide the wealth necessary both for subsistence and for civilization. Let us imagine, further, that in this society, every man, or every family, has a sufficient share in the private ownership of machines to derive sufficient subsistence from their productivity. In this automated industrial society, each man, as an owner of machines, would be in the same position as an owner of slaves in a slave society. As a capitalist, he would be an economically free man, free from exploitation by other men, free from destitution or want, free from the drudgery of mechanical work—and so free to live well if he has the virtue to do so.[9]

Such a society would be a truly classless society, and the very opposite of the class-divided society of the socialist state, in which a despotic bureaucracy constitutes a ruling and owning class as against the mass of the workers who have no economic independence or any effective political power. Even were we to accept at its face value the claim that the dictatorship of the proletariat creates a "classless so-

---

[9] The conception of the machine as an inanimate slave is a familiar thought in our industrial society. But the implications of this idea are seldom, if ever, followed through to their ultimate conclusion, which is that, like the few who were slave owners in the past, it is now possible for all men to be economically free by acquiring property in the automated machine slaves of the future. On the one hand, Norman Thomas, writing of the future of socialism, says, "Socialism believes that men may be free by making power-driven machinery the slave of mankind" (*After the New Deal, What?*, New York, 1936: p. 157). But in spite of the fact that the economically free men of the past derived their freedom from owning capital, often including slaves, Thomas as a socialist believes that universal freedom—economic independence and security for all—can be achieved without the private ownership of capital. On the other hand, in a recent speech, Roger Blough, Chairman of the Board of the United States Steel Corporation, cites a reference by the *London Economist* to machines as "inanimate slaves." He recommends multiplying them in order to produce more and to distribute more widely the greater wealth produced in the form of a higher standard of living for all; but he does not implement and expand this recommendation by proposing to make all men free by diffusing as widely as possible the individual and private ownership of our inanimate slaves.

ciety," it would be a classless society of propertyless workers. In contrast, the classless society of capitalism, the image of which we have projected from Aristotle's extraordinary fantasy, would be a classless society of masters not slaves, of propertied men able to enjoy leisure, not of propertyless men still engaged in toil.

Such a classless society fulfills the ideal of economic democracy. All its members would be economically free and equal, even as in a political democracy all men enjoy political freedom and equality. Just as the status of citizenship conferred upon all has achieved political democracy, so the individual and private ownership of capital by all households would achieve economic democracy.

This ideal can become a practical reality to whatever extent an actual society is able (1) to reduce human toil to the minimum through a proper use of automation; (2) to approximate a universal diffusion of private property in the capital instruments of production; and (3) to educate its members to devote themselves not only to the wise management and productive use of their productive property, but also to the pursuits of leisure and the production of the goods of civilization.

3 SOME PROBLEMS
TO BE SOLVED

Three problems confront us when we try to think through what is involved in creating an economically free and classless society.

THE PROBLEM OF ORGANIZING PRODUCTION

How shall industry be organized so that no man works primarily for the good of another, and so that each man has some voice in the conduct of economic affairs analogous to the voice he exercises in political affairs as a citizen?

Even if most of the purely subsistence work is done by machines, it is still possible for men to be used and managed as if they were machines or slaves.

How can this be avoided without, at the same time, sacrificing efficiency in the management of large-scale industrial enterprises?

THE PROBLEM OF DIFFUSING OWNERSHIP

How shall the ownership of productive property be so diffused that every man or family obtains subsistence, for the most part, as a result of his or its participation in the production of wealth by means other than, or in addition to, toil?

THE PROBLEM OF LIBERTY AND EQUALITY

Here we face a number of questions.

How shall the whole sphere of economic activity be properly subordinated to political institutions and the affairs of government in such a way that the false extremes of totalitarianism and individualism are both avoided?

What must be done to avoid the concentrations of political and economic power which threaten freedom? Must not Montesquieu's principle of the separation of the powers of government be applied above all to the separation of economic and political power? How shall we achieve the requisite political regulation and direction of economic processes and yet avoid state ownership of the means of production and political control of the distribution of wealth?

In order to understand these problems; beyond that, in order to understand how the two most revolutionary societies in the world today, the United States and Soviet Russia, have thus far failed to solve these problems; and finally, in order to understand how the capitalist revolution can solve them, it is necessary to consider the basic elements in the production and distribution of wealth, together with the role of property and the rights of ownership in the organization of an economy.

In Chapter Four, we shall, therefore, present what we regard as an elementary analysis of (1) the factors in the production of wealth;

(2) the role of man as a factor in the production of wealth; (3) the productivity of labor; (4) the forms of property; and (5) primary and secondary distribution. Then, in Chapter Five, we shall explain why property is the only basis for participating in the production and distribution of wealth; and in the light of that, we shall state the three principles of economic justice which are the ground plan of the capitalist revolution.

With this done, we shall present, in Chapter Six, a classification of all historic economies. In terms of that classification, we shall be able to describe the present stage of the American economy as wavering at the crossroads which leads either to the socialist or to the capitalist revolution.

FACTORS IN THE PRODUCTION OF WEALTH

The factors of production fall into three main categories: (1) natural resources, (2) human labor, and (3) inanimate instruments made by man. Each of these can be further subdivided as follows.

Natural resources include (a) agricultural and mineral land, the sea and air, and the raw (unprocessed) materials derived from them; (b) all sources of natural power, *e.g.,* water power, electrical power, solar power, atomic power, etc.; and (c) the power and skill of domesticated animals.

Human beings engaged in subsistence work contribute (a) physical power analogous to the power of animals or other sources of natural power, such as waterfalls; (b) mechanical skill, which consists in the *direction* or *control* of such power as is needed to produce wealth; and (c) creative skill, which consists in the invention or improvement of things, including the nonhuman factors in production, or in the organization and management of the productive forces derived from all the productive factors involved.

Inanimate instruments can be divided into (a) hand tools, which merely increase human productive power or skill; (b) power-driven machines, which replace men to some extent as sources of skill and which replace men and animals as sources of productive power, generally supplying more productive power than can be derived from animals and men; and (c) automatic machines, which not only replace men and animals as sources of productive power and provide vastly more power than either, but also replace men as sources of productive skill and, in addition, contribute to the productive process as a whole skills that are entirely beyond the capacity of men and animals to develop.

The fact that power-driven machines are a source of productive power vastly in excess of the power that can be supplied by animals and men makes possible the production of goods that cannot be produced by man power and animal power. The fact that automatic machines contribute skills entirely beyond the capacity of men and animals to develop enables capital instruments to produce forms of wealth undreamed of in pre-industrial societies.

This analysis of the factors in the production of wealth calls for two further comments. The first is that all these factors can be graded on a scale from *complete passivity,* at one extreme, to *complete activity,* at the other.

Thus, mineral land and hand tools are completely passive factors in production. In contrast, agricultural land, the various natural sources of power, the power and skill of domesticated animals, and power-driven machines are more or less active factors in production. This is indicated by the fact that agricultural land produces fruit and grain without man's help, and by the fact that the farmer, as an active worker, co-operates with nature as an active factor in production. So, too, the industrial worker or machine tender co-operates with the power-driven machine, which is an active factor in production to whatever extent it contributes power and built-in skills or controls to the productive process.[1]

At the other extreme, man is the only completely active factor in production, whether he contributes power alone, or both power and skill. Automatic machinery, which requires the least co-operation from men, is the closest approximation to man himself as an active productive factor on the level of subsistence work that is mechanical in quality. But, while automatic machinery can replace men in almost all productive tasks that are mechanical, and can perform productive tasks that men cannot perform at all, automata cannot perform even the simplest liberal task which involves creative intelligence; and so they cannot replace men who do work that is liberal in quality, even where its purpose is the production of wealth.

Theoretically, all mechanical work can be done by fully automated machines. This is a commonplace among students of automation. But as a practical matter, there will always be millions of mechanical tasks that will be performed by men, either because they are not especially difficult or because of the inherent cost or difficulty involved in technologically eliminating them. Nevertheless, as scientists and technicians extend man's ability to make capital instruments perform the tasks of producing subsistence, the relative number of uneliminated mechanical workers will diminish.

---

[1] In the Report on Manufactures, issued by the Secretary of the Treasury in 1791, Alexander Hamilton summarizes one of the arguments for the superior productiveness of agricultural labor as maintaining "that in the productions of soil, nature co-operates with man; and that the effect of their joint labor must be greater than that of the labor of man alone." He counters this by saying that in manufacturing, human labor co-operates with productive machinery, as in agriculture it co-operates with productive nature. Machinery, he says, "is an artificial force brought in aid of the natural force of man; and, to all the purposes of labor, is an increase of hands—an accession of strength, unencumbered, too, by the expense of maintaining the laborer." See *The People Shall Judge,* Chicago, 1953: Vol. I, pp. 404, 406.

THE ROLE OF MAN AS A FACTOR IN
THE PRODUCTION OF WEALTH

We have seen that man as a factor in the production of wealth is a source of physical power and mechanical skill (*i.e.,* control). While at one extreme the use of human productive power with little or no skill (*e.g.,* the slave turning a grinding wheel or hauling ore from a mine by hand) has now become quite rare, the opposite extreme has become less rare. We can find numerous examples of the use of human skill to control productive power which is wholly derived from nonhuman sources (*e.g.,* the control skill of those who operate power-driven machines). In the middle range of tasks that are mechanical in quality, the human worker contributes some power as well as some control. These tasks vary from one extreme, at which the contribution needed is mainly power, to the other extreme, at which it is mainly control.

In the process by which technological improvements shift the burden of production from workers to capital instruments, both the power and the skills previously contributed by workers are affected.

With respect to the power employed in production, a twofold change takes place. On the one hand, the physical or muscular power demanded of workers is reduced to a minute fraction of that required in pre-industrial production.[2] On the other hand, enormous sources of natural power which can operate only through capital instruments are harnessed.

With respect to skills, the earliest of our modern capital instruments—such as the spinning jenny, the sewing machine, and the calculating machine—eliminated certain skills. As machines became more complex, frequently through the process of coupling together several separate machines to perform related steps in a single process, the elimination of skills became more pronounced. Finally, in the

[2] It is estimated that human muscle power now accounts for approximately 1 percent of the energy used in production. See *America's Needs and Resources,* The Twentieth Century Fund, New York, 1955: p. 908.

application of the principles of closed-loop automation, the ultimate impact of technological advance upon human skill becomes clear. Through the use of a formidable array of devices, ranging from simple relay mechanisms to versatile analogue and digital computers, the skills contributed by workers in earlier production processes are totally eliminated; and, in addition, processes and products themselves may be redesigned to take advantage of a new order of electronic and mechanical "skills" lying far beyond the range of human competence.

We have seen one other thing that is of great significance here. In the production of wealth, men contribute some creative skills, such as those involved in the invention and improvement of machines and in the repairing of machines. Let us call these skills "technical." In addition, there are the skills which consist in the arts of organizing and administering the productive process as a whole, involving all the factors in production, including the employment and direction of technical skills, capital instruments, and the power and skill of operating personnel. Let us call these skills "managerial." In contradistinction to technical and managerial skills, we shall continue to use the word "mechanical" for all the noncreative skills that men contribute to the productive process.

With these distinctions in mind, we can construct a classification of all human work. It is set forth in the following table.

CHARACTER OF THE WORK	TYPE OF WORKER
I. *Work that is liberal in aim and creative in quality*	For example, pure scientists, philosophers, statesmen, clergymen, fine artists, teachers, etc.
II. *Subsistence work that is creative in quality*	Technicians and managers engaged in the production of wealth; and also lawyers, physicians, etc., whose services are incidental to the production of wealth. The tasks performed here are no more mechanical than the tasks per-

CHARACTER OF THE WORK	TYPE OF WORKER
	formed in the creative work that is productive of civilization rather than of subsistence.
III. *Work that is liberal in aim but mechanical in quality*	For example, clerical assistants to legislators, scientists, or teachers engaged in the performance of tasks for which machines can be substituted.
IV. *Subsistence work that is mechanical in quality*	Men who contribute muscular power or noncreative skills, or both, to the production of wealth, whether they do so exclusively by their own labor or work with hand tools or with power-driven machines.

Now let us focus our attention on all forms of mechanical work, in which noncreative skills or muscular power, or both, are the worker's predominant contribution to the production of wealth. What we are about to say applies to mechanical work that assists the production of the goods of civilization, as well as mechanical work that produces wealth; but it is of major interest to us in the sphere of the production of wealth.

There currently exists a great deal of loose talk about the increasing productivity of human labor, where by "human labor" is meant purely mechanical subsistence work. One of the basic contributions of the theory set forth in *Capitalism* consists in cutting through all this loose talk, much of which is self-serving on the part of labor, self-deceptive on the part of management, and fuzzy analysis on the part of theorists who have perpetrated or encouraged it.[3]

[3] *Capitalism,* to be published in the coming year, contains an analysis of the "increasing productivity" of workers which shows that in fact the inherent productiveness of labor, other than managerial and technical labor, has remained stable or has declined since the beginning of the industrial revolution, and that its economic productivity is far below the level indicated by the share of the national wealth received by workers.

The truth of the matter is simply that, over the whole period of man's historic life as a producer of wealth, "human labor" (*i.e.,* men engaged in purely mechanical work) is *either a constant or a diminishing source of productive power,* and a *diminishing source of productive skill.* The progressive diminution of man's productive skills as a mechanical worker is correlated with the progressive increase in the productive skills embodied in machinery. The constancy or decline of man as a source of productive power is an absolute fact. It has nothing at all to do with the harnessing or development of other forms of productive power. It merely reflects the inherent limitations of man as a physical organism allowing, of course, for variations from the average, as men are graded individually in strength and dexterity. Looking at mankind across the centuries, we see evidence that, on the average, man is a less powerful productive force today than he was in earlier times.

But though, *absolutely speaking,* the average unit of labor power must remain a constant quantity in the production of wealth (at least so long as the human physique remains what it is), the average unit of labor power is a *relatively* diminishing quantity in the course of progressive industrialization. Let us state this fundamental truth in another way.

In the industrial production of wealth, *i.e.,* in machine production, there are, as we have seen, three main types of human workers: (1) mechanical workers; (2) technical workers; and (3) managerial workers. Of these three, the first perform purely mechanical tasks. The last two perform tasks most of which are not mechanical and cannot be mechanized.

Just as the individual productive contribution of mechanical workers accounts for less of the total wealth produced in a highly industrialized economy than it does in a nonindustrialized economy or in one which represents a primitive stage of industrialization, so the individual productive contribution of technical and managerial workers accounts for more of the total wealth produced in a highly industrialized society than it does under primitive industrial conditions. Proportionately more technical and managerial man-hours are required, and more highly developed managerial and technical skills are called for, as industrialization becomes technologically more advanced. The available evidence further indicates that the economic productivity of managerial and technical workers—at least under conditions of relatively full employment—is higher today than at any previous time in our economic history.

The primary reason for the latter fact is undoubtedly that technical and managerial skills are responsible for the invention, improvement, and efficient operation of the machinery which, relative to other factors, has become more and more productive with progressive industrialization.

It follows, therefore, that with progressive industrialization and with the increasing productiveness of the economy as a whole, the relative productiveness of mechanical work diminishes and the relative productiveness of technical and managerial work increases, as measured by the contribution each makes to the total wealth produced.[4]

A TECHNICAL NOTE ON THE PRODUCTIVITY OF LABOR

In particular cases, new highly skilled workers are frequently called upon to replace greater numbers of relatively unskilled workers. But, in proportion to the wealth produced, the aggregate of skills eliminated

[4] It is entirely possible that, in a period of extensive unemployment, the economic productivity of managerial and technical labor (*i.e.*, the market value of managerial and technical services) might decline proportionately more than the economic productivity of mechanical labor. This could result from a widespread struggle on the part of mechanical workers to upgrade their qualifications for highly coveted managerial and technical positions. The resulting increase in the number of qualified managerial and technical workers, by affecting the supply side of the equation, would lower the managerial utility of the services rendered by these types of workers, and so would lower their economic productivity or distributive share.

is invariably greater than the new skills called into existence. Concurrently, the relative expenditure of human energy, as compared with the inanimate energy employed in production, constantly diminishes. Since these are the elements which submanagerial and subtechnical workers contribute to production, the annual increase in "productivity," or output per man-hour, has consistently represented a relatively increasing physical contribution by capital instruments and a relatively decreasing physical contribution by workers to the total product.[5]

When we consider that this change has been going on since the first century, and has been proceeding at a rapid pace since the end of the eighteenth century, it is clear that the actual physical contribution of labor to the production of wealth is now extremely small as compared with that of capital instruments. It is, if anything, an underestimation rather than an exaggeration to say that the aggregate physical contribution to the production of wealth by workers in the United States today accounts for less than 10 percent of the wealth produced, and that the contribution by the owners of capital instruments, *through their capital instruments,* accounts in physical terms for more than 90 percent of the wealth produced. All available statistical evidence tends to show that these figures greatly overestimate the extent to which labor contributes today to the production of wealth.[6]

---

[5] Labor today frequently comes close to acknowledging that it is not seeking to produce more in order to increase its distributive share, but that it is merely seeking to share in the increased wealth produced by capital instruments. The collective bargaining agreement in effect in 1957 between General Motors and the AFL-CIO United Auto Workers, for example, recites that "to produce more *with the same amount of human effort* is a sound economic and social objective." Nevertheless, the agreement provided for substantially increased compensation of workers over pre-existing wages and benefits.

[6] From 1850 to the present, the average rate of increase in output per man-hour, measured in terms of national income per man-hour in 1950 prices, has been in excess of 2 percent per annum. (See *America's Needs and Resources,* Table 14, p. 40.) Although statistical evidence is lacking for the period prior to 1850, many of the most spectacular advances in industrialization were made prior to that date. These included the use of water power for mass production, wind power for propelling vessels and pumping water, sewing machines, the flying

One further point remains to be mentioned. It appears that the economic productivity of labor has also declined, and that the decline is probably of the same order as the decline in inherent productiveness.

By "inherent productiveness" we mean the physical ability or capacity of a factor of production to produce goods or services. By "economic productivity" we mean the distributive share of the wealth produced that goes in a free market to an owner of a particular factor of production as a direct result of his contribution to production, its magnitude being evaluated through the mechanism of supply and demand in a freely competitive market. Thus the term "economic productivity" involves not only the physical contribution of the factor in question, but also the competitively determined market value of that physical contribution.

Where the value of labor is competitively determined (even allowing for true collective bargaining, which merely establishes a balance of the power as between the employed and the employer and leaves the employer free to employ others if he believes better terms can be made), the wage determination is automatically a determination of the value of labor's contribution to the final product. But since we live in an economy characterized by redistributive taxes, the combined power of unions and the countervailing power they receive from government, and various potent political devices that artificially stimulate consumer demand in order to provide full employment, there is no statistical evidence from which we can compute the actual economic productivity of labor in America today. We can only draw inferences from the magnitude of the means employed to prevent the competitive fixing of wages and to increase the employment of labor. We can also draw inferences of a negative sort, with regard to the relative economic productivity of capital instruments, by considering the incomes still received by the owners of capital *after* all the foregoing forces have

---

shuttle, steam pumping machines, the spinning jenny, the boring machine, the use of the steam engine as a prime mover, the gas engine, the cotton gin, the hydraulic press, etc.

diverted *from* the owners of capital and *to* the owners of labor a large portion of the wealth produced by capital instruments.[7]

THE FORMS OF PROPERTY

By property we mean that which a man possesses, together with a right to control it, use it, derive benefits from it, or dispose of it, in any lawful manner that he wishes. With regard to property, we would like to make two distinctions.

(1) The first distinction is between innate and acquired property. Innate property is that which a man possesses as part of his own nature, together with a right to its control. So far as property having economic significance is concerned, the only form of innate property is the productiveness that is inherent in a man's bodily strength and mental skill.

We shall use the word "labor power" for a man's productive abilities in the sphere of subsistence goods, without regard to the proportions of physical strength and mental skill that are involved, and without regard to whether, in the production of such goods, it is used to do work that is mechanical or creative in quality. Though all men are innately equipped with labor power, a chattel slave is a man who has been deprived of property in his own labor power, since the right to control it is legally vested in his master and owner, not in himself. The legal rights of the master are, of course, in violation of natural law, since every man has a natural right to his own labor power as well as to life and liberty.[8]

[7] An extensive analysis of these points is presented in *Capitalism*. That analysis explains the apparent divergence between the declining economic productivity of labor and labor's increasing distributive share of the wealth produced. For those who mistakenly suppose that present wage levels are an accurate index of labor's economic productivity, a brief summary of the explanation is given in the Appendix on the concealment of the declining productivity of labor in our present economy. See pp. 256–265, *infra*.

[8] In his second treatise *On Civil Government*, Locke uses the word "property" in a broad sense to designate all the things to which man has either a natural

Acquired property consists in all things external to a man's own person, which he not only possesses but also establishes his right to control. Writing with a pre-industrial economy in mind, John Locke enunciated the fundamental truth that it is a man's use of his own innate labor power which is the basis of his appropriation of the things which God gave to all men in common.[9] Locke's labor theory of property must never be confused with Marx's labor theory of value. Locke is concerned only with explaining the origin of *acquired property rights* at that starting point in human affairs when men first appropriated the land they tilled or the tools they made.

Starting with everything in common, men rightfully appropriated those things with which they mixed their labor power or which were exclusively the fruits of their own toil. In that original appropriation, it was a man's use of the only productive property he had (*i.e.,* his innate labor power) that gave him title to acquired property in the things he used his innate property to produce. Going beyond that original appropriation, it is possible to generalize Locke's theory by saying that, apart from gift or inheritance, a man's right to acquired property derives from the productive use of such property as he already owns, whether that is his own labor power, his land, or his stock of workable materials and working instrumentalities.

(2) The second distinction involves a threefold classification of the forms of productive property, *i.e.,* the ownership and control of factors productive of wealth. It is as follows:

---

or an acquired right: his natural right to life and liberty, on the one hand; and his right to the estate he has acquired, on the other. The word "property" in a narrow and economic sense is more frequently restricted to a man's estate, *i e.,* the property he has acquired by his own labor, by exchange, by gift or inheritance. When men are chattel slave the labor power inherent in them is a form of acquired property, owned by other men, just as the productive power of land, animals, and tools is owned. In contrast to chattel slaves, free men own their own labor power, to use and dispose of it, or its products, as they will. Hence to say that the subjection of men to slave labor is a violation of natural right is equivalent to saying that men have a natural right, not only to life and liberty, but also to the ownership of the labor power which is inherent in their bodily frame and mental competence.

[9] See *On Civil Government,* Ch. V, "Of Property."

(a) Property in natural resources (including mineral and agricultural land, resources reclaimed from the sea or air, raw materials, natural sources of power and domesticated animals).
(b) Property in instruments of production (including processed materials as well as hand tools, power-driven machines and automatic machines) and in productive organizations.
(c) Property in human labor power (including the acquired labor power of other men who are owned as slaves, as well as one's own innately possessed labor power).

With this classification in mind, we can now say how in the following pages we shall use the words "capital" and "labor." Excluding slave labor as having no place, by need or right, in a capitalist society, we shall use the word "labor" for the third form of productive property, *i.e.,* the property each man has in his own labor power; and we shall unite the first two forms of productive property mentioned above under the head of "capital." Capital thus represents all forms of *acquired* property in productive factors; and, excluding chattel slavery, labor represents the one form of *innate* property in a factor productive of wealth.[10]

Both capital and labor can either be widely diffused among the members of a society or highly concentrated in the hands of a few. In the slave societies of the past, the ownership of labor as well as the ownership of capital was concentrated in the hands of a small master class. With the abolition of chattel slavery, there can be concentrated ownership of capital alone; for the ownership of labor is universally diffused—each individual having property in his own labor.

Finally, it is of the utmost importance to recognize that property is not the same as private property. By *private* property we should

[10] The wealth of a society includes: (1) its fund of consumable goods; (2) its stock pile of combustible or expendable implements of war; (3) the cumulative fund of productive knowledge that its people have acquired or have ready access to, and which is the common possession of all members of the society except as it may be limited by patent or copyright laws; and (4) all the materials and instruments it has available to employ in the p.oduction of consumables and combustibles. The last of these, the so-called means of production, divides into the three forms of productive property mentioned above.

understand that which is owned and controlled by individuals, families, or private corporations, no matter how large. By *public* property we should understand that which is owned by the State and controlled by its officers or agencies—the persons through whom the State acts. As contrasted with property, private or public, there is that which is common (*i.e.,* not *proper* to any individual or corporation, including the State).

Common pasture land—as the Boston Common, for example—was owned by no one; no one had any right of control. The *common* represents the opposite of *property* (*i.e.,* that which is appropriated by someone who then exercises *exclusive control* over it), just as, within the sphere of the *proper, public* property represents the opposite of *private* property.

The Marxist program for the abolition of private property calls for the State ownership of capital (*i.e.,* all means of production other than labor power). It does not call for the abolition of property or for the diffusion of the ownership of capital, but rather for the transformation of private capital into public property and for the abolition of private property in everything except labor power and consumable goods in the hands of the consumer.

PRIMARY AND SECONDARY DISTRIBUTION

By "primary distribution of wealth" we understand the distribution of wealth to those who have produced it. In the simplest case of the solitary producer (*e.g.,* the Robinson Crusoe economy), this means that the individual directly and automatically acquires the wealth he has produced by his labor and by the use of whatever capital instruments he possesses. In the normal case of the economy of a complex society, in which large numbers of men are associated in the production of wealth and in which they exchange one kind of product for another, usually through the medium of money, the income each individual receives as a result of his participation in production represents his share of the primary distribution of wealth in that society. In a market economy in which the value of each contribution to production, whether in the form of land or raw materials, capital or labor, is evaluated objectively and impartially through the processes of supply and demand in freely competitive markets, primary distribution awards to each participant precisely the equivalent of what he would have received as a solitary producer: *the wealth which his participation in production created.*

As distinguished from primary distribution so conceived, we understand "secondary distribution of wealth" to include all transfers of wealth other than those which result from participation in production and the exchanges consequent thereto that take place in free markets. Secondary distribution, therefore, covers transfers of wealth within families or between friends by gift or by inheritance or by will, transfers through losing or finding, transfers from the public domain, transfers of previously produced property after it has come into the hands of an ultimate consumer, eleemosynary distributions of all sorts, etc.

To the extent that any of the contributions to production are not evaluated through the operation of supply and demand in a freely competitive market, the distribution which results from participation in production may be (1) less than the value of the contribution made, or (2) more than its value. In either case, the difference between the competitively determined value of the contribution and what is received for it (in wages, dividends, payments for materials, etc.) represents a secondary distribution of wealth in favor of the party who gets *more* than the value his contribution would have been determined to have in a freely competitive market.

The importance of this distinction between primary and secondary distribution will be seen in the next chapter where we shall set forth three principles of justice applicable to the production and distribution of wealth. None of these principles applies to secondary distribution. The only questions of justice with which we shall be concerned relate to the primary distribution of wealth—the distribution that is integrally connected with participation in the production of wealth.[11]

Before we turn to these questions of justice, one problem about the distribution of wealth remains to be considered. It has to do with the distribution of wealth to those members of society who are engaged in what we have called liberal work rather than subsistence work. We pointed out in Chapter Two that statesmen, fine artists, pure scientists, philosophers, members of the clergy, some lawyers, some physicians, some teachers, some journalists, etc., do not directly contribute to the production of wealth, *i.e.,* the goods of subsistence. The creative work they do is productive of the goods of civilization and of the human spirit—the liberal arts and sciences, the institutions of the state and of religion.

There are hundreds of thousands of such persons in our society and the great majority of them support themselves and their families by the incomes they receive in the form of honoraria, fees, and other payments for their services or for what they produce.

Is such income a part of the primary distribution of wealth in our society in spite of the fact that, in the light of our distinction between subsistence work and liberal work, these persons are not participating in the production of wealth?

At first glance, it would appear either (1) that we were in error in classifying the creative work of statesmen, fine artists, pure scientists, philosophers, etc., as something totally apart from the production of wealth, or (2) that the incomes received by a large number of liberal workers in our economy are not part of the primary distribution of our society's wealth, but fall rather under its secondary distribution. In the second alternative, the three principles of economic justice with which we are concerned would not seem to apply to their activities.

Neither of these alternatives leads us to the correct solution of the problem. In essence, those activities which we have called liberal, or

[11] There are, of course, other principles of justice that are applicable to the secondary distribution of wealth.

forms of leisure work, do lie totally outside the field of the production of wealth. A society is conceivable in which such activities would be carried on for the inherent satisfactions or intrinsic rewards to which they give rise, and without any need or desire for extrinsic compensation of the kind that must be given those who engage in the production of wealth, especially in such activities connected with it as are intrinsically unrewarding because they are in no sense creative. But for the most part our society does not operate in this manner, though the technological advances which are now foreseeable make it possible for it to become a society in which a great deal of the leisure work that is the work of civilization will be done without need for extrinsic compensation. The realization of that possibility is, as we shall see, one of the primary goals of the capitalist revolution.

In a free society, such as ours, wealth is anything that is regarded as wealth by a significant number of persons. Anything which is prized for its exchange value and which is bought, sold, exchanged, or systematically collected and exchanged among collectors, is thereby empirically determined to be wealth. This is true whether those who so treat the goods or services involved are motivated by the inherent qualities of these goods or services, their usefulness or ability to satisfy needs, their ability to produce wealth, or their ability to satisfy sentimental interests.

It is market demand which gives items of wealth their market value. It is the free play of the forces of demand upon the sources of supply that objectively and impartially determines the exchange value of whatever things are regarded as items of exchangeable wealth. But something further than a demand for particular goods or services is necessary for it to be regarded as an item of wealth rather than one of the goods of civilization which lies totally outside the sphere of wealth. It must be something which, by the common consent of those who own or furnish it and those who seek it, is regarded and treated as subject to purchase and sale, or exchange.

Let us illustrate this point. The charms of a virtuous woman are not an item of wealth, for no matter how highly and widely they are prized, they will not be sold and so they cannot be bought. The same holds true of works of art, scientific discoveries, the services of teachers, physicians, statesmen, etc., to whatever extent those who create such things or render such services refuse to *sell* them at any price. Under such conditions, they are not only in essence goods of civilization, but they are also kept from becoming items of wealth.

However, under other conditions, goods or services that are essentially goods of the spirit or of civilization and not at all goods of subsistence, do become items of wealth. Such things are bought and sold in our society for the simple reason that the creation of such goods or the rendering of such services is generally the sole or principal source of income for those engaged in these creative, liberal activities of leisure work.

However, there are a sufficient number of exceptions to confirm the fundamental insight that the goods produced or the services rendered by those engaged in liberal work are properly regarded as no part of wealth and, therefore, cannot be bought because they will not be sold. There are, for example, some artists, scientists, and philosophers who have enough income from their capital estates to enable them to engage in liberal work for satisfactions that are wholly above monetary compensation. There are men who are financially able to serve their country in political office without any compensation beyond the nominal pay of a dollar a year. There are teachers, physicians and lawyers who render services of various kinds to their society solely for the creative satisfaction it gives them, even where they might have sought pay and might have treated their creative work as if it were productive of wealth.

At the opposite extreme, we must recognize the fact that there are many men who possess adequate capital estates and who take such compensation as they can get for the liberal work they do as educators, scientists, criminal lawyers, physicians, highly paid public officials, etc. In addition, it is often the case that these men are able to retain little or nothing of such compensation because of their already being in a high income tax bracket. These men represent the ultimate in failure or refusal to distinguish between (1) items of wealth which are property subject to purchase and sale, and (2) the goods of civilization which should be entirely above the market place.

Therefore, the solution of this problem is not to be found in obliterating the essentially sound distinction between the goods of subsistence and the goods of civilization, nor in excluding the payments made to men who do essentially liberal work from the primary distribution of wealth, thereby making certain principles of economic justice inapplicable to liberal work that is extrinsically compensated. The ultimate solution lies rather in the transformation of our society that the capitalist revolution aims to bring about—a transformation that will enable an ever increasing part of the liberal work which creates civilization to be done without any extrinsic compensation for it.

5 ECONOMIC JUSTICE AND
ECONOMIC RIGHTS

PROPERTY AND JUSTICE

It has often been said that where there is no property, there can be neither justice nor injustice. The statement is usually meant to apply with complete generality to everything that belongs to a man by right —that which is his own or proper to him, whether innate or acquired.

As thus interpreted, the statement covers more than economic property and economic justice. We are here concerned only with the application of it to economic affairs, and especially to the distribution of wealth as that is related to the production of wealth. We are, therefore, excluding from consideration, as having no bearing on the justice of distribution, such wealth as a man obtains by charity or gift on which he has, prior to its receipt, no just claim, as well as the wealth he may obtain by seizure, theft, or other means by which he unjustly appropriates what does not belong to him.[1]

1 Since property in things includes the right of control and disposition in any lawful manner, the laws relating to the transfer of property at death bv will or

The question with which we are first of all concerned is how a man who already has some property—in the form of his own labor power, capital instruments, or both—can justly acquire additional property. This question presupposes that if a man has no property at all— that is, if in violation of his natural rights, he is a chattel slave deprived of innate property in his labor power—he may justly claim to have that innate property restored to him; but until it is restored, he has no property whereby he can justly acquire further property.

The underlying proposition is twofold: on the one hand, when a man has no property rights in factors productive of particular wealth, he can have no basis for a just claim to property rights in the wealth so produced; on the other hand, when he owns as his property all of the instruments of production engaged in producing particular wealth, he can lay just claim to all the wealth so produced.

From this it follows that if several men together employ their respective property in the production of wealth, each man's just share in the distribution of the total wealth produced is proportionate to the contribution each has made by the use of his property toward the production of that wealth. It must be repeated once more that it is only through his productive property—his capital instruments or his labor power—that a man can participate in the production of wealth as an *independent* contributor. The slave whose labor power is owned and used by his master is not an *independent* contributor; hence he cannot, as a matter of strict justice, claim any share in the distribution of the wealth produced.

Two hypothetical cases will help us to clarify this basic point. They

by intestate distribution are merely regulative of special types of transfers of property by an owner. It is frequently said that the right to inherit or to receive property by will is purely artificial or statutory, meaning that it is not based on natural right. While no one has a natural right to receive property by will or inheritance (because no one, as a matter of justice, has a right to receive a gift), the owner of property does have a natural right to control and dispose of it. The justice of laws regulating transfers by will, and therefore of the laws regulating inheritance (which are by custom relied upon as substitutes for affirmative disposition by will), must be measured by the standards governing the relations between the State and the owners of property.

are stated in terms of the so-called Crusoe economy, a device so often used in the literature of economics.

(1) Imagine first the economy of Robinson Crusoe, before the advent of Friday but after he has taken possession of the island, domesticated a few animals, devised some hand tools, etc. All the further wealth he produces comes from the productive use of Crusoe's own capital and labor power. Part of Crusoe's output may be additional capital goods; the rest, consumables. To whom does it all belong? No one would hesitate for a second to give the one and only right answer: Crusoe. *A man is justly entitled to all the wealth he himself produces.*

(2) Imagine next the same island economy complicated by two additional factors. One is Friday, who, for the purposes of the example, shall be Crusoe's chattel slave in violation of his natural rights. The other additional factor is another man, by the name of Smith, whom Crusoe does not enslave. Since Crusoe owns the island, all the capital goods thereon, and the one available slave, Smith enters into an arrangement with Crusoe whereby he will participate in the production of wealth by contributing his own labor power for which, after some bargaining, it is agreed that Smith shall receive some share in the distribution of the wealth produced.

The fact must be noted that the only way Smith can participate in the production of wealth is by using his own property—the only property he has, namely, his own labor power. Only by contributing his labor can Smith's participation in the production of wealth be the basis for a just claim to a share in the distribution of the wealth produced.

Crusoe's man Friday, his goat, his dog, his tools, and his land all more or less actively participate in the production of wealth. But since their participation does not involve any property on their part, it affords no basis for their claiming a share in the distribution of the wealth produced.

Crusoe gives his dog, his goat, and Friday enough to keep them alive and serviceable. Since they participate in production as Crusoe's property and not independently, he can rightfully claim as his all the wealth they produce. It is his to give them as he pleases or not. But since Smith participates in production, not as Crusoe's property used by Crusoe but independently and by the voluntary use of his own labor, he has a right to claim a share in the distribution, as Friday, for example, does not.

What is Smith's just share? Suppose, in this hypothetical case, that it could be known that the value of Smith's contribution to the total production of wealth was one-tenth of the value of the total final product, the other nine parts being contributed by Crusoe's own labor and capital (*i.e.,* all the forms of productive property he owns). On that supposition, can there be any doubt at all that Smith's share in the distribution should be one-tenth of the total? If it is evident that a man is justly entitled to all the wealth he produces, does it not follow with equal clarity that, when several men jointly produce wealth, each is justly entitled to a distributive share that is proportionate to the value of the contribution each makes to the production of the wealth in question?

The foregoing hypothetical cases exemplify the principle of justice with regard to the distribution of wealth to those who have participated in its production by the use of their own productive property —their capital or labor power, or both. They show us concretely what it means to say that each independent participant is entitled to receive a distributive share of the total wealth produced; and that in each case the distributive share, to be just, must be strictly proportional to the contribution that each makes toward the production of the total wealth by the use of his own property.

This is the only principle whereby the distribution of the wealth produced can be justly grounded on the rights of property engaged in the production of wealth. It is furthermore the only distributive principle that is based on the recognition of the rights of property in productive factors, for the essence of such property lies in the right of the owner to receive the portion (or proportionate share) of the wealth which the productive factor owned by him produces.[2]

In order to apply this principle, we must be able to assess the economic value of the contribution made by each of the independent participants in production. How can their economic value be impartially or objectively determined, and determined in a way that is consonant with the institutions of a free society? More specifically, what assesses the value of the contribution to production made by factors A, B and C, in terms of which the owners of such factors are entitled to receive proportionate shares of the total wealth produced?

Our answer, in brief, is: *free competition.*

FREE COMPETITION AS THE DETERMINANT OF VALUE

In the opening chapter of *Capital,* Karl Marx announces that, in elaborating on a theory advanced by Ricardo, he alone has solved a problem that Aristotle first raised but failed to solve; namely, the problem of finding an objective measure of the economic value of goods and services, so that a just exchange of commodities is possible.

Marx accepts Aristotle's principle of justice in exchange as requiring that the things exchanged be of equal value. He refers explicitly to the pages of Book V on Justice in Aristotle's *Ethics,* and especially to Chapter 5 where Aristotle raises the question of how we can equate the value of beds and houses so that a certain number of beds can be justly exchanged for a certain number of houses.

[2] There are other distributive principles not based on justice or property rights. One is the principle of charity. To continue with the example we have been using, suppose Friday had a sister who became Smith's wife and bore him five children. If Smith's contribution to the production of wealth in the Crusoe economy continued to be no more than one-tenth of the value of the total annual output, his annual income would probably become woefully insufficient for the support of his household of seven. In that case, Crusoe might give him something to supplement the income he earned. Since Smith had not earned this additional wealth, it would represent a charitable distribution on Crusoe's part.

Aristotle recognized, Marx says, that we cannot equate qualitatively different commodities, unless they can somehow be made commensurable; but lacking any objective and common measure of their exchange value, he found that there was no way to commensurate qualitatively different things. Marx quotes Aristotle as declaring that "it is impossible that such unlike things can be commensurable"; and then adds that Aristotle "himself tells us what barred the way to his further analysis; it was the absence of any concept of value. What is that equal something, that common substance which admits of the value of the beds being expressed by a house? Such a thing, in truth, cannot exist, says Aristotle." [3]

At this point, Marx offers his own solution of the problem which, he says, Aristotle failed to solve. The objective and common measure of exchange value is human labor. According to the labor theory of value, two qualitatively different things can be made commensurable by measuring both by the amount of human labor involved in their production, and when thus measured, things of equivalent value can be justly exchanged.

Turning now to Book V, Chapter 5, of the *Ethics,* we find Aristotle saying, as Marx reports, that a just exchange of qualitatively different things requires that they be of equivalent value; and that this in turn requires some way of commensurating their value. "All goods," Aristotle declares, "must therefore be measured by some one thing," and "this unit," he then says, "is in truth demand, which holds all things together; for if men did not need one another's goods at all, or did not need them equally, there would be either no exchange or not an equal

[3] *Capital*, Book I, Part I, Ch. 1, Sect. 3. "The brilliancy of Aristotle's genius," Marx tells us, "is that he discovered, in the expression of the value of commodities, a relation of equality. The peculiar conditions of the society in which he lived alone prevented him from discovering what, 'in truth,' was at the bottom of this equality." Living in a society that "was founded upon slavery, and had, therefore, for its natural basis, the inequality of men and of their labor powers," Aristotle, Marx thinks, was "prevented from seeing that to attribute value to commodities is merely a mode of expressing all labor as equal human labor."

exchange." [4] Aristotle admits, as Marx says, that it is impossible for the qualitatively heterogeneous to be made perfectly commensurate; "but," he immediately adds, "with reference to demand they may become so sufficiently." [5]

So far as we know, Marx and Aristotle offer the only recorded solutions to the problem of how to commensurate the value of heterogeneous things in order to determine equivalents for the purpose of justice in exchange. If Marx's labor theory of value is false, as we contend it is, then Aristotle's solution is the only one available; and, as he says, it is sufficient for all practical purposes even if, under actual market conditions, it falls short of perfection.

The exchange value of goods and services is, in its very nature, a *matter of opinion*. Only where free and workable competition exists does the value set on things to be exchanged reflect the free play of the opinions of all, or at least many, potential buyers and sellers. Any other method of determining values must involve the imposition of an arbitrary opinion of value, an opinion held by one or more persons or an organized group; and such a determination of value, to be effective, must be imposed by force. We submit that the human mind can conceive of no other accurate, objective, and impartial determinant of economic value, once the fallacious labor theory of value has been discarded.

What has just been said about free competition as the only accurate, objective, and impartial means of measuring the equivalence of values for the purpose of justice in the exchange of heterogeneous commodities is equally applicable when the purpose is one of measur-

[4] *Nicomachean Ethics*, Book V, Ch. 5, 1133ª27–29. We would say today not "demand" but "supply and demand," or "free competition." However, these are merely different expressions for the same thing.

[5] *Ibid.*, 1133ᵇ19–20. We might add that any variance between the absolutely just relative values of two things being exchanged and the values at which they are in fact exchanged in a particular market merely reflects variances from *perfect competition* in the market. Aristotle is in effect saying that the free and workable competition that is attainable in a market exempt from all monopolistic restraints results in a determination of values which makes goods and services sufficiently commensurable and makes just exchange possible.

ing the relative contribution of different factors in the production of wealth, in order to allocate a just distribution of the wealth produced among the owners of these productive forces.[6]

One further point should be observed in passing. If the labor theory of value were true—that is, if labor and labor alone were the source of all value in economic goods and services—then labor would be entitled, in strict justice, to the whole of the wealth produced. According to this theory, labor, either in the form of living labor or, as Marx suggests, in the form of "congealed labor" (*i.e.,* the labor that is accumulated and congealed in machines), contributes everything to the production of wealth except what nature itself affords. Hence, everything produced would belong to labor as a matter of just requital.[7]

Hence if the labor theory of value were true and if a just distribution of wealth were to be based upon it, there would be no problem of how to divide the wealth produced as between the owners of property in capital and the owners of property in labor power. Marx might then be right in arguing that capital property in private hands should be expropriated, and in recommending that the State, having "expro-

[6] In a money economy, the unit of measurement of value is, of course, the unit of money employed.
[7] Twenty years before the *Communist Manifesto,* the Preamble of the Mechanics' Union of Trade Associations (Philadelphia, 1827) declared that labor was the source of all wealth, but instead of demanding all the wealth labor produced, they asked only for an equitable share of it, *i.e.,* that which could be "clearly demonstrated to be a fair and full equivalent" for the productive services they rendered. That they did not think of a "fair and full equivalent" as *all* the wealth they produced is indicated by the following passage: "We are prepared to maintain that all who toil have a natural and unalienable right to reap the fruits of their own industry; and that they who by labor (the only source) are the authors of every comfort, convenience, and luxury are in justice entitled to an *equal participation,* not only in the meanest and coarsest, but likewise the richest and choicest of them all" (italics added). Equal participation left something for the owners of capital who did not, under this theory, contribute anything to the production of wealth. Marx was more consistent and thorough. He carried the labor theory of value to its logical conclusion; namely, that any return whatsoever to owners of capital who do not themselves work is *unearned increment* on their part, obtained unjustly by the exploitation of labor.

priated the expropriators," should operate all capital instruments for the general welfare of the working masses, to whom all the wealth produced should then be distributed according to their individual needs.[8]

Since, as we maintain, the labor theory of value is false, and capital is a producer of wealth in the same sense that labor is, all the consequences drawn from the labor theory are wholly without foundation. We are therefore confronted by a problem to be solved—one which, so far as we know, has not yet been solved. That is the problem of achieving a just distribution of the wealth produced in an industrial society, while at the same time (1) preserving the prosperity of the economy, (2) securing economic welfare by a satisfactory general standard of living for all, and (3) maintaining the economic and political freedom of the individual members of the society.

To that problem we now turn.

THE PROBLEM OF JUSTICE AND WELFARE IN AN INDUSTRIAL ECONOMY

If the increasing productiveness of labor were the sole source of the increasing output of wealth per man-hour employed, labor could justly claim a larger and larger distributive share of the total wealth produced, by virtue of contributing more and more to its production. An objective evaluation of the services of labor through free competition among all relevant factors in production would automatically award ever increasing wages as a just return for the services of la-

---

[8] It should be pointed out that even if the labor theory of value were true, and even if it justified placing all capital instruments in the hands of the State so that the wealth produced by "congealed labor" could be shared by all living laborers, it would not provide a just principle of distribution, useful in solving the problem of what shares individual workers would be entitled to receive relative to one another. This explains why Lenin argued against any system of distribution that is based on the rights of workers—equal rights or unequal rights—instead of upon their needs. See his tract entitled *The State and Revolution,* Moscow, 1949: Ch. 5, especially Sects. 3 and 4.

bor. As the total wealth of the economy increased, the standard of living of those who worked for a living would rise.

But as we have already pointed out, the productiveness of submanagerial and subtechnical labor is a relatively diminishing quantity as the productiveness of the whole economy increases with the introduction of productive forces other than human labor. If a competitive evaluation of the contribution of labor were then to set wages at a level which labor could justly claim as a return for its services, labor's standard of living might dwindle to bare subsistence or even fall below it.

Hence in an economy in which the wealth produced is distributed in accordance with the one principle of justice we have so far considered, that principle of distributive justice might work against the welfare of the great mass of men who work for a living, whose only income-bearing property is their own labor power, and whose only income takes the form of wages.

Such conflict would not necessarily occur in a pre-industrial economy, in which human labor was the chief productive factor and in which each man had property in his own labor power (*i.e.,* no man being owned by another as a chattel slave). But the case of an industrial economy is exactly the opposite. As the machines of an industrial economy become more and more efficient in the production of wealth, the problem of the conflict between distributive justice and the welfare of workingmen becomes more and more aggravated.

Before we examine the problem further, let us be sure that the truth about the relatively diminishing productiveness of human labor is clearly seen. The comparison of two slave economies, one more and one less productive, will help us to compare pre-industrial with industrial economies, and less advanced with more advanced industrial economies. In each of these comparisons, the greater productiveness of one economy over the other will clearly be seen to result from productive factors other than mechanical labor.

Let us first consider the hypothetical case of a slave economy in which every man is either a master or a chattel slave. Let us further suppose that each slave owner participates in the production of wealth without any use of his own labor power, but only through the use of his capital property, including the slaves he owns. On this supposition, the total wealth produced would belong to the slave owners; and, other things being equal, more would go to a slave owner who used more land and slaves than to one who had less of such property to use in the production of wealth. Here we see a just distribution of wealth based on participation in production through the use of one's property, no part of which is one's own labor power.[9]

Now let us consider two slave economies, *Alpha* and *Beta,* and let us imagine them as differing in one respect and only one. The slave owners in *Alpha* own beasts of burden as well as human slaves, while the slave owners in *Beta* have slaves to use but no animals. All other productive factors are equal in the two economies, *i.e.,* both have the same natural resources, the same hand tools, and the same type of slaves (*i.e.,* the slaves in the two cases have equal strength and skill); and, in addition, the slaves who are household stewards and supervise the work of other slaves are equally diligent and efficient.

In which of the two economies is more total annual wealth likely to be produced—*Alpha* with beasts of burden, or *Beta* without them? The answer is *Alpha,* of course.

Since the reason for this answer is that *Alpha* involves a productive factor (animal power) not involved in *Beta,* it is perfectly clear that one economy can be more productive than another without that

[9] Questions about how the slave owner acquired the property he has at the beginning of a particular year may be relevant to other considerations, but not to the matter at hand. We are concerned here only with the total wealth produced in that particular year, at the start of which two slave owners differ in the productiveness of the capital they own. During that year, let us suppose that each employs his property to its fullest productive capacity, and neither contributes his own labor. At the end of that year, the man with the more highly productive capital employed is entitled to a larger share of the total wealth produced than the man with less productive capital involved, for his property has made a larger contribution toward its production.

greater production of wealth resulting from the greater productiveness of its human labor. And if that is clear, is it not equally clear, according to the principle of justice stated, that the distributive share to which labor would be justly entitled does not necessarily increase with every increase in the total productiveness of the economy?

Now, then, substitute machines for animals; and for slaves, substitute men with property in their own labor power. With these substitutions, let *Alpha* be an industrial economy and *Beta* a nonindustrial one. All other factors being equal, *Alpha* will annually produce more wealth than *Beta;* but the contribution of labor, as compared with all other forms of property, will be no greater in *Alpha* than in *Beta.*

The same relationships will hold if *Alpha* is an advanced industrial society with powerful and automatic machinery, and *Beta* is a relatively primitive industrial economy, with few machines and poor ones.

Hence we see that the greater productiveness of one economy as compared with another can be attributed to labor only if, all other productive factors being equal, one economy employs more man power than another, or if, with equal amounts of man power employed, there is some difference in its average skill or strength.

Where it cannot be attributed to mechanical labor, and where, in fact, such labor power makes a relatively diminishing contribution as compared with all capital instruments of production, men who participate in production only through the use of such labor power may be justly entitled to so small a share of the total wealth produced, and would receive on a competitive evaluation of their contribution so small a share, that it may become necessary for them to use the power of labor unions, supported by the countervailing power of government, in order to obtain a reasonable subsistence or, better, a decent standard of living.

Laboring men may thus get what they need, even if it is more than they have justly earned by their contribution to the production of the society's total wealth. And if they do get more than they have justly earned, the distributive share paid out to the owners of capital must necessarily be less than the productive use of their property has justly earned for them. When this occurs, the rights of private property in capital instruments have been invaded and eroded, just as much as the rights of private property in labor power are invaded and eroded whenever the owners of such productive property are forced to take less than a competitively determined wage.

We are, therefore, confronted with this critical problem. In an industrial economy such as ours, is it possible to order things so that (1) all families are in a position to earn what amounts to a decent standard of living, (2) by an organization of the economy which preserves and respects the rights of private property in capital instruments as well as in labor power, and which (3) distributes the wealth produced among those who contribute to its production in accordance with the principle of distributive justice stated above?

We know that Soviet Russia claims or hopes eventually to be able to give all its families a decent standard of living. But we also know that its economy is based on the abolition of private property in capital instruments, and that it violates the principle of distributive justice insofar as it gives to each according to his needs, not according to his deserts. State ownership of all capital instruments and the governmental distribution of wealth in a charitable fashion may be able to achieve human welfare so far as the general standard of living is concerned, but such concentration of economic and political power in the hands of the officials who manage and operate the machinery of the State cannot help infringing, thwarting, or destroying the freedom of all the rest.

We know that in the United States we have already accomplished what Soviet Russia eventually hopes it can do to provide a generally high standard of living. But we also know that the distribution of wealth in this country has largely been effected by the power of labor unions supported by the countervailing power of government, by redistributive taxation, and by government spending to promote full employment. While more than 90 percent of the wealth is produced by capital instruments, about 70 percent of the resulting income is distributed to labor. Hence while private property in capital instruments still exists nominally, property rights are attenuated or eroded by withholding from the owners of capital the share of the wealth produced that is proportionate to the contribution their property makes.

The economy of the United States, or what some of its enthusiastic exponents call our "welfare capitalism," is hardly a system based on property rights and distributive justice. We may have succeeded in meeting requirement (1) of the three *desiderata* stated on the preceding page, but only at the expense of sacrificing requirements (2) and (3).

Can the problem be solved? We think it can be, in spite of the fact that, in an advanced industrial economy, the contribution of mechanical labor to the production of wealth has diminished to the point where the return to which it is justly entitled and which it could obtain in a freely competitive market might well fall below mere subsistence, not to mention a decent standard of living.

With every future phase of technological progress, the discrepancy between (a) the contribution of labor to the production of wealth and (b) the income needed by workers to maintain a desirable standard of living must necessarily widen. But with every technological advance, the increasing productiveness of capital instruments also makes the solution of the problem more feasible.

That solution is based on full respect for property rights and on principles of economic justice which not only respect such property rights but also recognize that each man (or, more accurately, each household) has a natural human right to participate in the production of wealth through the ownership and application of productive property (either property in labor or in capital instruments or in both) to a degree sufficient to earn for that household a decent standard of living.

So far we have stated only one of the three principles of justice that constitute the solution of the problem. By itself, it is inadequate, as will be seen when we show why it needs to be supplemented by the other two.[10]

THE THREE RELEVANT PRINCIPLES OF JUSTICE

Justice, in its most general formulation, imposes the following moral duties or precepts upon men who are associated for the purposes of a common life: (1) to act for the common good of all, not each for his own private interest exclusively; (2) to avoid injuring one another; (3) to render to each man what is rightfully his due; and (4) to deal fairly with one another in the exchange of goods and in the distribution of wealth, position, status, rewards and punishments.

[10] An industrial economy faces another problem, which is neither one of justice nor of charity in the distribution of wealth. It is the problem of maintaining a level of consumption adequate to ever increasing levels of productiveness. If it fails to solve this problem, an industrial economy is prone to cycles of boom-and-bust in a mounting series of economic crises of the sort that Karl Marx predicted would bring about the eventual and inevitable collapse of capitalism. His prediction that capitalism will sow the seeds of its own destruction is based, of course, on his assumption that what he called the "capitalistic exploitation of labor" would persist in keeping wages at a bare subsistence level. Since the few who were capitalists could consume only a small portion of the goods an industrial society was able to produce; and since the laboring masses kept at a bare subsistence level did not have enough purchasing power to consume the residue, Marx argued that mounting crises of overproduction and underconsumption are inevitable. Only the widely diffused purchasing power that represents a generally higher standard of living can solve this problem. No plan for the organization of an industrial economy, no matter how just, has any practical significance unless it also solves this problem of the economy's self-preservation. Granting that, we are confronted with these alternatives: (1) Can an industrial economy be saved from self-destruction by adopting principles of economic justice, with full respect for all human rights, including those of private property in capital as well as in labor? Or (2) must it resort to principles of charity and welfare in order to effect a generally higher standard of living, and in doing so violate certain principles of justice by invading the rights of private property in capital (as in the United States) or by abolishing them entirely (as in Soviet Russia)? We think that the first alternative is not only possible, but that it is also morally and humanly better than the second, because by a just organization of the economy it preserves political liberty and gives men individual freedom as well as the economic welfare that is necessary, though not sufficient, for a good life. But it will take the capitalistic revolution we are advocating to bring this about.

The one principle of justice already stated in this chapter is a special application of the fourth precept to the distribution of shares in the wealth produced among those who have participated in its production. When, according to this principle, the distributive share rightfully due a participant in production is determined, the third precept becomes applicable, for it commands us to render unto a man whatever is his due.

As we pointed out, two more principles are needed to solve the problem stated in the preceding section. The second principle is a special application of the third precept alone for, quite apart from particular exchanges or distributions, it is concerned with the economic rights of individuals and with the obligation of society to see that every family gets its due in accordance with such rights. The third principle calls for whatever legislative regulation of economic activity may be needed to prevent some individuals from injuring others by pursuing their private interests in a way that violates the economic rights of others. It is a special application of the second precept of justice given above, and indirectly of the first as well.

As applicable to the production and distribution of wealth, these three principles of justice can be briefly stated in the following manner:

1. THE PRINCIPLE OF DISTRIBUTION
   Among those who participate in the production of wealth, each should receive a share that is proportionate to the value of the contribution each has made to the production of that wealth.

   (It will be seen that this is another way of saying that each participant in production is rightfully entitled to receive the wealth he produces. Where all exchanges, including those which are part of the process of production and distribution itself, are impartially evaluated through free competition, the share received by each participant, paid in money, is the equivalent in value of the contribution he has made.)

2. THE PRINCIPLE OF PARTICIPATION

Every man has a natural right to life, in consequence whereof he has the right to maintain and preserve his life by all rightful means, including the right to obtain his subsistence by producing wealth or by participating in the production of it.

(It will be seen that this is another way of saying that everyone has a right to earn a living by participating in the production of wealth. Since a man who is not a slave can participate in the production of wealth only through the use of his own productive property, *i.e.,* his own labor power or capital, the right to earn a living is a right to property in the means of production. The principle of participation, therefore, says that every man or, more exactly, every household or consumer unit must own property in the means of production *capable,* if employed with reasonable diligence, of earning by its contribution to the production of wealth a distributive share that is equivalent to a viable income.)

3. THE PRINCIPLE OF LIMITATION

Since everyone has a right to property in the means of production sufficient for earning a living, no one has a right to so extensive an ownership of the means of production that it excludes others from the opportunity to participate in production to an extent capable of earning for themselves a viable income; and, consequently, the ownership of productive property by an individual or household must not be allowed to increase to the point where it can injure others by excluding them from the opportunity to earn a viable income.

(It will be seen that this is another way of saying, first, that chattel slavery is unjust, for it makes men propertyless and thus deprives them of their natural right to earn a living by their ownership of any means of production; and, second, that, in an economy in which the private ownership of capital as well as labor is the basis of an effective participation in the production of wealth, injustice is done when the ownership of capital is so highly concentrated in the hands of some men or households that others are excluded from even that minimum degree of participation in production which would enable them justly to earn a viable income for themselves.)

If the meaning of these three principles is clear; if the relation of the second to the first and of the third to the second is also clear; if their special significance for an industrial as opposed to a nonindustrial economy is seen; and if it is understood how the operation of these three principles would solve the problem stated in the preceding section, the reader does not need the amplification which follows in the remainder of this chapter. It is offered to provide a commentary that may be needed. It sets forth, in the light of the foregoing principles, the conditions requisite for the just organization of any economy, and especially of a capitalist economy.

THE ORGANIZATION OF A JUST ECONOMY

To show how the first principle is supplemented by the second, and the second by the third, we will discuss the three principles in the order named.

(1) *The Principle of Distribution.*   While the fourth precept in the general formulation of justice is almost exclusively concerned with economic transactions so far as exchanges are concerned, it has both political and economic application with regard to distributions.

Exchangeable goods are largely economic goods—commodities and services which have exchange value. Here the rule of justice is the simple rule of equality: that in the exchange of heterogeneous goods, the things exchanged should be of equivalent value. On the other hand, as the fourth precept indicates, wealth is not the only thing that is subject to distribution among men.

Political status and position can be justly or unjustly distributed. The rule of justice here is that equals should be treated equally, and unequals unequally in proportion to their inequality. The application of this rule depends on the ascertainment of the facts of equality and inequality.

The fact that all men are by nature equal makes the democratic distribution of citizenship—universal and equal suffrage—just.[11] From this fact it also follows that all oligarchical restrictions of citizenship and suffrage are unjust for, in restricting this fundamental political status, to which all men are entitled, oligarchies treat equals unequally.

The other fact, that men are individually different and unequal in their innate talents and acquired virtues, calls for an unequal distribution of political offices or functions. Some men by their individual merits are better qualified than others to perform the special functions of government above the basic plane of political participation on which all men are equally entitled to operate as citizens. To the extent that a democracy selects men for its hierarchy of public offices or functions according to their merit, it distributes these posts justly; for it thereby treats unequals unequally and proportionately, placing men of greater ability in positions of greater responsibility. What we have called a "rotating aristocracy of leaders" is as essential to the political justice of a democracy as is the institution of equal suffrage for all men.

The foregoing brief statement of the principle of distributive justice, as applied to the basic political status of citizenship and the hierarchy of public offices, prepares us for the statement of an analogous application of the principle to the distribution of wealth among the households of a community.

Considering *only* those who are engaged in the production of wealth, and relying on free and workable competition as the only way to ascertain the facts about the equal or unequal value of the contributions made by each of a number of independent participants in production, distributive justice is done if the share (whether in the form of wages, dividends, rents, etc.) received by each participant in production is proportionate to the value of his contribution to production.

[11] The assertion that all men are by nature equal means that all are alike in their natural possession of the dignity of being human and, as persons, of having the natural endowments of reason and freedom which confer on all the capacity for active participation in political life.

Concretely stated, this means that if A, B, C and D are four persons or families in a society having only four independent participants in the production of wealth; and if, through the use of the productive property they own, A, B and C contribute to the total wealth produced in the ratio 3, 2, 1, then the distributive shares they should receive, according to their just deserts, should also be in the ratio of 3, 2, 1. And if the contribution of D, the fourth member, is equal to that of A, B or C, his distributive share should in justice be equal to that of A, B or C.

We can now explain why this principle is by itself inadequate to solve our problem or to set up a just economy.

As stated, the principle does not take account of every man's natural economic right to share in the distribution of wealth as a result of participating in its production. It looks only at the actual facts of participation without questioning whether the existing state of affairs is just in other respects, *i.e.,* whether it provides every household with the opportunity to participate in production to an extent capable of earning thereby a viable income.

Thus, for example, the principle of distributive justice might be operative in a pre-industrial slave economy even though that economy were unjust in other respects. It would be unjust insofar as it deprived the men whom it enslaved of their natural right to earn a living and, consequently, of their right to life itself. It would also be unjust insofar as the concentrated ownership of labor power by a small class of slave owners prevented other men who were not slaves from earning by their own labor a viable income for themselves or families. Nevertheless, under such unjust conditions, distributive justice would still be done if the slave owners, who were also the major landowners and owners of hand tools and beasts of burden, received the major share of the wealth produced because the major portion of that wealth had been produced by their property, *i.e.,* the means of production (land, tools, labor, etc.) which they owned.

Before we turn to the second and third principles of justice—the principles of participation and limitation—it is necessary to remind the reader of something said at the end of Chapter Four; namely, that these three principles of justice apply only to primary distribution, and not at all to secondary distributions, for it is only the primary distribution of wealth that directly results from participation in its production. It is also necessary to deal with a problem which may have arisen in the reader's mind with respect to the principle of distribution that we have been considering. Facing this problem here may not only prevent certain misunderstandings of that principle, but may also contribute to the understanding of the other two principles which are still to be discussed.

The problem to be faced arises from the consideration of those aspects of human society which contribute to the production of wealth where such contributions are not paid for. The most obvious of these things, especially from the point of view of an industrial society, is accumulated scientific knowledge together with the dissemination of it through the educational system. But other things can also be mentioned, such as good public roads, an efficient postal system, adequate care of public health, and other services of government which protect or facilitate productive activity.

If certain factors enter into the production of wealth for which no one is paid because these factors do not represent private property for the productive use of which anyone can justly claim a return out of the primary distribution of the wealth produced, then how can it be said that each participant in production receives a distributive share that is proportionate to the competitively determined value of his contribution? Is there not a leak here?

If in the primary distribution of the total wealth produced, that total is divided among those alone who, by their labor or capital, have participated in its production, do they not inevitably receive some portion of the wealth that unpaid-for factors have contributed to producing? And do not these unpaid-for contributions especially benefit the owners of capital instruments which embody scientific discoveries or inventions that have not been protected by copyrights or patents or upon which the statutory copyright or patent protection has lapsed? Does not the income they receive for the contribution made to production by such capital instruments contain and conceal an "unearned increment"—a payment to them for something they did not contribute? If it does, then there is something wrong or inadequate in our principle of distributive justice which asserts that the distributive shares should in every case be proportioned to the value of the contribution made by those who actually participate in production through their ownership of currently active productive property, whether capital or labor or currently furnished raw materials.

We contend that the principle of distributive justice as stated is neither wrong nor inadequate. To begin with, this can be clearly shown with regard to the contribution that scientific discoveries and inventions make to the inherent productiveness of a technologically advanced industrial society. What can be said on that score applies to all the other unpaid-for factors that have been mentioned as grounds for questioning the justice of the distributive principle which should be operative in the primary distribution of wealth in a free society.

It is true that the construction and use of capital instruments and related techniques of production do involve the appropriation, from mankind's funded knowledge, of ideas without which we would still be obtaining our subsistence in the most primitive manner. It should be noted, in the first place, that the ideas thus appropriated come from knowledge that is the achievement of the human race as a whole, not just our own society; and noted, in the second place, that even where some specific new discovery or invention has been recently made within our own society, and is then technologically applied to the production of wealth, that recent discovery or invention invariably involves the appropriation and use of innumerable "old ideas" or elements of applicable knowledge that have been in mankind's possession for centuries, *e.g.,* the wheel.

The present inventor of an electronic control instrument which would eliminate the human control of some widely used productive machinery may contribute something quite novel. It may even be patentable under existing patent laws which, if the inventor takes advantage of them, would give him for a limited length of time a right (*i.e.*, a property right) to charge a royalty for the use of his invention; after which time, the idea becomes "public domain" and can be appropriated by anyone without payment of royalty to the inventor or his heirs. But this new invention, even if it is capable of being patented, depends of necessity upon the contributions of thousands of scientists, mathematicians, discoverers and inventors in the past.

Readily granting the importance and propriety of laws that encourage inventors by enabling them to obtain, for a limited time, a property right in their contribution to production, there can be no question that all the technologically applicable knowledge that lies back of inventions, which can be protected by patent laws, properly belongs, upon the expiration of statutory patent rights and copyrights, in the public domain. It is the common inheritance of all men simply because they are men; *and precisely because it is common, all have an equal right to use it just as all have an equal opportunity to add to it.*

The equal right of every man to appropriate and use knowledge that belongs to all men in common certainly does not entitle those who make no use of such knowledge to share equally in the wealth produced by those who take advantage of their right to use it by putting it to work in a productive instrument or process. Yet that is the only distributive effect which could follow from supposing that, since the knowledge is the common possession of all, all should stand to profit equally from its use.

To recognize that injustice would be done by thus treating equally those who, with respect to knowledge in the public domain, have not made an equal effort to use it productively is to see that the principle of distributive justice, *as stated,* is neither wrong nor inadequate, even when we take into account the contribution to production that is made by the technologically applicable knowledge that is the common possession of mankind.

The equality of men with regard to useful knowledge is an equal right to the opportunity to master it, use it, and take advantage of it. Men who use the common knowledge that spoiled food may be poisonous do not share the illness of those who remain ignorant or fail to apply such knowledge. It is said that one of the great technological feats of mankind was the domestication of animals. Once that was achieved, did the men who had the opportunity to take advantage of it, but did nothing about it, have a just claim for sharing equally with those who captured and domesticated animals for use as instruments of production?

Society and the State may well have a duty to all men to afford them an equal opportunity to make use of the funded common knowledge of mankind. A system of universal, free public schooling goes a long way toward creating such equal opportunity for all. The existence of free public libraries is another step in the same direction. But Society and the State cannot have a moral responsibility to see that those who take advantage of such opportunities to acquire knowledge which they then subsequently put to use in the production of wealth should share in the proceeds of production on an equal basis with those who, having the same opportunities, make no use of them. That would not be justice but rank injustice.

The production of wealth is a current activity for a current result. If a man produces something by his labor and sells the product in a free market, he has currently received the return for his efforts and has no further claim on any return from the use that is later made of the thing he has sold. If, subsequently, the purchaser makes a productive use of it, then it is the purchaser of the thing, not the original producer of it, to whom the current return must be made.[12] He acquired

[12] Of course, specific contractual arrangements, such as provisions for royalty payments on tools embodying patented inventions, may be the basis of a duty of an otherwise outright owner to pay for using his property in production.

property rights in it, and so long as these are vested in him, he has sole right to claim a distributive return for contributions to production made by the employment of his productive property, even as, at an earlier moment, the original producer of the thing in question had sole right to claim a distributive return for the use of his labor power in producing it.

Hence those who take advantage of the common knowledge of mankind and use it in the production of wealth by capital instruments that incorporate such knowledge, as well as those who acquire by legal means property rights in capital instruments of this sort, have no obligation whatsoever to share their current returns from the economic productivity of their capital property even with those who made the discoveries therein incorporated (assuming they could be identified), except to the extent provided by patent laws or by specific contractual arrangements between those who made the discoveries or inventions and others who wish to make use of them.

There is even less of an obligation on the part of those who own capital instruments that incorporate elements from the funded common knowledge of mankind (which all capital instruments do) to share with all members of society all or even some portion of the wealth produced by these instruments. Justice is done if the benefit that each participant in production derives from the funded common knowledge of mankind depends on the specific use he makes of that knowledge in the current production of wealth. Those who currently contribute to the fund of man's technologically applicable knowledge can derive a current benefit from their contribution to whatever extent they can take advantage of the existing patent laws or enter into special contracts of advantage to themselves.

What has been said on the subject of useful knowledge holds for other aspects of man's social life which contribute to the production of wealth, but which are in the public domain and which, therefore, all men are equally entitled to use to their advantage. Those who do are then entitled to derive a benefit corresponding to the productive use they have made of the factor in question. But in the case of the economically useful services of government another consideration enters. Such services, *e.g.,* road building and maintenance, postal service, etc., which promote the production of wealth, are among the functions of government the costs of which are paid for by taxation.

Under an equitable system of taxation, all members of society contribute to defray the costs of government. All are equally entitled to take advantage of those services performed by government which are helpful to anyone engaged in producing wealth. Hence, here as before, there is no ground for maintaining that those who make use of this right are not entitled to the benefit derived from the use they have made. To think otherwise is either (a) to assert that all who pay taxes should share equally in the economic benefits derived from the services of government, regardless of whether they take advantage of them in the production of wealth, or (b) to admit that the availability of such useful services in the production of wealth can have no definite effect on its distribution.

(2) *The Principle of Participation.* In the fourfold formulation of the general meaning of justice with which we began, the third precept called for rendering to each man what is his due by right. When it is declared that life, liberty, and the pursuit of happiness are among man's natural and inalienable rights, criteria are laid down by which to measure the justice of the political and economic institutions of a society.

A just society is one which, by its constitutions, laws and arrangements, recognizes and protects all of man's natural rights; and to the extent that society violates one or more of these, it is unjust in its organization. Some of these rights belong to man as a human being, *e.g.,* the rights of life, liberty and the pursuit of happiness; some belong to man as a civic person or member of the political community, *e.g.,* the right to suffrage, the right of association, the right to form political parties; and some belong to man as an economic person or member of the economy, *e.g.*, the rights of man as an owner of property and as a producer or consumer of wealth.[13]

We are here concerned with man's economic rights. Among these, two are of paramount importance for the just organization of an economy.

One is man's right to property in his own labor power. As we have seen, the injustice of chattel slavery or forced labor consists in the violation of this right. But while an economy which has abolished chattel slavery or forced labor grants all men the right to be independent participants in the production of wealth through the use of their own labor power, that by itself is not enough in any economy in which men who wish to *earn* a living by the use of their property are unable to do so.

We are thus brought to the consideration of a second basic right, which is complementary to man's right to produce the wealth he needs, or, what is the same thing, to share in the distribution of wealth as a result of earning his share.

This second right derives immediately from the most fundamental among all of man's natural rights—his right to life or existence. The right to life involves more than a right not to be murdered or maimed. Since a man cannot live for long without having the means of subsistence, the right to life is meaningless unless it involves a right to acquire subsistence by rightful means.

This right has sometimes been referred to as the "right to a living wage." [14] As that phrase indicates, it is a right to *earn* a living, not to receive it as a gift or to obtain it by theft. To say that it is a right to *earned* income is, therefore, to say that the share of wealth received must be proportioned to the contribution made.

The chattel slave may be given subsistence; but since he is deprived of all property—property in his life and liberty as well as labor power

[13] For an enumeration and classification of natural rights, see Jacques Maritain, *The Rights of Man and Natural Law*, New York, 1951: Ch. II, esp. pp. 73–114.
[14] See Msgr. John A. Ryan, *A Living Wage: Its Ethical and Economic Aspects*, New York, 1906.

—he has, under these unjust conditions, no way of earning his living. A man who cannot find employment may be kept alive by private charity or by the public dole; but he, too, is unable to earn a living so long as he is unable to use the only property he has, his labor power, to participate in the production of wealth and thereby have a just claim upon a share in its distribution.

Thus we see that there are two conditions under which a man's life may be preserved and yet his right to subsistence denied, *i.e.,* his right to obtain a living through the use of his own property. One is the condition of slavery, in which a man lacks any property through which he can participate in the production of wealth. The other is the condition of those who have productive property but whose property, under the prevailing economic circumstances, is rendered ineffective as a means of obtaining a viable income.

We are, therefore, required by justice to do more than abolish chattel slavery. We are required to organize the economy in such a way that every man or family can use his or its property to participate in the production of wealth in a way that earns a living for that man or family.

This principle of justice, which is based on the right of every man or family to obtain a viable income by *earning* it, is integrally connected with the principle of distributive justice already stated. The latter declares the right of every independent participant in the production of wealth to receive a share of that wealth proportionate to his contribution. It indicates that a man's right to an earned income is a conditional right; for it imposes upon him the duty to contribute by the use of his property to the production of wealth. Unless he does so, he cannot rightfully claim a share.

Unless a man exercises his right to earn a living by actual participation in production, he is not entitled to any distributive share. But the right to earn a living by participating in the production of wealth would be a wholly illusory right if the only means by which it could be exercised were in fact incapable of producing wealth or of making a large enough contribution toward its production to earn a viable distributive share. Hence the principle of distributive justice does not operate to guarantee the right to earn a living unless the economy is so organized that every man or family has or can readily obtain property which can be effectively used to participate in the production of wealth to an extent that justifies the claim to a share which constitutes a viable income for that man or family.[15]

When, relative to the increasing productive power of capital instruments, labor as a whole makes a progressively diminishing contribution to the production of wealth, the full employment of those whose only property is such labor power, even if that is accompanied by a just distribution to them of what they earn through the contribution they make, would not provide such men and their families with a viable income.

Hence in an industrial economy, and especially in one that is technologically advanced, the right to obtain subsistence by earning it involves more than the right to work and the right to a just return for work done. It involves the right to participate effectively in the production of wealth by means consistent with the existing state of technology and with the greatest technological advances of which the economy is capable.

As labor becomes less and less productive of wealth, the ownership of nothing but labor power becomes less and less adequate to satisfy

[15] In any society, there cannot help being marginal cases of economic failure or economic incompetence. After justice has been done, private or public charity always remains as the remedy for those who are in dire need through no moral fault of their own. In the organization of the economy, justice takes precedence over charity. Only after every step has been taken to see that justice is done, and only after every rightful claim is requited, should charity become operative in response to those pressing human needs which even the most just organization of the production and distribution of wealth may fail to provide for. On this point, see W. Stark's essay *The Contained Economy* (Blackfriars Publications, London, 1956: Aquinas Paper No. 26). Stark points out that "however desirable a spirit of charity may be in social life, society can yet survive without it. But justice is not just an embellishment of human co-existence, it is the very basis of it, an indispensable precondition." Declaring that "a sin against justice is an attack on the social bond itself," Stark maintains that "a sin against justice is a very much more serious affair than a sin against charity" (*op. cit.,* p. 18).

the principle of participation, on condition, of course, that the share of wealth labor receives is equivalent to the value of its contribution as competitively determined. When, for example, the state of automated production reaches a point where, at current levels of consumer demand (free from artificial stimulants designed to create "full employment"), the demand for labor is substantially less than the number of those whose only means of participating in production is through their labor, then for a large number of men the mere ownership of labor power may give them insufficient income-earning property to satisfy the second principle of justice. *When the great bulk of the wealth is produced by capital instruments, the principle of participation requires that a large number of households participate in production through the ownership of such instruments.*

To assert that every man has a right to obtain his living by earning it is not, therefore, the same as asserting everyone's right to a living wage. Under pre-industrial conditions, it might have been possible for those who had no property except their own labor power to have earned a living wage if their contribution to the production of wealth had been justly requited. But in an advanced industrial economy, in which most of the wealth is produced by capital and in which the ownership of capital is concentrated so that all but a few households are entirely dependent upon their ownership of labor for participation in production, it is apparent that labor—at least mechanical labor—would not earn a living wage if the contribution it makes, relative to that made by capital instruments, were justly requited; that is, if instead of being overpaid, the value of its services were objectively and impartially evaluated under conditions of free competition.

To contend that, under all conditions, men are justly entitled to a living wage is, therefore, equivalent to saying that men have a right to the continuance of the conditions under which wealth is produced primarily by labor. There is, of course, no such right; nor would men wish to see it implemented or enforced if there were. To speak of the right to a living wage is, therefore, an inaccurate statement of the right to earn a viable income by effective participation in the production of wealth. The principle of participation entails a right to produce wealth in a manner consistent with the way wealth is in fact being produced, taking full advantage of the existing state of technology.

In an industrial economy, there are two basic ways in which a man or a household may participate in the production of wealth to an extent sufficient to earn thereby a viable income. One is through the productive employment of one's own labor power. The other is through the productive employment of the capital instruments in which one has property (normally represented by shares of capital stock, but capable of being represented by other forms of securities or by partnerships or other proprietary interests). A household may also participate in production through combinations of these two means.

In all three cases, the income is *earned* income, for it is earned by the productive use of one's private property, whether that is property in capital instruments or property in labor power.

The right to earn a viable income is thus seen as the right of every man or family to own property which, under the prevailing system of producing wealth, is capable of enabling its owner to contribute to the production of wealth to an extent that justly entitles him to receive in return an earned income to support a decent standard of living.

(3) *The Principle of Limitation.* This third principle is implied by the first and second, *i.e.,* the principles of distribution and participation.

Capital instruments are productive of wealth in exactly the same sense that labor power is productive of wealth. In the absence of chattel slavery, the ownership of labor cannot be concentrated; on the contrary, it is completely diffused, each free man having proprietorship in his own labor. But it is possible for the ownership of capital to become highly concentrated. Such concentration is capable of reaching the point at which some men or households are either totally excluded from participation in production or excluded from participating to an extent sufficient to earn them a viable income or, as we sometimes say, a decent standard of living. It is at this point that the principle of limitation must become operative to prevent such concentrations of capital ownership as are injurious to the economic rights of others, *i.e.,* their right of effective participation in production and to earn thereby a viable income in the form of the distributive share to which they are justly entitled by the value of their contribution.

This principle of limitation has significance only for an economy based on the institution of private property in the means of production and on the joint participation of a number of independent contributors to the production of wealth. If the size of the distributive share an individual receives bears no relation to the value of the contribution he makes; if, in other words, the principle of distribution is "from each according to his ability, and to each according to his needs," then the principle of limitation is without significance. On the contrary, if the distribution of wealth is based on a principle of charity divorced from property rights, instead of on a principle of justice in acknowledgment of property rights, then the distribution of wealth may be more effectively accomplished through the greatest possible concentration of capital ownership, *e.g.,* its total ownership by the State.

As the methods by which an economy produces its wealth call for proportionately more capital and less labor, the opportunities to participate in the production of wealth increasingly rest on individual ownership of capital and decreasingly on individual ownership of labor. The concentration of capital ownership—a wholly normal process where the inherent productiveness of one factor is constantly increasing in relation to that of the other—will tend at some point to become a monopolization of the principal means of production by some members of the economy. When this happens, others will be excluded from opportunities to which they have a natural right.

To whatever extent the concentrated ownership of a society's capital stock excludes any portion of its members from effective participation in the production of wealth (*i.e.,* effective in the sense of earning a viable income through the productive employment of their own property), such concentrated ownership is intrinsically unjust. It not only violates the common good but also does direct injury to those individuals who are deprived of their natural right to earn a viable income under a system of production in which it is impossible for them to earn a living wage by forms of labor whose contribution, competitively evaluated, would not justly entitle them to a decent standard of living for themselves or their families.

Accordingly, the concentration of ownership in the hands of some men or families must not be allowed to go beyond the point where, under a just system of distribution, it would prevent other men or families from earning a viable income by participating effectively in production. When the preponderant portion of the wealth is produced by capital, participation in the production of wealth must be preponderantly through the ownership of capital—a requirement which at some point, to be empirically determined, imposes a limit upon concentration in the ownership of capital.[16]

It is not our purpose here to anticipate the legislative deliberations which must precede the determination of the point at which, under given technological conditions and for any given general standard of living, the concentrated ownership of capital becomes destructive of the opportunities of others to participate effectively in the production of wealth. In the second part of this book, devoted to outlining a practical program for accomplishing the capitalist revolution, we will suggest what we believe to be a number of feasible ways of making the principle of limitation operative.[17] Suffice it to say here that *the principles of distribution and participation cannot be observed in the*

---

[16] It should be noted that the principle of limitation calls for no upper limit to the private ownership of nonproductive property, *i.e.,* consumer goods.
[17] This is done in Chapter Thirteen.

absence of laws designed to make the principle of limitation effective.

The liberty of each man to pursue his private interests, so far as this can be done without injury to others or to the common good, would not be infringed by legislation preventing individual accumulations of capital from exceeding the amount at which they tend to prevent others from effectively participating in the production of wealth by their ownership of capital. If any line can be drawn between liberty and license, it is certainly at the point at which one individual seeks to do as he pleases even though he thereby invades the rights and liberties of other men. In his essay *On Liberty,* John Stuart Mill circumscribed the sphere of actions in which the individual is justly entitled to be free from interference or regulation on the part of society or government, by excluding from that sphere actions which injure others or work against the public interest.[18]

In Mill's terms, the principle of limitation we are here discussing calls for a justifiable limitation on individual liberty to acquire wealth in the form of capital goods. It limits such liberty by a just concern for the rights of others. It simply says, to paraphrase Mill, that no man's ownership of the most productive form of property in an industrial economy should be so extensive as to exclude others from an economically significant participation in the production of wealth, or as to reduce their participation below that minimum level where their competitively evaluated distributive share is a viable income for themselves or their families.

---

[18] "The object of this Essay," he declared, "is to assert one very simple principle, as entitled to govern absolutely the dealings of society with the individual in the way of compulsion and control. . . . That principle is, that the sole end for which mankind are warranted, individually or collectively, in interfering with the liberty of action of any of their number, is self-protection. That the only purpose for which power can be rightfully exercised over any member of a civilized community, against his will, is to prevent harm to others. . . . The only part of the conduct of anyone, for which he is amenable to society, is that which concerns others" (*op. cit.,* Ch. I). And in Chapter V he reiterated that "for such actions as are prejudicial to the interests of others, the individual is accountable, and may be subjected either to social or legal punishment, if society is of opinion that the one or the other is requisite for its protection."

In a democratic polity, political freedom and justice are as widely diffused as citizenship. If one wishes freedom and justice, the thing to be in a democracy is a citizen. As one cannot now effectively participate in democratic self-government without suffrage, so in the fully mature industrialism of the future it may be impossible to participate effectively in the industrial production of wealth without owning capital.

It should not come as a surprise, therefore, that in a truly capitalist economy, economic freedom and justice will be as widely diffused as the ownership of capital. The thing to be in a capitalist democracy is a citizen-capitalist.

6 ECONOMIC HISTORY: THE CLASSIFICATION OF ECONOMIES

FIRST STAGE: FROM THE BEGINNING TO THE NINETEENTH CENTURY

Until the emergence of industrial production in the nineteenth century, all the economies of the past were *laborist* economies. Many were in fact slave economies, because a large portion of the human labor used to produce wealth was drawn from men who were owned as chattels. But a laborist economy need not be a slave economy. In fact, the primitive form of the laborist economy involved no slaves at all. It was only in its civilized form that slavery was introduced and became indispensable to the development of civilization.

We define an economy as *laborist* if labor (*i.e.,* human productive power and skill) is the chief force in the production of wealth, and is either the sole form or the principal form of productive property entitling its owners to shares in the distribution of the wealth produced.

The primitive laborist economy was that of the isolated family or the small village or tribe, in which there was some division of labor among the members of the group, in which each family owned its own labor power, its tools and its animals, in which land was usually common rather than appropriated, and in which few were hirelings, *i.e.,* dependent for their subsistence on payments made by others.

In some primitive laborist economies, including some that exist today, the distribution of the total wealth produced was and is accomplished by gift and apportioned to need rather than determined by right and apportioned to earning. In such cases, the institutions of the market and competitive evaluation by demand were and are also absent.[1]

However, where in a primitive laborist economy the distribution was by right rather than by gift (as, for example, in isolated colonies or frontier settlements), that distribution was also *laboristic* in form. It could hardly have been otherwise if it tended to approximate a just distribution; for in an economy where labor is the chief productive force, the distributive shares of the wealth produced, to be justly apportioned, must be largely determined by the different amounts of labor—both power and skill—whereby men contribute to the production of wealth.

In certain primitive laborist economies—again the frontier settlement affords a good example—the ownership of productive property was widely diffused. Each man or family owned his or its own labor power, tools, and animals. An almost universal diffusion of this sort will not be achieved again until the capitalist revolution is fully accomplished; for in most of the civilized forms of the laborist economy, certainly in all that were built on slave labor, there was highly concentrated ownership of labor as the chief form of productive property; as, in the first hundred and fifty years of the capitalist economy, there

[1] On this point, see Karl Polanyi, *The Great Transformation,* New York, 1944: Ch. 4.

was and still is highly concentrated ownership of capital as the chief form of productive property.[2]

What has just been said calls attention to the critical difference between the primitive and civilized forms of a laborist economy. The latter form usually involves chattel slavery or feudal serfdom. Hence it concentrates in the hands of the slave owners or feudal lords the ownership or control of the chief form of productive property, *i.e.,* human labor or skill.

The civilized form of the laborist economy arose with the emergence of cities and with a division of society into a leisure class of free men and a working class of chattel slaves, mechanics, and artisans. The slave owners, or feudal lords, were also the landowners and the owners of the tools, animals, raw materials, etc. Hence the ownership of almost all productive property was concentrated in the hands of the few and with that, of course, went a great concentration of political power. The leisure class was the ruling class. The working masses were without political status, rights, and liberties; and, except for bloody uprisings, such as the Peasants' Revolt at the time of the Reformation, they had no way of exerting any political power.[3]

In the civilized form of the laborist economy, there was not only a division of labor in the sphere of subsistence work, but, what is more important, there was also a sharp division of human activity itself into subsistence work and leisure work. While slaves and toilers produced the wealth on which the whole society subsisted and prospered, the propertied men of leisure, at least those who were virtuous as well as free, produced the goods of civilization. It was generally thought that

[2] It reaches the absolute limit of concentration in Soviet Russia where the State owns all capital instruments and so is the only capitalist. It was slightly less concentrated in the "*laissez-faire* capitalism" of England and the United States in the nineteenth century. It is still less concentrated in the "welfare capitalism" of England and the United States today.
[3] The "Bloodless Rebellion" in England in 1688 and the French Revolution a century later were uprisings of the new merchant class against the feudal aristocracy of king and court. The condition of the working masses remained unchanged by this change in the character of their masters.

slavery, serfdom, or their equivalents in submerged human labor, were necessary for the emancipation of the few to do the work of civilization.

SECOND STAGE: FROM 1800 TO THE PRESENT DAY

We defined a *laborist* economy as one in which human labor is the sole or chief productive force, entitling the owners of labor (their own or that of chattel slaves) to shares in the distribution of the wealth produced.

With the invention and improvement of power-driven machines, labor began to lose its place as the chief form of productive property. As society passed from handicraft production to machine production and from nonmechanized to mechanized agriculture and mining, labor progressively contributed less and less to the wealth produced; capital instruments, more and more. As the efficiency of the machines increased, the burden of production gradually shifted from men to machines. With that change, capital replaced labor as the principal form of productive property.

When labor is the chief productive force in the economy, it must be combined, of course, with other productive factors, such as natural resources and hand tools. Similarly, when machines constitute the chief productive force, they must also be combined with other productive factors, such as natural resources and labor. The main difference between a nonmechanized system of production and an industrial system, therefore, lies in the substitution of machinery for labor as the principal form of productive property.

As we have already seen, capital consists of property in all the means of producing wealth except one, *i.e.,* labor. Hence, by the substitution of machinery for labor as the principal form of productive property, we pass from a *laborist* to a *capitalist* economy.

The distinctive character of a capitalist economy is thus indicated.

It can be defined as an economy in which capital instruments are the chief productive force and, together with natural resources, constitute the principal form of productive property entitling its owners to shares in the distribution of the wealth produced.

THE CLASSIFICATION OF ECONOMIES

All economies are either economies in which labor is the chief productive force and the principal form of productive property, or they are economies in which capital rather than labor occupies that place. The primary division among all economies is thus based on mode of production. By this criterion, all economies are either laborist or capitalist.

Subordinately, economies which are either laborist or capitalist in mode of production can be further divided by reference to mode of ownership and form of distribution. We have already made such subdivisions among the laborist economies of the past.

We have seen that the ownership of labor power was either (a) universally diffused, as in primitive laborist economies in which slavery did not exist, or (b) relatively concentrated, as in civilized laborist economies in which large amounts of human labor were owned by a small slave-owning class. We have also seen that the form of distribution was either (a) by right, *i.e.,* based on amount of contribution to production, or (b) by gift, *i.e.,* based on needs rather than on rights.

In those cases in which all, or a major portion, of the wealth produced is distributed among those who by their labor produced it, we call the form of the distribution "laboristic." The principle of such distribution may be either justice or charity depending on whether it is based on rights or needs. Labor receives what labor earns when shares of the wealth produced are apportioned among those who produce it by a competitive evaluation of the contributions workers make to its production.

The slave economies present us with what at first appears to be an anomalous case. They were laborist in mode of production, but they were not laboristic in mode of distribution, inasmuch as the major portion of the wealth produced went to the slave owners who were also owners of land, tools, and animals. If we can call the slave owners "capitalists," even though labor was the principal form of productive property that they owned, we can describe the form of distribution as "capitalistic," thereby signifying that the major portion of the wealth produced was distributed to those who earned it, not by their own labor power but by the use of other instruments of production which they owned.

So far the terms we have used to describe the various forms of the laborist economy are purely descriptive. They describe the way in which the wealth of a society is produced, the way in which its principal productive property is owned, and the way in which the wealth produced is distributed. *But when we pass from the form of distribution to the principle of distribution, we cannot avoid questions of justice.* Thus, for example, we have seen that, in an economy that is laborist as to mode of production, either justice or charity (*i.e.,* either rights or needs) may be the principle of a distribution that is laboristic in form.

We are also confronted with the anomalous case of the slave economies that are laborist as to mode of production but are "capitalistic" rather than "laboristic" in the form of their distribution. The basic fact that slavery is intrinsically unjust, because it violates each man's natural right to property in his own labor power, underlies the anomalous character of the slave economies. It explains how they can be capitalistic in form of distribution, even though they are laborist as to mode of production. Wherever we find such discrepancy between the mode of production and the form of distribution, we have good reason to suspect that the economy is not organized in accordance with all three of the relevant principles of economic justice—the principles of distribution, participation and limitation.[4]

Nevertheless, if we judge the slave economies in terms of only one of these principles, *i.e.,* the principle of apportioning distributive shares on the basis of contributive shares, then the capitalistic form of distribution in a slave economy did observe one principle of justice while violating the other two. This amounts to saying that if we do not question the highly concentrated ownership of human labor (which violated the principles of participation and limitation), then slave owners, in receiving the major portion of the society's wealth, received what the productive use of their property earned for them.

THE FORMS OF CAPITALISM

With these criteria of classification clear, we turn to economies that are capitalist in mode of production, in order to classify them further by reference to (1) mode of ownership, (2) form of distribution, and (3) principle of distribution. We will try to present a purely descriptive classification first; but while a description of the forms of capitalism can be separated from questions of justice and liberty, the human significance of the forms described cannot be judged except in the light of such questions.[5]

What follows, then, is a classification of economies that are all forms of capitalism in the basic descriptive sense of that term. In our judgment, the primary division of economies should be made by

---

[4] In fact, it can be stated as a general rule that the more closely the form of distribution matches the mode of production, the more nearly an economy approaches justice in distribution. A capitalistic form of distribution in a laborist economy (*e.g.,* ancient slave economies) is unjust; and similarly, a laboristic form of distribution in a capitalist economy.

[5] In what follows, the reader will be aided by remembering that we have adopted the adjectives "laborist" and "capitalist" to designate an economy by reference to its mode of production, and that we shall use the adjectives "laboristic" and "capitalistic" in designating an economy by reference to its form of distribution.

reference to mode of production rather than mode of ownership or form of distribution. What we are about to describe as the various forms of capitalism are all economies that are clearly capitalist rather than laborist in their mode of production.

(1) *The Mode of Ownership.*   The capital instruments of a society can be (a) privately owned and operated by individuals, families, and corporations; or (b) publicly owned by the State and operated by its governing bureaucracy.

(a) Under a system of private ownership of capital, the ownership may be highly concentrated in the hands of the few at one extreme, or widely diffused among the population at the other extreme; or its degree of concentration or diffusion may fall somewhere between these two extremes. Insofar as it is highly concentrated, it gives the few economic power with which they can exert undue influence on the organs and personnel of government. Insofar as it is widely diffused, it gives the people generally the economic independence they need to bulwark their political liberty.

(b) Under the system of public ownership of capital, the ownership is completely concentrated in the corporate personality of the State, which means that, for all practical purposes, it is highly concentrated in the hands of the policy making office-holders who exercise the political power of the State. Only if those persons were completely responsible to the electorate and subject to all the checks of popular sovereignty could the operative control of the capital instruments owned by the State be widely diffused, even though the ownership of them is not. But where, in a capitalist economy, private persons and corporations do not own property in capital instruments, they are without the leverage of economic power to exercise control over those who have political power; and so, where the State is the only capitalist, both economic and political power tend to become concentrated in the organs or bureaus of government. The bureaucrats who act in the name of the State are beyond check and cannot be made responsible. Under such conditions, democratic processes are fictitious, and the economic as well as political freedom of individuals is all but extinguished.[6]

(2) *The Form of Distribution.*   In economies in which capital instruments are the chief productive force and the principal form of productive property, the form of distribution is either (a) capitalistic or (b) laboristic. We are using these terms here in the same descriptive sense that we used them before in connection with economies in which human labor is the chief productive force and the principal form of productive property.

(a) The distribution is capitalistic in form if the major portion of the wealth produced goes to the owners of capital. In an economy in which the private ownership of capital prevails, and in which that ownership is highly concentrated in the hands of a small class, the

---

[6] In his *Economic Policy for a Free Society,* Chicago, 1951, Henry C. Simons summarizes the case for the diffused ownership of property as indispensable to both political and economic freedom. "Private property in the instruments of production," he writes, "is an institutional device both for dispersing power and for securing effective organization of production. The only simple property system is that of a slave society with a single slave owner—which, significantly, is the limiting case of despotism and of monopoly." (He might have said the same of a capitalist economy with a single owner of capital—the State.) "Departure from such a system," Simon continues, "is a fair measure of human progress. The libertarian good society lies at an opposite extreme, in the maximum dispersion of property compatible with effective production. . . . Basic to liberty are property rights in labor or personal capacities. The abolitions of slavery and serfdom are the great steps toward freedom—and, by the way, are striking reconciliations of apparent conflict between productional and distributional considerations. Property in one's own services, however, is a secure, substantial right only where there are many possible buyers. It thus implies private property in other resources and freedom of independent sellers of labor to choose and to move among autonomous, independent organizations or firms. It also implies a distinctively modern institutional achievement, namely, the separation or dissociation of the economic and the political—a political order that sustains formal rights and a largely separate economic order that gives them substance." Simon then goes on to say that all property rights—both in capital and in labor —are integral aspects of personal capacity, and that "a society based on free, responsible individuals or families must involve extensive rights of property," presumably in capital instruments as well as in labor. See "A Political Credo" in *op. cit.*, pp. 27–28.

residue which remains to be apportioned among the laboring masses will inevitably be less than is needed for a decent standard of living, or in some cases even for a meager subsistence.[7]

(b) The distribution is laboristic in form if all or the major portion of the wealth produced goes to those who contribute to its production only by the use of their own labor power; and it is partly laboristic and partly capitalistic in form if the distributive share which goes to the owners of capital is less than the major portion of the wealth produced, being the residue that remains after a substantial portion of that wealth goes to labor in order to provide a majority of the population with a decent standard of living.[8]

In an economy in which the ownership of capital is completely concentrated in the hands of the State, the form of distribution is purely laboristic, and necessarily so.[9]

In an economy in which capital is privately owned, but in which that ownership is concentrated in the hands of the few, the form of distribution cannot be purely laboristic without completely violating the rights of private property in capital. A purely laboristic distribution of industrially produced wealth is inconsistent with the effective private ownership of capital. It nullifies a productive use of such property in order to obtain the share of the wealth which it produced. But under a system of private ownership, and one in which that ownership is highly concentrated, it is possible for the form of distribution to be either purely capitalistic or partly capitalistic and partly laboristic.

We cannot describe the difference between these two alternatives without considering the principles that control these two forms of distribution—on one hand, the principle of justice together with

[7] British capitalism throughout the nineteenth century is the classic example of a capitalistic economy in which the form of distribution was purely capitalistic.
[8] British or American capitalism in the middle of the twentieth century is the classic example of a capitalistic economy in which the form of distribution is mixed, *i.e.*, partly capitalistic and partly laboristic.
[9] The capitalism of Soviet Russia is the classic example of a capitalistic economy in which the form of distribution is purely laboristic.

respect for human rights; on the other hand, the principle of charity together with concern for human needs.

(3) *The Principle Underlying the Form of Distribution.* The principle underlying the form of distribution is either (a) one of strict justice, based on the rights of private property in capital and labor, as well as on other human rights; or (b) one of charity.

When the principle is one of charity, concern for human needs or welfare may lead to only a limited invasion of the rights of private property in capital, in which case the form of distribution will remain partly capitalistic; or the principle of need may completely replace the principle of rights, in which case private property in capital will be completely abolished and the form of distribution will become purely laboristic.

The capitalist economy of Soviet Russia represents one in which a purely laboristic distribution is avowed to rest entirely on the principle of human needs or welfare. The substitution of needs for rights is of a piece with the abolition of private property in capital. Both together express the view that since the State should take possession of all capital instruments for the welfare of the people, the wealth produced by capital should be distributed to them according to their needs and not apportioned on the basis of the varying contributions which individual men make by their labor.[10]

We said above that the purely laboristic distribution in Soviet Russia is *avowed* to rest entirely on the principle of human needs or welfare. From recent reports, it would appear that actual practice deviates from Marxist theory, insofar as a much higher standard of living is accorded by the State to managerial and technical labor than

[10] According to Lenin's interpretation of it, in *State and Revolution*, the Marxist principle—"from each according to his ability, to each according to his needs"—replaces and transcends all considerations of justice and rights. The communist ideal, according to Lenin, will not be fully realized until such bourgeois considerations are as completely abolished as the institution of private property in capital, with which they are connected. See *op. cit.*, Moscow, 1949: Ch. V, Sects. 3 and 4.

to mechanical labor. This might be thought to be an atavistic revival of some concern for rights, in view of the fact that in any capitalist economy managerial and technical labor contributes much more than mechanical labor to the production of society's wealth. But if the establishment by the State of wide differentials in living standards springs solely from a wish to provide the necessary incentives or inducements to get certain kinds of work well done, then the controlling principle is neither one of justice nor of charity, but of expediency. It aims at the survival of the economy itself, or at its greater productivity and prosperity.[11]

The present capitalistic economy of Great Britain or the United States represents one in which a partly laboristic distribution is sometimes mistakenly avowed to rest on the principle of human rights. The mistake is a profound one. To correct that mistake, it is necessary to re-examine the capitalistic economy of Great Britain or the United States before the power of labor unions, supported by the power of government and by the legislative regulation of wages and hours and the policy of full employment, raised the general standard of living to its present level.

We have already observed that in an economy in which the private ownership of capital prevails and in which that ownership of capital is highly concentrated in the hands of a small class, a capitalistic form of distribution necessarily gives the major portion of the wealth produced to a few men or families, and leaves for the majority of the population a residue so small that their standard of living is at a subsistence level or less.

Is the principle underlying such a capitalistic distribution just? And, we cannot help asking also, is it expedient?

We have already indicated the answer that must be given to the

---

[11] The principle of charity or welfare is thus qualified by a principle of expediency in Soviet Russia's purely laboristic form of distribution. We shall see presently that a principle of expediency may enter into other forms of distribution, as, for example, in the partly laboristic and partly capitalistic form of distribution which has developed in Britain and America in the last forty years.

first question. We pointed out in the preceding chapter that one principle of justice, *i.e.,* the principle of distribution, can be operative in a society that is unjust in other respects, *i.e.,* by violating the principles of participation and limitation. We also pointed out earlier in this chapter that an economy achieves justice in distribution when its form of distribution matches its mode of production. Thus, if an economy that is capitalist in its mode of production has a capitalistic form of distribution, it achieves justice in respect to distribution, but it may nevertheless be quite unjust in other respects.

A capitalist economy in which large numbers of men cannot effectively participate in the production of wealth because the ownership of capital is concentrated in the hands of the few is hardly a just economy. Though its capitalistic form of distribution is based on full respect for the property rights of the few who are capitalists, the economy violates two of the three principles of justice—the principles of participation and of limitation.

The economic hardship, or, worse, the abject misery of the great mass of men, was the immediate consequence of the injustice that was done in the capitalist economies of Great Britain and the United States during the nineteenth century. The cause was not the private ownership of capital, which is as just as the private ownership of labor power; nor was it the purely capitalistic form of distribution, which is also in itself quite just in an economy that is capitalist in its mode of production. *The cause was the highly concentrated ownership of capital.*

In addition to being unjust, with deplorable consequences for the welfare of the masses, the capitalist economy we have just been describing would have "sowed the seeds of its own destruction," as Marx predicted, had its capitalistic form of distribution continued without modification. With the major portion of the wealth going to the one-tenth of the population who were the owners of capital, the residue that went to the remaining nine-tenths gave them insufficient purchasing power to support a high level of production.

Only by raising the general standard of living and creating a widely diffused purchasing power can the consumption of wealth support mass production in a capitalist economy. Hence if it was nothing else, the transformation of the form of distribution from a purely capitalistic one into a partly laboristic one was highly expedient. It kept the economy going, and saved it from the disastrous climax of the cycle of boom-and-bust.

There is ample evidence of such motivation in the explicitly stated policies of the New Deal, as well as in the declarations of those union leaders who picture labor as in partnership with capital to make capitalism a prosperous economy for the welfare of all concerned.[12] But the action of labor unions and the effort of government regulation to create a partly laboristic form of distribution were not entirely motivated by considerations of expediency with an eye to keeping the economy afloat. The original, abiding, and deeper interest was in alleviating human misery and improving the lot of the masses.

Without excluding or minimizing a concern for the stability of the economy, the controlling principle in the transformation of the form of distribution stemmed from deeply humanitarian motives—concern for pressing human needs and the economic welfare of the "forgotten man." These good purposes, as well as the efficiency and prosperity

[12] See Philip Murray's Annual Report for 1952. "Our mass production economy," he wrote, "can expand on a healthy basis in the long run, only if it is based on rising levels of consumption of the output produced by expanding productive facilities." He argued that high levels of production and employment, high wages, high volume sales in mass markets and narrower profit margins are to the common interest of capital and labor. It is interesting to observe that more than a hundred years earlier, in 1827, the Preamble of the Mechanics' Union of Trade Associations in Philadelphia argued in a similar vein: "If the mass of the people were enabled by their labor to procure for themselves and families a full and abundant supply of the comforts and conveniences of life, the consumption . . . would amount to at least twice the quantity it does at present, and of course the demand, by which alone employers are enabled to subsist or accumulate would likewise be increased in an equal proportion. . . . All are dependent on the demand which there is for the use of their skill, service, or capital, and the demand must ever be regulated by the ability or inability of the great mass of people to purchase and consume" (reprinted in *The People Shall Judge*, Chicago, 1953: Vol. I, pp. 580–583).

of the economy itself, were served by creating a mixed form of distribution which over the years has become more and more laboristic, less and less capitalistic.[13]

These good ends were served, however, without correcting the injustices of the nineteenth-century capitalism which was self-destructive as well as inhumane because, with a highly concentrated private ownership of capital, it maintained a purely capitalistic form of distribution. On the contrary, the mixture of a laboristic with a capitalistic form of distribution in a capitalist economy, especially in a technologically advanced one in which nine-tenths of the wealth is produced by capital instruments, does serious injustice to the owners of capital. It invades, attenuates, or erodes their property rights in capital in proportion as it makes a larger and larger cut in the distributive share which should be theirs by right of earning it in order to increase the distributive share given to the owners of labor power, *which is for the most part not earned* by them.

The present capitalist economy of Great Britain and the United States, therefore, not only fails to correct the injustices that it inherits from the last century, but also adds thereto the injustice of a form of distribution that has become more and more laboristic, as measured by the increasing portion of the wealth that is rightly due to the owners of capital but goes to labor The fact that this transformation in the distribution of wealth can be "justified" by the ends it has served, *i.e.,* the general welfare of our people and the prosperity of our economy, may make it humane or expedient, but it does not make it just.

To be just, the production and distribution of wealth must be organized so that all human rights are fully respected—the right of everyone

[13] We have referred to the principle of distribution that rests on a concern for human needs as one of charity. It can also be called the "welfare principle" or the "principle of socialism." The present capitalist economy of Great Britain and the United States, which we have described as one in which the form of distribution is mixed (partly laboristic, and partly capitalistic) can, therefore, also be described as "welfare capitalism" or "partly socialized capitalism."

to receive the full share of what his productive property produces as well as the right of everyone to participate in production through the use of property which, under a capitalist mode of production, is capable of earning a viable income or a decent living.

To correct the injustices that were present in capitalism in its first stage and still exist as a result of the highly concentrated private ownership of capital, and to correct in addition the injustice that has recently been introduced by an increasingly laboristic form of distribution under the principle of charity, welfare, or socialism, it is necessary to reinstate a purely capitalistic form of distribution, with full respect for the rights of private property in capital, and at the same time to innovate a widely diffused private ownership of capital.

Only in that way can all relevant economic rights be safeguarded. Only in that way can all three principles of economic justice be embodied in a capitalist economy. Only in that way can a capitalist economy be justly organized. Only in that way can the prosperity of a capitalist economy be preserved or augmented, and the economic welfare of the population be cared for, without recourse to expedients that are not only unjust because they invade property rights but are also inimical to freedom because they involve concentrations of political and economic power in the same hands.

The so-called communist revolution established the complete socialization of a capitalist economy. Completely socialized capitalism may be able to operate with enough efficiency to ensure some measure of economic prosperity. It may be able, by a purely laboristic form of distribution, to take care of human needs and even to provide a gradually improved standard of living for all. But if it succeeds in these respects, it can do so only at the sacrifice of justice and liberty, of personal rights and individual freedoms—all of which are bound up with the institution of private property and the right of a man to live on what he earns by property over which he has exclusive control.

What is called for is the capitalist revolution, a revolution which not only serves the cause of justice and liberty, but also has the power to create, more surely and fully, an efficient and prosperous economy, and a standard of living that amply provides for the economic welfare of all.

The path the capitalist revolution will take faces in exactly the opposite direction from that taken by the communist revolution. It seeks to diffuse the private ownership of capital instead of abolishing it entirely. It seeks to make all men capitalists instead of preventing anyone from being a capitalist by making the State the only capitalist.

The capitalist revolution also turns away from the mixtures and confusions of economies that are partly socialized or laboristic capitalisms. But it does not turn back to the unjust and inhumane capitalism of the nineteenth century. It moves forward to the full fruition of the principles of justice that were possible under capitalism from the beginning. It seeks to make an economy that is capitalist in its mode of production one that is also purely capitalistic in its mode of distribution, *as it should be.* And by seeking to make all men capitalists, it strives to make effective their right to live on what they can earn by their capital property as well as by their labor, *as men should be able to live in a society where capital instruments produce most of the wealth.*

7 THE ECONOMIC FUTURE

THE FOUR CAPITALISMS

In the preceding chapter, we distinguished four forms of capitalism. Of these, three belong to the past or present. One belongs to the future. It is the object of the capitalist revolution to bring that one into being.

We have so far identified the three forms of capitalism that belong to the past or present by referring to historic examples of them. For ease of reference, we would now like to substitute tag-names that will serve as shorthand devices for remembering their salient characteristics. We propose the following nomenclature.

(1) *The form of capitalism which existed in Great Britain during the nineteenth century and which persisted in a waning state until the end of the First World War.* In view of the fact that this was the original form taken by capitalism with the emergence of industrial

production, we think it is fitting to call it "primitive capitalism." It represents the least developed stage of industrial production as well as the first stage in the organization of an economy in which power-driven machinery and other capital instruments slowly became the chief productive force.

The distinguishing characteristics of primitive capitalism are: (a) private ownership of capital instruments; (b) no limitation on, and hence undue concentration of, such ownership; (c) a capitalistic form of distribution with full returns to the owners of capital of what their productive property earns; (d) a bare subsistence standard of living, or worse, for the laboring masses in the population.

(2) *The form of capitalism which exists in Soviet Russia today.* Two names suggest themselves as appropriate: "completely socialized capitalism" and "State capitalism." The first points to the form of distribution, the second to the mode of ownership which prevails. We will use "State capitalism" because it is briefer.

The distinguishing characteristics of State capitalism are: (a) public ownership of capital instruments; (b) complete concentration of such ownership in the hands of the State, or in what for all practical purposes become the hands of the bureaucrats who wield the political power of the State; (c) a laboristic form of distribution, controlled and administered by the State for the economic welfare of the workers; (d) a much improved basic standard of living for the masses, with a scale of differential incomes added to provide incentives, not earned rewards, for the most highly productive types of labor.

(3) *The form of capitalism which exists in the United States and Great Britain today and which has been developing since the end of the First World War and the rise of labor unions to power with the help of the countervailing power of government.* This form of capitalism has been called "collective capitalism," "managerial capitalism,"

and "laboristic capitalism." [1] It can also be called "mixed capitalism," "partly socialized capitalism," or "welfare capitalism." All these names point to the fact that the form of distribution is partly capitalistic and partly laboristic. The last two, in addition, point to the controlling principle of the distribution insofar as it is laboristic—concern for the needs of those who participate in production through labor alone, not for what they are justly entitled to by such participation as measured by its contribution. We will use "mixed capitalism," (and sometimes "the mixed economy") as the tag-name for this form because it calls attention to the mixture of conflicting elements, some of which are vestiges of primitive capitalism and some of which are halfway measures whose tendency, if they continue unchecked, would push this economy further and further toward completely socialized or State capitalism.

The distinguishing characteristics of mixed capitalism are: (a) vestigial or nominal private ownership of capital instruments; (b) no limitation on, and hence still undue concentration of, such ownership, though that concentration is somewhat less than in primitive capitalism; (c) a form of distribution that is partly capitalistic and partly laboristic, according to which owners of capital receive some share of what their property produces but much less than they are entitled to as measured by its contribution, and according to which those who

[1] In a paper entitled "Administered Prices and All That," delivered before the Western Economic Association on August 28, 1957, Professor Edwin G. Nourse employed such phrases as "corporate capitalism" and "managerial capitalism" in order to distinguish the present form of capitalism from what he called the "traditional" or "proprietary capitalism" of the nineteenth century. He attributed to Professor Sumner Schlicter the description of our present economic system as a "laboristic economy," but felt that it was more accurate to describe it as a "laboristic capitalism," because, as he said, "what we have is not fully laborism but merely modified capitalism." See *Hearings before the Subcommittee on Antitrust and Monopoly of the Committee of the Judiciary, U. S. Senate*, July 9–16, 1957, Government Printing Office, Washington: pp. 188–190. The phrase "collective capitalism" was coined by Professor Gardiner C. Means and employed in a lecture entitled "Collective Capitalism and Economic Theory," delivered at the Marshall Whythe Symposium, College of William and Mary, Williamsburg, Virginia, March, 1957. This lecture is also reprinted in the Senate Hearings cited above: see pp. 104–114.

participate in production through mechanical labor alone receive a much larger share than such participation earns by its contribution; (d) a generally high standard of living for the laboring masses in the population.

(4) *The form of capitalism which will exist, probably in the United States first, after the capitalist revolution has brought into being the first justly organized capitalist economy.* This is the only one of the four forms for which it is difficult to find a readily appropriate name. As contrasted with primitive capitalism, it might be called "mature capitalism" or "fully developed capitalism" to indicate its highly advanced stage of industrial production; but both State capitalism and mixed capitalism will also enjoy the advantages of the technological advances to be made in the next fifty years. As contrasted with State capitalism, it might be called "private property capitalism," but that does not distinguish it from mixed capitalism in which capital instruments are, nominally at least, still privately owned. As contrasted with mixed capitalism, it might be called "pure capitalism" to indicate that its form of distribution is purely capitalistic, *i.e.,* without any admixture of a socialized laboristic form of distribution; but primitive capitalism can also be called "pure" in the same sense.

"Just capitalism" would be appropriate and distinctive because, of the four forms of capitalism, this is the only one that embodies all the relevant principles of economic justice. But the phrase "just capitalism" is open to misinterpretation, and it would be burdensome to be sure each time that "just" carried the connotation of "justice." Hence we have decided to adopt the word "Capitalism," with a capital "C" but without any qualifying adjectives, as the name for the capitalist economy to be created by the capitalist revolution.[2]

---

[2] The phrase "People's Capitalism" is currently used in a sense that is vaguely suggestive of what we mean by Capitalism. But those who use it often fail to acknowledge explicitly that what they mean by "People's Capitalism" does not yet exist in the United States; nor do they explicitly recognize all the changes that would have to take place in our present mixed capitalism in order to bring

The distinguishing characteristics of Capitalism are: (a) the private ownership of capital instruments, restored to full effect from its present nominal condition and attenuated rights; (b) the widest possible diffusion of such ownership to provide effective participation in the production of wealth for all members of the economy; (c) a capitalistic form of distribution with fully paid out capital earnings to owners of capital, and with an ultimate reduction of the wages of labor to what labor's contribution earns, as measured by demand under freely competitive conditions; (d) a high standard of living for all, based on a minimum viable income for individuals or families, derived, in most cases, from participation in production as owners of capital or as owners of labor and capital.

A quick comparison of the four forms of capitalism will reveal that certain characteristics are common to two or more.

Calling all four "forms of capitalism" implies that all are alike in being capitalist as to mode of production. But primitive capitalism differs from all the rest in respect to industrial development. With the coming of the second industrial revolution, of which automation is only one harbinger, State capitalism and mixed capitalism, if they survive another half century, will exceed the productivity of the most advanced industrialism that exists today to a much greater extent than the productivity of the United States or Soviet Russia today exceeds that of primitive capitalism at the end of the nineteenth century. On this score we think that Capitalism, by its unchecked pursuit and promotion of technological advances, will be able to go further than either State capitalism or mixed capitalism. It will most fully realize the productive potentialities of capital instruments.

State capitalism, mixed capitalism and the Capitalism of the future are alike in another and related respect, in which they all differ from primitive capitalism; namely, with regard to the economic welfare of

it into existence. The phrase is, therefore, almost as much an advertising slogan, and as empty of real content, as the one on which it is modeled—"People's Democracy," the term used by the Communist countries to claim for themselves a non-capitalistic form of democracy which does not exist and cannot.

the whole population or the general standard of living. Though they achieve that desirable objective by different means and under the aegis of different controlling principles, they all are able to remove the economic hardships and widespread misery that existed under primitive capitalism. Given foreseeable advances in productivity, both State capitalism and mixed capitalism, continuing along their present lines, will be able to go much further in this direction; but here as before we think that Capitalism will be able to go furthest by reason of its principles, precisely because they are principles of justice rather than of charity or welfare.

In one further respect, State capitalism, mixed capitalism and Capitalism have some affinity, and one that is not shared at all by primitive capitalism. Where primitive capitalism was doomed to self-destruction by a mode of ownership and a form of distribution that prevented mass consumption from supporting mass production in the open market, State capitalism is able to avoid the problem by controlling consumption as well as production; mixed capitalism has found that the operation of its welfare principle is also able to create effective mass purchasing power at the same time that it creates a generally high standard of living for the masses; and the Capitalism of the future will be able to avoid the orgy of overproduction and its resulting monetary inflation that are entailed by mixed capitalism's misguided pursuit of full employment. All three, by quite different means, can operate a capitalist economy for a time at least with the minimum efficiency that is necessary for its survival; but here, once again, we think that Capitalism can attain a higher level of efficiency, and stability as well, without the human waste and moral corruption that is involved in mixed capitalism's needless overproduction of wealth and without State capitalism's suppression of freedom. Once a decent standard of living is achieved for all, and as soon as military and defense expenditures can be kept from increasing or can perhaps even be reduced, an economic balance can be achieved under which our technology can advance and our standard of living can be raised to any reasonable limit without the simultaneous waste involved in the production of surpluses for the mere sake of providing full employment.

On the three points we have so far considered, Capitalism is more like State capitalism and mixed capitalism than like primitive capitalism. The only respect in which Capitalism resembles primitive capitalism is in giving full effect to the private ownership of capital through a capitalistic form of distribution which operates solely under the principle of apportioning distributive shares of the wealth produced on the basis of contributions to its production, the value of which is measured by demand in a freely competitive market.

With regard to the institution of private property, mixed capitalism somewhat resembles primitive capitalism and the Capitalism of the future. On this score, it is unlike State capitalism. But in certain essentials mixed capitalism has a much deeper affinity with State capitalism; for, while it involves the nominal private ownership of capital instruments, it does not give full effect to the rights of such ownership under its partly capitalistic and partly laboristic form of distribution. As partly socialized or welfare capitalism, it has strong leanings toward the completely socialized welfare state of State capitalism. A serious economic crisis, which might be precipitated by uncontrollable technological advances, or by monetary inflation necessarily resulting from its policy of full employment, would unquestionably bend it further in that direction.

Finally, there is the one crucial respect in which Capitalism stands completely by itself. It is the only form of capitalism which is built on the diffused private ownership of capital instruments. And it is for that reason the only form of capitalism that is a justly organized economy.

THE THREE ALTERNATIVES

The industrial economy, *i.e.*, capitalism, in one form or another, is here to stay. Except for some major cataclysm that would reduce the world to rubble, destroy civilization as we know it, and condemn the scattered survivors to primitive modes of existence, there is little or no chance of a return to the laborist economies of the past. Nor would anyone in his right mind wish to give up the benefits of industrial production. Only those who are deluded by hallucinations of a golden age that once existed can be so blind to the potentialities of a civilization built on the utilization of machines and other capital instruments rather than on the enslavement of men as to think that the past can hold a candle to the future.

It is true that the pre-industrial class-divided societies of the past achieved for the few certain refinements and permitted those few to achieve certain excellences that seem to be threatened by the emergence of a mass, or one-class, society in the twentieth century.[3] But when we compare a mass society with civilizations built on the slavery of the submerged masses, we must remember that the ultimate measure of a society's worth is its potentiality for development. This applies to the capitalist economy as compared with the laborist and slave economies of the past.

If it was a great step forward in the history of man for the rise of civilization to permit a small class of free men to engage in the liberal pursuits of leisure and to advance civilization itself by their efforts, how much greater is the step that can be taken by our emergent mass society when it sees how to turn the twin institutions of democracy and capitalism into a school for the good use of the political and economic freedom they confer on all men alike.

[3] With prophetic vision, Alexis de Tocqueville foresaw in 1835 most of the social, political, economic and cultural problems that would confront a mass society as it developed under what he called "conditions of equality." But de Tocqueville also faced the future with the faith that Providence, in decreeing the inexorable progress of society from conditions favorable for the few to conditions favorable for all, challenged man to solve the problems incidental to such progress, and thereby make it thoroughly benign. He closed *Democracy in America* with these words: "The nations of our time cannot prevent the conditions of men from becoming equal; but it depends upon themselves whether the principle of equality is to lead them to servitude or freedom, to knowledge or barbarism, to prosperity or wretchedness."

Like the industrial production of wealth, the classless organization of society is here to stay—in one form or another. Our only choice is as to form. But we do have a choice. The totalitarian state with a regimented population of equal and uniform puppets is no more the inevitable crystallization of the mass society than State capitalism is—as Marx thought it was—the one form toward which an industrial economy inevitably tends.

With capitalism here to stay, we are confronted with three alternatives, and only three. For most of the English-speaking peoples, who would not think for a moment of exchanging life in the United States or in the British Commonwealth for life in Soviet Russia, these quickly reduce to two.

We can choose to perpetuate the mixed capitalism we have created in the last quarter century, with the hope that we can keep it mixed, or we can undo the mixture by eliminating the laboristic and socialistic aspects of our economy, with their tendency toward State capitalism, and replace them with the principles of justice that would create Capitalism. Our choice, in short, is between the *status quo* and the capitalist revolution.[4]

The case for the capitalist revolution may be sufficiently clear from what has already been said. It should be for those who understand the principles of economic justice and who see that the just organization of a capitalist economy is not only desirable in itself but, more than that, indispensable to economic freedom, to political democracy, and to the fulfillment of the promise of a good human life for all men. Thus persuaded, they may wish only for a summary statement of the theory

---

[4] Though we have treated primitive capitalism as one of the four forms of capitalism, it does not present a real alternative in the twentieth century. The successive waves of the scientific-industrial revolution exclude it from sensible consideration, just as much as the development of our conscience excludes the slave economy. Furthermore, it is morally almost as repugnant to us as a slave economy, both on the grounds of justice and on a humanitarian concern for human welfare. If all this were not enough to eliminate it forever from our thought, its self-destructive tendencies would by now have removed it from the running.

of Capitalism as the ground plan of the revolution, and for a projection of the practical program by which it can be accomplished.

A brief summary of the theory will be given in Chapter Eight; and a feasible, though tentative, program of practical steps will be outlined in Part II, which follows Chapter Eight. In the rest of this chapter, we shall address ourselves to those who may not yet see that our choice is between a socialist revolution, on the one hand, and the capitalist revolution, on the other. They may not realize that mixed capitalism as well as State capitalism is a product of the socialization of an economy that is capitalist in its mode of production. The same errors underlie both, and the same threats to freedom are present in both. What the completed socialist revolution has done to man and society, the creeping socialist revolution is in the process of doing.

THE TWO SOCIALIST REVOLUTIONS

(1) *The Completed Socialist Revolution.* We said that State capitalism is not a real alternative for us. Even if it could show itself to be the most productive, prosperous, and powerful of the forms of capitalism, and even if it could create the highest standard of living for all, we would have none of it. An American socialist like Norman Thomas, and an English socialist like John Strachey, reject it as vigorously as those among us who would not regard themselves as socialists.

The attitude all of us share springs from our devotion to democracy and from our wish to preserve and strengthen our individual freedoms and our free political institutions. We are all convinced that State capitalism cannot operate except in a totalitarian state. But the socialists among us, together with those who have leanings toward socialism whether they know it or not, do not see that an advanced capitalist economy without the private ownership of capital instruments and without full respect for the rights of such ownership cannot be operated without one or another type of bureaucratic management which inevitably concentrates economic and political power in the hands of a small clique.

Hence even though State capitalism, as exemplified in the completed socialist revolution, repels rather than attracts us, it is useful for us to look at it a moment longer. It does more than offer us the clearest example of what we are trying to avoid. If we are trying to avoid certain tendencies carried to the extreme by the completed social revolution, we should recoil from those same tendencies manifested in the process of the creeping socialist revolution which our mixed capitalist economy has been quietly carrying on.

Orthodox defenders of the Marxist faith may argue that State capitalism as currently practiced in Soviet Russia does not represent the *completed* socialist revolution, but only the penultimate stage in the process that leads to the ultimate creation of the truly communist society. They believe that the "dictatorship of the proletariat," administered by the Communist Party, is a necessary step in the process of expropriating private property in capital and putting it to social use; but that it is only a step in the revolutionary process, not its culmination. That will inevitably be reached when the State itself withers away and, in place of the oppression that any form of political government involves, the only government will consist in the people's co-operative management of things rather than in the rule of men over men.

The Marxist thinks that the withering away of the State follows as inevitably from the dictatorship of the proletariat as that in turn follows from the forces at work in any capitalist economy. With the rise of capitalism, it is maintained, the class war reaches the point at which the owners of capital and the propertyless (or rather capital-less) owners of labor power are aligned against one another in a death struggle which can have only one outcome. According to Marxists, the resolution of the class war leads to the ideal classless society, but its route takes it through a temporary interregnum, which they call "the dictatorship of the proletariat," and we call "the totalitarian State."

Prophecies that do not give dates can never be refuted by facts. But they do become incredible in proportion as the things we know make what they predict look improbable. It is, to say the least, improbable that the leaders of the Communist Party, who administer the dictatorship of the proletariat and hold in their hands the greatest concentration of economic and political power ever consolidated on earth, will ever voluntarily divest themselves of such power in order to bring about the withering away of the State and to make way for the ideal classless society.

Even if they were dedicated and holy men before they became bureaucrats, the power they then acquired would corrupt them, and being almost absolute would corrupt them almost completely. The peaceful transformation of the State capitalism of the totalitarian state into the communist-capitalism of the whole community co-operatively managing its capital without any need of coercive regulation by political government is, therefore, highly improbable.

A violent uprising of the Russian people may overthrow the dictatorship of the Communist Party, but it will not, because it cannot, foment the withering away of the State or transform the totalitarian state into the communist classless society. A peaceful community without the institutions of government is impossible and will remain impossible, to paraphrase Hamilton, as long as men are not angels.

Marx was right in his abhorrence of all the class-divided societies of the past and of his own day. He was right in his condemnation of the bitter class war in all its phases. He was right in his hope, and we hope he was right in his prediction, that the ultimate outcome of this long struggle of class against class would be the classless society—not only politically classless but also economically classless. But he was *wrong* in his mythical or utopian dream of the form the classless society would or could take.

This is not the only point on which Marx finally went wrong after being partly right. He was right in his condemnation of the injustice of primitive capitalism. He was right in his moral indignation over the human misery that its injustice caused; and though he was not a lone voice in his outcry against it, he, perhaps more than any other man, so forcefully stated the case that no one thereafter could ever make light of it. He was right in his enthusiasm for the unqualified superiority of the new capitalist economy over all the laborist economies of the past so far as its sheer power of producing wealth is concerned. He was also right in his sense that the injustice of a system in which close to nine-tenths of the wealth produced went to about one-tenth of the population (*i.e.,* those who owned the capital instruments of production) somehow stemmed, not from the capitalist mode of production, but from the mode of capital ownership together with a capitalistic form of distribution.

In all this he was right, but he was *wrong*—crucially wrong—when he finally put his finger on the root of the trouble. He thought the root cause of the injustice of primitive capitalism was the private ownership of capital. Private property in capital, he thought, operating under a capitalistic form of distribution, inevitably resulted in the maldistribution of wealth with all its consequences: human misery, almost slavery, for the submerged masses, and a concentration of economic and political power in the hands of a small class of capitalists.

Though he came very near to putting his finger on the right spot, he missed it. But for that fatal error, Marx might have advocated the capitalist revolution instead of the socialist revolution. The root of the trouble was not the *private* ownership of capital, but the *highly concentrated* private ownership of capital. That being the cause, the remedy lies not in abolishing private property in capital, as Marx recommended, but rather in diffusing the private ownership of capital by bringing into existence new capitalists at a rate commensurate with the shift in the burden of production from human toil to capital instruments. When that is accomplished under Capitalism, a capitalistic distribution of wealth will produce results the very opposite of those produced under primitive capitalism.

Marx's fatal error in diagnosing the cause of the injustice in primitive capitalism was intertwined with all the other errors he made, both in his theory of capitalism and in his revolutionary program.

His labor theory of value, which is pivotal in his theory of capitalist production, served to rationalize or "justify" the expropriation of private property in capital; for if, as he claimed, labor and labor alone produces all wealth, even in a capitalist economy (machines, he said, represent nothing but accumulated or "congealed" labor), then all the wealth produced should in justice be distributed to those who produce it. Since, in his view, the owner of capital produces nothing, simply by owning machines and raw materials and allowing them to be used by labor, any return to the capitalist, Marx argued, is unearned increment obtained by the exploitation of labor. He therefore concluded that the only way to prevent such exploitation and unearned increment is to have society as a whole, organized as a State, take over all capital instruments and control them for the benefit of the producers of wealth, to whom all the wealth should go. To accomplish a laboristic distribution of wealth, the State must not only control the capital instruments; it must also control the distribution of the wealth that a society of laboring men produces. Thus the labor theory of value, with its consequences, reaches the result at which Marx aimed from the beginning—from the moment he made his mistaken diagnosis that the private ownership of capital was the root cause of the trouble.[5]

At this point, however, Marx departed from one concern with which he began. That he began with a concern about justice is plain in the light of such words as "exploitation" and "unearned increment." But

---

[5] Since that diagnosis was wrong, there is no need here to expose all the fallacies in the labor theory of value. That is amply done in *Capitalism*, which will soon be published. A chapter of this book, entitled "Karl Marx: The Almost Capitalist," was in *American Bar Association Journal*, March, 1957. It is important here, however, to point out that economists who claim to reject the labor theory of value nevertheless swallow its central error whenever they translate the increased productiveness of the capital of a capitalist economy into assertions about the increased productiveness of labor. They sometimes even talk as if the machines were not themselves active factors in production but passive instruments that derive all their productivity from labor. It is not surprising, therefore, that such economists should be exponents of the laboristic and socialistic forms of distribution adopted by our mixed economy or welfare capitalism.

it is equally clear that he ended by substituting charity for justice. His famous formula—"from each [laborer] according to his ability, and to each according to his needs"—totally divorces distribution from contribution. It cannot, therefore, be a principle of distributive justice. Since it is determined by need rather than by earning, it is a principle of charity, more often referred to as a principle of "social welfare."

Charitable distributions may be necessary in any economy. We know that the injustice of primitive capitalism made them necessary in the nineteenth century in order to relieve human beings in dire distress and to preserve those whose very existence was at stake. But it makes a considerable difference whether charity is accomplished by private gifts or by a public distribution of wealth, as under State capitalism; and whether charity is auxiliary to the economy's system of distribution or is its central principle, as it is under socialism.[6]

The fact that under State capitalism the distribution of wealth, as well as the production and consumption of wealth, is controlled by the State illustrates the ancient truth that a little error in the beginning can lead to enormous ones in the end. The crucial error Marx made about the precise cause of the malfunctioning of primitive capitalism led him to recommend a system which is more unjust and more inimical to human freedom than the one it proposed to supplant. For if the cause of the injustice and the danger to freedom in primitive capitalism came from the concentration of economic and political power in the hands of a small group of private capitalists, how much more serious is the threat to freedom when all economic power is concentrated in the hands of the men who also hold all political power as representatives of the monolithic State. And how much more far-reaching is the injustice that results from the abolition of private property in capital in order

---

[6] It also makes a difference whether the charitable distribution, as in Robin Hood's case, is made from funds obtained unjustly. The partly laboristic distribution of wealth in our mixed economy comes to that, since it cannot be accomplished without cutting deeply into that portion of the wealth which should go to owners of capital as a just return for the wealth their capital produces.

to avoid the injustice that results from the concentration of its private ownership.[7]

However great was the political power that private capitalists wielded under primitive capitalism, the political power of the bureaucrats is far greater under State capitalism, because they control all capital property in the name of the State. Under such conditions, the society may be *nominally* classless in an economic sense, according to the fiction that all men are proletariat and none owns capital property. But, the fiction aside, the facts are clearly the very opposite. State capitalism creates a class-divided society, in which there is a ruling class (the bureaucrats or leaders of the Party) and a subject class (the mass of the workers). In addition to being the ruling class, the bureaucrats are in fact the owning class; for, by having complete control of the capital owned by the State, they are in effect its possessors.

As we are writing, Milovan Djilas, formerly vice-president of Yugoslavia and a top functionary in its Communist Party, has just been tried and sentenced to seven years' imprisonment for having the courage to publish a book in which he proclaimed that the *effective* ownership, *i.e.,* the *control,* of productive property under State capitalism is vested in the leading members of the ruling party—*the new class.* In that book, Djilas wrote:

As defined by Roman law, property constitutes the use, enjoyment, and disposition of material goods. The Communist political bureaucracy

---

[7] In an article in *Reader's Digest* in 1941, Max Eastman, who had been a socialist, offered his version of the Marxist paradox of good intentions leading by mistake to results the very opposite of those intended. He wrote: "It seems obvious to me now—though I have been slow, I must say, in coming to the conclusion—that the institution of private property is one of the main things that have given man that limited amount of free and equalness that Marx hoped to render infinite by abolishing this institution. Strangely enough Marx was the first to see this. He is the one who informed us, looking backwards, that the evolution of private capitalism with its free market had been a precondition for the evolution of all our democratic freedoms. It never occurred to him, looking forward, that if this was so, these other freedoms might disappear with the abolition of the free market."

uses, enjoys, and disposes of nationalized property. . . . The new class obtains its power, privileges, ideology, and its customs from one specific form of ownership—collective ownership—which the class administers and distributes in the name of the nation and society.[8]

The tragic consequences of the fatal flaw of Marx's initial error have not yet been fully stated. The deepest reversal of all lies in the fact that Marx, recognizing that a capitalist mode of production had the power to emancipate men from toil, nevertheless made "the equal liability of all to labor" a cardinal tenet of the socialist revolution. He should have insisted instead upon the participation of all in the production of wealth by means of capital property, so that all could enjoy a decent standard of living with as little labor as possible.

Marx recognized this when, comparing the condition of capitalists and workers under primitive capitalism, he claimed that the capitalists had all the advantages and privileges that made life worth living. Yet under State capitalism the State is, nominally at least, the only capitalist, and so all men are, in theory, *forced to be laborers.* Even were State capitalism to create a classless society, it would be the wrong kind of classless society, for the ideal that is indicated by capitalist production is a classless society of capitalists.[9]

---

[8] *The New Class,* New York, 1957: pp. 44–45. Immanual Kant, John Adams, Alexander Hamilton, and even John Stuart Mill doubted that a man was in a position to exercise political freedom unless he had a minimum degree of economic independence, *i.e.,* unless he did not depend for his subsistence on the arbitrary will of others. The laboring classes during the first century of capitalism, before they secured the protection of unions and of government, were frequently thought not to deserve suffrage because they did not have the requisite economic independence to use the political freedom it conferred. Clearly, under State capitalism, those who depend for their very existence, not to mention their livelihood, on the arbitrary will of the State or its bureaucrats have as little or less freedom than those who, under primitive capitalism, depended for their subsistence on the arbitrary will of the factory owners.

[9] The goal of capitalism first appeared in the life of leisure that was built on slavery in the laborist economies of civilized antiquity. It was previsioned in occult fashion in Aristotle's dream of complete automation, which suggested the picture of a society in which all men would have the leisure of slave owners because all would own the inanimate automatic slaves that produce the society's wealth.

The Marxist error here is flagrant. If we recognize that a republic in which only a few men are citizens is politically unjust, we can also see that the remedy is to make all men citizens, not to abolish citizenship. Hence when we recognize that an industrial economy in which only a few men are capitalists is economically unjust, we should be able to see that the obvious remedy is to enable all men to become capitalists, not to make it impossible for anyone to be a capitalist.

(2) *The Creeping Socialist Revolution.* The transformation of the American and British economies during the last half century, and especially in the last thirty years, has frequently been celebrated by its apologists as revolutionary. To quote the titles of some of their books on the subject, this revolution has been called "the managerial revolution" (by James Burnham) and "the twentieth-century capitalist revolution" (by Adolph Berle). The product of the revolution has been called "modern capitalism," or "American capitalism," by John Kenneth Galbraith and other American economists.

In our view the most accurate description of the changes now in progress in the United States and Great Britain is that suggested by the English socialist, John Strachey. He shows that the changes in our economy, which the theories of R. H. Tawney and John Maynard Keynes gave direction to, have progressively socialized it by introducing a form of distribution that is more and more laboristic and less and less capitalistic. Such progressive socialization, accomplished with little violence, mainly by law, and still going on, is aptly called a "creeping socialist revolution" in contrast to the completed one that has produced State capitalism in Soviet Russia. And the present product of this incomplete or partial socialist revolution is the partly socialized economy of mixed capitalism.

This is not the place to show by detailed analysis how the economic theories of Keynes, Tawney, Berle, and Galbraith rest on an unwitting acceptance of Marx's labor theory of value in spite of explicit protestations to the contrary.[10] Our interest here is not in the theories on the basis of which these economists have recommended the erosion of property rights in capital, the policy of full employment, administered wages and prices, the welfare principle in distribution, and the laboristic form of distribution. Our interest is in comparing the mixed capitalism that has put these recommendations into effect, with the State capitalism that has put into effect Marx's more radical recommendations—recommendations, let it be said, that are more rigorously consistent with the labor theory of value.

First of all, let us compare the motivation of the two socialist revolutions. Both tried to correct the deplorable consequences which followed, in primitive capitalism, from a capitalistic form of distribution operating under conditions of highly concentrated private ownership of capital. Both were instigated by a deep sense of the injustice that must somehow be responsible for so grievous a maldistribution of wealth as existed in the first century of capitalist production. But they differ in their diagnosis of the cause.

As we have seen, the program of the completed socialist revolution took its departure from the error that private property in capital itself was the root cause of the injustice; and so it proceeded to abolish private capitalists and to make the State the only capitalist. In contrast, the program of the creeping socialist revolution took its departure from the error that a purely capitalistic form of distribution was the root cause of the injustice; and so, while perpetuating private capitalists, it proceeded to invade and erode their property rights by mixing an increasingly attenuated capitalistic distribution of wealth with an ever enlarging laboristic distribution of it.

Neither revolutionary program proceeded from the right premise—that the root cause of the injustice was the *highly concentrated* private ownership of capital. The completed socialist revolution does

10 Such analysis is given in *Capitalism* in a series of chapters devoted to exposing the Marxism that is implicit in the economic theories of the most eminent advocates of the revolution which has produced mixed or partly socialized capitalism.

not remedy this by creating a public ownership of capital that is even more highly concentrated. On the contrary, it multiplies the injustice by violating all three of the principles on which a capitalist economy, to be just, must be organized.

So, too, the creeping socialist revolution does an injustice in order to correct the results of an injustice. It tries to offset the consequences of the concentrated private ownership of capital, which still exists in our mixed economy, by introducing an injustice which has the opposite effect. It introduces a laboristic form of distribution which is unjust in an economy that is capitalist in its mode of production, but which has the effect of raising the general standard of living. It does this as a countermeasure to the concentrated ownership of capital which violates the principles of participation and which, until counteracted, has the further effect of imposing serious economic hardships on the mass of the population.

So far as their effects are concerned, one injustice can thus act as a countermeasure to another. But it is one thing to remedy the deplorable consequences of an injustice by any means—just or unjust—and quite another to get at the root of the trouble and correct the injustice itself.

That primitive capitalism needed to be reformed, no one can doubt. Nor can anyone criticize the two revolutions which, in trying to reform it, were soundly motivated by considerations of justice and welfare. But the trouble with the two socialist revolutions—the one in Russia and the other in Britain and the United States—is that they achieved welfare but did not establish justice; or worse, that they achieved economic welfare (to a higher degree in the United States than in Russia) by countermeasures that were themselves unjust (to a lesser degree in the United States than in Russia). Neither was the right revolution. The capitalist revolution seeks to rectify the injustices of primitive capitalism and is calculated to achieve economic welfare to a high degree. It does both without committing the injustices of State capitalism and mixed capitalism.

In both State capitalism and mixed capitalism, the general economic welfare of the population is achieved by a laboristic distribution of wealth. Though in one case the distribution is purely laboristic and in the other only partly so, both quite obviously must accomplish the distribution in some way other than by giving to labor the declining proportion of the total wealth of the economy which it produces.

The laboristic distribution of wealth in our mixed economy therefore takes on the charitable aspect that it has in State capitalism. True, the apologists for mixed capitalism talk *as if* labor were justly entitled to all the wage increases it has received. But this soon becomes double talk, for they acknowledge, on the one hand, that technological improvements in machinery are mainly responsible for the increased productiveness of our economy but, on the other hand, continue to assert that labor itself becomes more and more productive as the capital instruments with which it co-operates become more powerful productively and have more built-in skill for their own self-control.

Having introduced a laboristic and charitable form of distribution, while preserving some of the rights of private property in capital by partly retaining a capitalistic distribution of wealth, our mixed economy is a halfway house on the road to complete socialism. In State capitalism, the distribution, as well as the production and consumption of wealth, is controlled by the State. In mixed capitalism, it is mainly the distribution of wealth that is controlled by the State. Whereas in Russia that control is exerted by direct political action, in the United States it is accomplished only in part by the State—directly through taxation, subsidies, full employment schemes, welfare programs, and public works—and, in part, indirectly through legislation and administrative procedures that support the demands of organized labor for a larger distributive share than labor actually earns.

For the most part, the value of labor is not determined by bargaining in the United States any more than it is in Russia, although all our talk about "collective bargaining" sometimes deceives us into thinking so. Bargaining implies a freely competitive market of sellers and buyers. It implies the right to buy elsewhere if better terms can be found. The laboristic distribution which organized labor, with the help of government, has managed to effect has been achieved by the exercise of political and economic power, not by bargaining. In Russia, the governing bureaucracy is exclusively vested with such consolidated economic and political power. In the United States, the countervailing power of government is in varying degrees wielded in support of the demands of labor, of farmers, and even of industries where it will promote "full employment," even though that results in unneeded surpluses.

Hence while the actual operation of State capitalism entails an almost total loss of economic and political liberty, the actual operation of mixed capitalism has so far resulted in much less drastic reductions in our fundamental freedoms. Since mixed capitalism involves a combination of principles that tend in opposite directions, it can be said, of course, that in proportion as mixed capitalism tends to become more laboristic in the form of its distribution and more socialistic in the method of effecting such distribution, it also tends to cause encroachments on economic and political liberty.

The whole story is not told, however, unless we remember that the creeping socialist revolution and the mixed capitalism it has produced are now congratulated for having "saved capitalism," even by many who once opposed the policies that initiated this revolution in the early thirties.

We have pointed out in an earlier chapter that, quite apart from considerations of either justice or charity, the measures which reformed primitive capitalism were necessary to prevent the collapse that Marx had predicted it would suffer. His prediction, it will be recalled, was made on the assumption that an economy based on private property in capital, and with highly concentrated ownership of capital, would persist in maintaining a purely capitalistic form of distribution. On that assumption, his prediction would have come true.

The mass of the population would be forced to live at a bare subsistence level, and so would be unable to pay for the goods and services that a progressively industrialized economy is able to produce in ever increasing quantities. For a while the exploitation of colonial markets might offset the inadequacy of purchasing power in the domestic market. But this, too, would eventually be exhausted, and then the periodically recurrent crises of overproduction and underconsumption would reach the point where the cycle of boom-and-bust would end in one last bust.

All the modifications of primitive capitalism that have occurred gradually in England and the United States between 1850 and 1950 have tended to prevent the predicted collapse of capitalism, understood as a system of industrial production based on private property in capital. These reforms were effected by the growth of trade unions; by legislation in support of "collective bargaining"; by governmental regulation of wages and hours and of the prices of many goods and services; by government spending for welfare, public works programs and the promotion of full employment; by policies of taxation which facilitated a laboristic distribution of wealth; by all sorts of protection, for society itself and its members, against the excesses of *laissez-faire*—a system which operated, for a short while, to the immense benefit of the owners of capital property.

It is probably the case that these reforms could not have been effected by due process of law, had not the political battle, *i.e.,* the battle for the extension of the franchise, first been won. It was the gradual emergence of political democracy during the last half of the nineteenth century and the first decades of the twentieth that made it possible for primitive capitalism to be overthrown without widespread violence; as the absence of political democracy made recourse to violent revolution almost a necessity in Russia.

The chief human effect of all these reforms was to raise the standard of living of the masses; and, at first, that was the only, or at least the chief, purpose of the effort. But when the cycle of recurrent economic depressions began to give urgent credibility to Marx's prediction of the inevitable collapse of private-property capitalism, another motive for adopting, extending, and accelerating these reforms came into the picture. It was the motive underlying Henry ʔord's voluntary recommendation of the five-dollar day, which other capitalists gradually came to see as eminently expedient.

One way of preventing the threatening collapse, and of correcting the imbalance between mass production and individual consumption, was to build up mass purchasing power by raising real wages. Henry Ford did this in his "revolutionary proposal" to his fellow capitalists, which subsequently became, in the "revolutionary policies" of Franklin Roosevelt, a concerted effort on the part of the government to "save capitalism" (*i.e.,* capitalism based on private property in capital) by closing the circuit of production and consumption.

Capitalism, as a system of industrial production, could not help becoming more and more productive. If private capitalists could not bring themselves *quickly enough* to adopt a laboristic distribution of wealth, then direct governmental action and the action of trade unions with governmental support had to be resorted to, in order to assure consumer demand of such a magnitude as to exert continual pressure on production in the interest of obtaining a rising standard of living. As between Henry Ford's "revolutionary proposal" and Franklin Roosevelt's "revolutionary policies," there was no difference so far as the adoption of a laboristic principle of distribution is concerned. The difference—and it is a crucial one—lies rather in the fact that the intervention of government in the distributive process makes the distribution socialistic in method as well as laboristic in form; and so, in the process of trying to "save" a capitalism that is based on private property in capital, it may have introduced the germ of its destruction.

There is a better and surer way of "saving capitalism" that has not yet been tried. The general standard of living can be raised to the point where mass purchasing power, widely diffused among individuals and families, supports whatever level of production of goods and services we may desire within the limits of our resources. This can be done without recourse to a laboristic distribution of wealth. It can be done by a capitalistic distribution of wealth, if that is based on a widely diffused ownership of capital instruments.

Some may suppose that the difference between these two ways of "making capitalism work" is of no significance, because all that matters is avoiding the collapse that Marx predicted or assuring all men of a decent standard of living. They will not understand the seriousness of the choice we face.

That choice, we repeat, is between the creeping socialist revolution we have been carrying on and the capitalist revolution which remains to be tried. We must not allow our acceptance of the immediate and surface benefits of mixed capitalism to blur our sense of the radically different directions in which these alternatives take us. The distance which our partly socialized economy has traveled along the road to the completely socialized economy of State capitalism may not be great enough yet to frighten us. But we should remember that it is difficult to stand still, especially in an economy that is subject to constantly accelerated technological improvements, *i.e.*, one in which the contribution to production by capital is constantly growing as that of labor is diminishing.

If we try to perpetuate our mixed capitalism, but cannot keep it stabilized in its present state by keeping the conflicting elements in the mixture in their present proportions, in which direction will we move?

Forward to a more and more socialized economy with the specter of State capitalism at the end of the line? As soon as that prospect becomes real for them, most Americans will recoil from it.

Backward, then, to a less and less socialized economy but without any positive solution of all the problems of primitive capitalism? That way lies self-destruction.

The only way out is not to try to perpetuate our mixed economy but to transform it into the unmixed one of Capitalism by extirpating the socialist elements in the mixture. To do this without falling back into primitive capitalism, we must go forward along another path— the path of the capitalist, rather than the socialist, revolution.

We said earlier that our choice lay between perpetuating mixed capitalism and establishing Capitalism—that these were the only real alternatives for Britain and America. But it may be that we do not really have a choice at all.

If mixed capitalism cannot check the inflationary process of the last thirty years, if it cannot resolve the conflict between its policy of full employment and the technological advances that lie ahead, if by the very nature of the elements in the mixture the laboristic aspect of the distribution tends to expand and the capitalistic aspect to contract (just as in primitive capitalism the accumulation of capital tended to expand in the hands of its owners), then, perhaps, mixed capitalism, like primitive capitalism, contains the seeds of its own destruction.

In that case, our only choice is the capitalist revolution. Before we try to show that in that direction lies our salvation as a free society, we will advance some reasons for thinking that our mixed economy cannot solve its problem of inflation and full employment.

MIXED CAPITALISM'S INSOLUBLE PROBLEM: INFLATION

Inflation is a natural and necessary process in an economy that is capitalist in its mode of production and laboristic in its form of distribution. Over 70 percent of the wealth produced is distributed to labor, but over 90 percent of that wealth is produced, not by labor, but by capital instruments. Quite apart from the manifest injustice of this imbalance, it is in this ulcerous gap that the spiral of inflation breeds.

The ulcer cannot be healed without reversing the policies of full employment and laboristic distribution, upon which any attempt to perpetuate our mixed economy must rely. Upon them depends the widely diffused purchasing power that produces a balance between mass production and mass consumption. They are the shot in the arm that keeps our mixed economy functioning. It is precisely that shot in the arm which also produces the disease of inflation—a chronic and progressive disease which cannot be prevented without endangering the health of mixed capitalism.

When our fixed national policy of full employment collides with the irresistible moving force of technological progress, something must give. That something is the virtue of the monetary system—its stable value. The result is inflation. The relation between inflation, as it occurs in our mixed economy, and the policy of full employment can be concretely illustrated in the following manner.

The civilian labor force at the present time is approximately 66,000,000 workers. There are various estimates of the current rate of "productivity increase," i.e., the rate of increase in output in terms of man-hours of input. The most conservative is about 3 percent per year for the economy as a whole. Assuming for the economy an overall productivity increase of 3 percent per year, 1,980,000 workers each year become technologically disemployed (at any given level of production). Estimates of the number of new entrants into the labor market each year also vary, mainly because of the relatively incalculable factor of the increasing number of young and middle-age wives, even mothers of school-age children, who are entering the labor market. A median of the various estimates would be a net increase of 800,000 workers in the labor force each year, with the tendency to increase rather than decrease.

To comply with its policy of full employment, which, under a laboristic form of distribution, is essential to widely diffused purchasing power, our mixed economy must employ each year, under conditions of higher output with progressively less labor input needed, an additional 2,780,000 workers. The best thinking about the present state of the "increasing productiveness of capital" (as it should be called) holds that the newest developments in automation in the years immediately ahead will technologically disemploy workers at a rate substantially exceeding 3 percent a year.[11] For present purposes, however, let us face the problem of how our mixed economy can provide full employment for an additional 2,780,000 workers a year in an industrial system that turns out an ever increasing amount of wealth with a constantly diminishing use of labor.

One solution of this problem would be for the government to assign a quota of increased employment to each business firm each year, and to order each firm to employ fully, at prevailing or increased rates of pay, the additional number of workers through increasing their output, and at the same time to make all reasonable efforts to utilize the most productive machinery available. *Only a totalitarian state could enforce such measures.* In addition, if they were carried out by coercion, their effect would be extremely deflationary; for they would result in staggering increases in output without regard to the effect on business costs.

Absurd as the solution just proposed may be as a theoretically possible means of implementing a policy of full employment, since it is totally impracticable in a free society, it nevertheless helps to illustrate why the methods we must use to implement our policy of full employment are necessarily inflationary.

In order to maintain as much freedom as possible in our economy and still bring about full employment, it is necessary for us continuously to raise output in a constantly accelerating orgy of production, yet without rigid government control of wages, prices or methods of production. But in the face of the increasing productiveness of our capital, there is no way of constantly raising output to a level commensurate with full employment, while leaving the economic partici-

---

[11] See, for example, *The Scientific-Industrial Revolution,* a study published in 1957 by the New York investment banking house of Model, Roland & Stone; and also the report of the hearings before the Subcommittee on Economic Stabilization of the Joint Economic Committee, on *Automation and Technological Change* (1955) and on *Instrumentation and Automation* (1956).

pants relatively free, except by constantly increasing our artificial stimulation of purchasing power.

We have ceased to think of many of these stimulants in connection with the problem of providing full employment, but that is one of the principal ways they function. A mere enumeration of some of the devices now in use to overstimulate purchasing power will indicate how far we have gone in this direction. It will also show how radical our future steps must become to keep pace with the relentless advance in the increasing productivity of capital. The following are some of our more potent stimulants to purchasing power.

1. *Constant union pressure upon wage levels, supported by extensive grants of the countervailing power of government.* Largely as a result of these forces, wages are raised well above their competitive levels.

2. *Defense spending, which now amounts to about 40 billion dollars a year.* While spending on defense increases production—and therefore employment—it satisfies no consumer desires. The defense products, therefore, do not absorb any of the purchasing power arising out of their production, thus leaving this purchasing power to be used in the further stimulation of production, and therefore of employment in other industries.

3. *A governmentally encouraged system of easy construction mortgage credit, giving a vast stimulation to the high-employment building trades.* At the present time there is outstanding some 103 billion dollars in housing mortgage credit, 36 billion dollars in multi-family and commercial mortgage credit, and around 10 billion dollars in farm mortgage credit.

4. *A governmentally encouraged system of easy consumer credit for durable goods, of which some 42 billion dollars is now outstanding.*

5. *Governmental subsidization of farm production, and therefore of farm employment, with about 8 billion dollars of farm surpluses in government hands today, notwithstanding gifts or sales below cost of vast quantities of these stores in recent years.*

6. *Defense stock-piling of minerals and strategic materials, with the effect of stimulating production and employment in the mining and processing industries.* About 8 billion dollars of such materials are now on hand and, notwithstanding the passing of the strategic goals, great pressure is building up to continue these programs.

7. *Foreign aid subsidies, frequently taking the form of credits for purchase of goods in the United States.* Over 40 billion dollars of such subsidies have been granted since 1948.

8. *The "emergency facility" rapid amortization program, heavily used during World War II and initiated again after the outbreak of hostilities in Korea in 1950.* Between November, 1950, and June, 1957, 21,946 certificates of necessity have been granted by the Office of Defense Mobilization upon 38.3 billion dollars of new construction, of which 23.1 billion dollars has been certified for rapid write-off against corporate income taxes. This is, in its economic effect, an aggregate of 23.1 billion dollars of governmental interest-free loans for the purpose of stimulating the construction of over 38 billion dollars of new plants and equipment.

9. *The steady expansion in the number of civilian employees of federal, state, and local governments.* From 1949 to 1957, the aggregate number of governmental employees rose from 5,856,000 to 7,388,000. Of these, nearly 2,400,000 were civilian employees of the federal government.

10. *Social Security payments in excess of those actuarially supportable by the social security fund.* There are many actuaries who believe that the social security fund is but a fraction of liabilities already accrued against it. If so, current social security payments may be considered as partly, if not largely, overstimulation of consumer demand in excess of the payments which would be actuarially proper on the basis of the reserves against such liabilities. In effect, this would be simply a rapidly increasing but unrecorded national debt currently incurred to support mass purchasing power.

11. *The very persistence of the federal government's debt in the face of unprecedented economic prosperity.* This represents nothing but the overstimulation of consumer purchasing power. Rather than reduce our debt during an era of prosperity, the best we have been able to do is to prevent it from increasing beyond 275 billion

dollars. The failure of the government to reduce its debt during the decade since the end of World War II without question reflects an unwillingness to incur the shrinkage in consumer purchasing power which such debt retirement would cause.

Each year, as it becomes more and more difficult to maintain full employment in an economy in which the output of wealth is expanded by the constantly higher productiveness of capital, the orgy of production must be stimulated to ever higher peaks. The pace of technological advance itself accelerates the process.

The stimulation of production by the creation—through credit, wage raises, etc.—of sufficient purchasing power in excess of that generated through the normal distribution of wealth is now the accepted policy of both political parties in the United States. Both have espoused the national policy of full employment as formulated by the Full Employment Act of 1946.

Under this policy, progressive and increasing inflation is a normal and necessary result of the overstimulation of production through constantly increasing mass purchasing power.[12] The productive system is capable of expanding its output to untold limits—to levels not now contemplated in our wildest dreams—provided the purchasing power, the fuel of this mighty engine, is applied in ever increasing quantities. But the system needs a constantly diminishing proportion of labor, through whose ranks the mass purchasing power must be diffused

[12] Lord Beveridge, who, through his book *Full Employment in a Free Society*, New York, 1945, was one of the intellectual pioneers of laboristic distribution, in a speech on October 20, 1956, in London, noted that one of the disastrous results of simultaneous attempts to have both *full employment* and a *free society* is inflation. Lord Beveridge said: "Most of my working life was spent in University service. When I left that service to become a politician in 1945, I was able to take with me for superannuation enough thousand pounds to feel fairly happy for my future. Now each of those pounds is worth about 6s. 8d. Like many other healthy people in the seventies I am in danger of living longer than I can afford to live. Our plans for useful old age are all going hay-wire. The underlying reason for that is the claim of each industry to fix its own money wages by sovereign action. Under full employment, that is leading to destruction of the value of money, and is spreading wide-spread poverty among all who are trying to live on savings or fixed pensions."

by full employment. Out of these conflicting tendencies is born the paradox that our economy, characterized by the greatest assembly of labor-eliminating machines and devices on earth, has the highest proportion ever reached of both men and women engaged in paid employments. A constantly increasing proportion of the population must enter the labor market if the laboristic distribution of wealth is to keep pace with the increasing productiveness of capital.

Another solution of the problem has been proposed. It is offered as a means of providing full employment through the pressure of generating excessive quantities of purchasing power, *while at the same time preventing inflation.* It is strongly advocated by some of our most prominent labor leaders and by many political exponents of the theory of "full employment without inflation."

This theory proposes the observance by business—voluntarily, if possible; otherwise involuntarily, under government coercion—of two policies. One is a policy of limiting wage increases to so-called productivity increases. The other is a policy, to be pursued by business, of abstaining from raising prices in response to increases in wages where such increases are limited to "productivity increases." [13]

With regard to the second of these policies, we should note first that it calls upon business to abandon the competitive setting of prices, just as our mixed economy has long since abandoned, or suppressed, the competitive setting of wages. Regardless of the competitive forces at work in the market, the application of the second policy would arrest the prices of products and services, while the application of the first would automatically increase the wages of labor at a rate commensurate with the increasing productiveness of capital instruments.

We must look deeper, however, to see the ultimate significance of the theory of full employment without inflation.

---

[13] For a clear statement of these two policies, see Philip Murray's Annual Report for 1952, reprinted in the Supplement to *The People Shall Judge,* Chicago, 1956: pp. 278–294. For what closely resembles an affirmation of them, see President Eisenhower's State of the Union message delivered to Congress, January, 1957.

As we have already noted, one essential right of private property in an instrument of production is the right to receive the wealth produced by that instrument, *i.e.,* a return proportionate to the value of the contribution it makes to the production of wealth. The only impartial determination of the value of that contribution is one made through the operation of supply and demand under conditions of free competition. We estimate that the productive power of capital instruments accounts for over 90 percent of the wealth produced, but that over 70 percent of that wealth is distributed to labor in accordance with our mixed economy's partly laboristic and partly capitalistic form of distribution.[14] This means that one of the most essential rights of private property in capital has already been greatly attenuated. It also means that effective and highly concentrated ownership of capital in about 5 percent of the households of our economy is incompatible with the production of some 90 percent of the wealth by capital instruments.

Now the proposal by advocates of "full employment without inflation," translated into language which recognizes that increased "productivity" is the increased economic productivity of capital, comes to this: that wages should be allowed to increase in proportion to the increase in the wealth produced by capital. In point of fact, these "productivity increases" are increases in output that result from additional investment in capital instruments. Hence the essence of the proposal is that a large portion, if not all, of the increased wealth produced by the new or improved capital instruments should be passed on to the workers employed in industry.

The ultimate meaning of the theory of full employment without inflation is, therefore, that future capital formation should be subject to a process of socialization; for it is only through government regulation or through the countervailing power of government in support of organized labor that such an unjust distribution of wealth can be effected. If technological advance is not arrested, and if

14 See pp. 40–43, *supra,* and also the Appendix, pp. 256–264, *infra.*

labor should continue to receive a larger and larger portion of the wealth produced by newly formed capital, then the rate of socialization—or, what is the same, the degree of attenuation of the right of private property in capital to receive a full return on what such property earns—will conform to the rate of technological progress.

Here, then, is the perilous dilemma that confronts our mixed capitalist economy.

On the one hand, to continue to carry out the policy of full employment without controlling prices or otherwise rigidly regulating the economy would be to allow inflation to reach the point where public confidence in the monetary system is gravely weakened. When that happens, controls equivalent to full public ownership of capital by the state will most certainly ensue.

On the other hand, to adopt the theory of full employment without inflation is to initiate at once a process of further socialization and to project it at a rate which will be governed by the rate of technological progress. This, too, can only end in the complete socialization of our economy.

In either case, our mixed economy seems to be sowing the seeds of its own destruction. Even if we wished to perpetuate our system of mixed capitalism instead of dissolving its mixture in favor of Capitalism, we almost certainly would not be able to do so. When its inherent and incurable weakness becomes fully apparent to us, we may realize that, if we wish to avoid the complete socialist revolution of State capitalism, a capitalist counterrevolution is our only choice.

OUR ONLY CHOICE—CAPITALISM

It is one thing to have no choice because of inexorable necessities, and quite another to have only one choice when one thing is clearly seen to be the best means to the end we have in view.

We are under no necessity to choose the path of the capitalist revolution. Nothing compels us to make every feasible effort to establish a capitalist economy based on a widely diffused private ownership of capital, instead of allowing the creeping socialist revolution to push us further and further in the direction of a capitalist economy based on the public ownership of capital and the complete control by the State of the production, distribution, and consumption of wealth.

Only when the organization of an economy is seen by us as something which by its justice or injustice either serves or defeats the ends of a free society and a good human life for all men, does Capitalism, as opposed to State capitalism, become our only choice. If we were not devoted to the institutions of political democracy, because through their intrinsic justice they afford all men the freedom and dignity essential to the pursuit of happiness, if we were not deeply imbued with the democratic faith in human equality, if we did not firmly believe that equality of opportunity in a truly classless as well as free society held out the promise of the fullest development of the potentialities of the human spirit—if these things did not constitute the ideal goal of our aspirations, we would be under no necessity to undertake the capitalist revolution. But given these ends, we have no other choice.

That being the case, we should not look upon the capitalist revolution as something forced upon us by the instability of our mixed economy and by the grave risks we would incur of ultimate consequences that we abhor, should we try to perpetuate it. Even if it were possible to perpetuate mixed capitalism in its present condition, with no more socialization and no greater concentration of political and economic power in the hands of government than now exists, we *ought* still elect to undo the mixture and try to create Capitalism. The obligation expressed in that word "ought" is both one of justice and one of prudence—one of justice insofar as Capitalism represents a justly organized economy as mixed capitalism does not, one of prudence insofar as Capitalism is clearly the better economic means to the political and human goods that constitute our ideal goal.

We need not argue the case for Capitalism on the basis of economic justice. That has already been sufficiently done in Chapter Five. What must be done is to show that Capitalism, of the various forms that an industrial economy can take, is the economic counterpart of political democracy and that, together with political democracy, it is the best means to the ideal of a classless society of free and equal men whose freedom and equality gives them all the opportunity for a truly human life.

However, a brief summary of the intrinsic justice of Capitalism is necessary for the purpose of showing how such justice creates an economic democracy that is the counterpart of political democracy, and how together they serve the cause of freedom and human happiness.

Of all forms of government, democracy is the most just or the only perfectly just constitution of a political society. Tyranny enslaves men. Despotism, even when benevolent, degrades them to the level of children; for though it paternalistically takes care of them, it allows them no voice in their own government. Only constitutional or republican government grants men the political status of citizenship through which, with suffrage, they can participate in self-government. But some republics are constituted as oligarchies. These violate the natural right of all men to be citizens by conferring on the few, and refusing to the rest, the political liberty to which they are all equally entitled. Only the democratic constitution of a republic, with its basic principle of universal equal suffrage, grants all men citizenship, and so gives all of them the political liberty that comes from having a share in the sovereignty and from being able thereby to participate in self-government. Hence democracy is the only perfectly just form of government.

In like manner, Capitalism is the only perfectly just form of an industrial economy. By its preservation of private property in capital as the chief means whereby men can, in an industrial economy, participate in the production and distribution of wealth; by its principle of proportioning distributive shares of the wealth produced on the basis of the contributions made to its production, as measured impartially by supply and demand in a freely competitive market; by its limitation of undue concentrations in the ownership of capital; and by its correlative effort to diffuse that ownership as widely as possible among the persons or families in the economy, Capitalism embodies all the principles of justice with regard to the distribution of wealth and protects the right of every man to subsistence, and its inseparable right to private property as a means of earning that subsistence. A purely capitalistic distribution of wealth in a highly productive capitalist economy gives full effect to these basic rights.

Thus it is clear that Capitalism will produce economic democracy or the counterpart in the economic order of democracy in the political order. As democracy is a polity in which it is possible for all men to participate as citizens, so Capitalism is an economy in which it is possible for all men to participate as capitalists. As their participation in government through the suffrage of citizenship gives them political liberty, so their participation in the production of wealth through the ownership of capital will give them economic freedom.

Furthermore, it is in respect of their all being citizens alike that men enjoy political equality. They are not divided into a ruling and a subject class. So it is in respect of all having alike the opportunity to participate in production as capitalists that men will enjoy economic equality. They will not be divided into an owning and a laboring class (*i.e.,* capitalists and proletariat). Hence the establishment of Capitalism as the economic substructure of democracy will produce for the first time in history the ideal classless society in which the whole mass of humankind will constitute a single class—one that is truly privileged and justly so.[15]

15 It is often said that the institution of private property provides the economic basis for democracy. That is not the case; or rather, it is a misleading half-truth. The institution of private property may be necessary for economic freedom, but by itself it is hardly sufficient for the diffusion of such freedom among all who

We just referred to Capitalism as providing the requisite economic substructure for democracy. That statement is intended to convey not only the subordination of the economic to the political order as a whole, but also the necessity of economic freedom for the protection and vitality of political liberty.

The second point needs further comment. We have pointed out several times the reluctance or refusal of our ancestors to extend the franchise to workingmen, or to grant equal suffrage to propertied men of leisure and to those who were dependent for their subsistence on toil and had to work twelve hours a day or more from childhood to the grave. One reason they gave for this, as expressed by John Adams and Alexander Hamilton, was that no man who was dependent for his subsistence on the arbitrary will of others (as propertyless laborers were in those days) had the economic independence requisite for citizenship and the use of political liberty.

There were other reasons, too. It was felt that since the propertied and the propertyless did not belong to the same economic class, neither should they belong to the same political class. Furthermore, it was thought that the owners of property, by reason of their property, had more at stake than the propertyless workers; and in a sense they did. This led to the maxim that the country should be run by those who owned it. Finally, John Stuart Mill pointed out, as Aristotle had before him, that the trouble with making workingmen citizens is that they had neither the education to fit them for the duties of citizenship nor the leisure in which to exercise citizenship by an active participation in government. As a simple matter of fact, this was as true when Mill wrote his essay on *Representative Government* in

---

should be citizens in a democracy. In primitive capitalism, the small capitalist class, in whose hands the private ownership of capital was concentrated, were among the most strenuous and obstinate opponents of all efforts to move toward political democracy by extensions of the franchise to the nonpropertied working masses Hence it is Capitalism—the diffused ownership of capital, not just the private ownership of it—that creates the economic substructure appropriate to democracy.

1863 as it was when Aristotle wrote the *Politics* in the fourth century B.C.

The good sense in all of this would seem to point to the conclusion that the universal ownership by individuals of wealth-producing and income-bearing property, which is capital in an industrial economy, is needed as the economic basis for the universal possession of political rights and privileges which come with citizenship in a republic. Nevertheless, it may be argued that it is not necessary for all men to be capitalists in order for them to be made citizens, to be trusted with political liberty, or to be relied on to take an active and responsible interest in public affairs because they have a serious stake in the results of self-government.

In support of such objection, it may be argued that we have universal suffrage now and that it is working reasonably well even though under our mixed capitalism only a relatively small number of citizens are also capitalists in any significant sense of that term. It is working well, it may be contended, because the spread of universal public schooling with the extension of the franchise until one has become as universal as the other, has provided the education prerequisite for citizenship. That, together with the steady reduction in the hours of work which industrial production has made possible and which organized labor and government regulations have made actual for the working masses, provides them not only with the training for political life but with ample opportunity, in the time that has been freed for leisure, to participate actively in the affairs of government.

All this has been done in support of democracy by our mixed capitalist economy and without making all men capitalists in order to enable them to be good citizens. Why, then, is Capitalism required as the economic substructure for democracy?

The answer is to be found in two considerations. Neither has to do with education or time for leisure; for it must be admitted that these prerequisites of citizenship can be provided without making all men capitalists. But these are not the only prerequisites.

One of the additional considerations is the kind of economic independence which can be had in a capitalist economy only by being a capitalist. In our mixed economy, those who are neither capitalists nor members of labor unions do not gain their subsistence without dependence on the arbitrary will of other men. And those who enjoy such economic security and independence as they have through the power of organized labor, together with the power of government in support of organized labor, do not have their economic security and independence in function of their own property, but only by a struggle for power in the war of class against class.

Even if every labor union were organized and operated in the image of democracy, its members would still not be as economically free as men who had a grasp on their livelihood as independent individuals rather than as members of a group, and had it as a matter of personal right rather than as a matter of organized might. Since the power of labor unions depends upon the countervailing power of government, to have a grasp on one's livelihood through organized might is to be dependent for it on the power of government. This is the second of the additional considerations mentioned above.

Both of these considerations entered into Thomas Jefferson's argument that an agrarian, as opposed to an industrial, economy provided the economic basis for republican government. He pictured an agrarian economy as one in which the great majority of families obtained their subsistence from farms they owned and worked, instead of being dependent on wages and employers as were the families of the workers in the manufacturing cities that were just beginning to arise. The land-owning farmer had the kind of economic independence which, according to Jefferson, was the ideal basis for citizenship and for a vigorous as well as virtuous use of political liberty.

Such men were not beholden to government for their subsistence or their independence. Their hold on both was integral to their ownership of income-bearing property. Consequently, they were in a position to participate in government as independent persons. They did not seek to endow government with extraordinary powers in order to give them freedom. On the contrary, because they had their freedom in their own property and in their citizenship, they sought to limit the powers of government to such as were necessary to protect their property and safeguard their rights as citizens.

What Jefferson said in terms of a laborist agrarian economy, what Aristotle had said before him in terms of a similar economy, holds true of a capitalist industrial economy. We need only transpose the terms. In place of the slave-owning aristocrat who was the ideal citizen in Aristotle's day, or in place of the land-owning farmer who was the ideal citizen in Jefferson's day, we need only substitute the capital-owning *common* man as the ideal citizen in our own day. In all three cases, such men have the kind of independence that is needed for self-government; and since they have their economic and political freedom by right, not by might, they will try to limit the powers of government to those necessary for the protection of their rights.

But while Capitalism will thus serve democracy, and while together they will create an economically and politically classless society, that is not the ultimate contribution which Capitalism can make to human life. Under Capitalism, as the participation of men in the production of wealth through the employment of their labor diminishes, their participation through their ownership of capital will increase. Under Capitalism, men will be saved the waste involved in all the unnecessary forms of toil that our present mixed economy imposes.

It requires no special insight to see that labor spent in the production of agricultural and industrial surpluses is wasted toil; nor to understand the mystery of why, as hours are shortened under the pressure of organized labor, increasing numbers of workers hold two and three jobs and an increasing number of married women with growing children enter the labor market. A laboristic distribution of wealth requires labor, whether or not it is needed for the production of desired wealth. Only Capitalism invites all men to go beyond the production of wealth to what is essential to their happiness once their subsistence is assured—engagement in the liberal pursuits of leisure which produce the goods of civilization and of the human spirit.

In this respect Capitalism, as a justly organized industrial economy, has a marked advantage over the most justly organized laborist economy of which the past can boast. In a just laborist economy, where no man was a slave, all men had to spend most of their life and energy in toil for subsistence. No man enjoyed the leisure of purely liberal work.

In the laborist economy that was built on the grievous injustice of chattel slavery, some men—the members of the leisure class—were able "to live well by engaging," as Aristotle said, "in philosophy and politics," or, in other words, by spending most of their life and energy in purely liberal work productive of the goods of civilization: the liberal arts and sciences, the institutions of the state and of religion.

Any capitalist economy, by its very nature as a system of industrial production, can be the most potent source of time for leisure work that the world has ever seen. The *possibility* of leisure for all men is equally present in a State capitalist economy, such as that of Soviet Russia, and in a mixed capitalist economy, such as ours. But both State capitalism and mixed capitalism involve a laboristic distribution of wealth which makes both of them erect false ideals about human work for subsistence. The liability of all to labor is one of the tenets of State capitalism. The goal of full employment is a central objective in the scheme of mixed capitalism. Neither of these is a sound ideal according to the principles of Capitalism.

The ultimate goal of Capitalism is not full employment on the level of subsistence work but rather the fullest employment of one's time in leisure work. Far from its being morally sound for all men to be liable to labor, the moral truth is rather that all men are obligated to spend as much time as they can in liberal pursuits. And if it is possible for them to spend most of their time in liberal activities, because they obtain a viable income from the productive use of their property in capital, there is nothing immoral about their not spending any time or energy in doing subsistence work, especially that which is mechanical in quality. Capitalists, of course, must devote time and effort in the management and husbanding of their property, but this is an activity that is at least liberal in quality.

When we refer to liberal pursuits, we have two things in mind. One is purely liberal work of the sort that is exemplified in the activities of statesmen, philosophers, scientists, artists, teachers, etc. The other is the kind of work that is done by technicians and managers who, even though they are engaged in producing wealth rather than the goods of civilization, are nevertheless performing activities which are liberal in quality though employed in the production of subsistence.

Men who enjoy such activity, as compared with philosophy, pure science, the fine arts, and teaching, may have a lower aim so far as an absolute order of goods is concerned. But so far as the human quality of the work is concerned, they are engaged in creative activity that has all the essential characteristics of leisure.

In addition, those who are engaged in the management of large-scale industrial enterprises are, within their own corporations, performing the quasi-political functions of legislation, adjudication, and administration. And in the relation of private corporations to one another and to the agencies of government, the managers of business and industry, like the heads of private universities, hospitals, and foundations, should function as statesmen.

With this important qualification in mind, it should now be possible to say, without misunderstanding, that the ultimate aim of Capitalism, beyond the establishment of economic justice and freedom, is the enjoyment of leisure by all men in the major portion of their life's time. Thus it aims to do for all men what a primitive laborist economy could do for none, and what a civilized laborist economy based on slavery succeeded in doing only for the few. By substituting machines for slaves, under conditions of advanced industrial production, both State capitalism and mixed capitalism are in a position to do for all men what the slave societies of the past did for the few. But because of their fundamental errors and confusions about the disposition of capital and labor in the production and distribution of wealth, they do not clearly and consistently aim at this result. On the contrary, they often tend in the opposite direction. Only Capitalism, by the soundness and consistency of its principles, aims at the right human result—the good life for all men.

8 THE THEORY OF CAPITALISM

THE ECONOMICS OF CAPITALISM

We think it may be useful to summarize the theory of Capitalism, in this concluding chapter on the idea of the capitalist revolution, before we turn to the practical program by which it can be accomplished. That theory involves more than the economics of the production and distribution of wealth. It involves basic considerations of political economy, concerning government's role in relation to the economy as a whole. It also involves some fundamental ethical judgments about wealth in relation to more important goods, and about subsistence work in relation to more important activities.

The economics of Capitalism has been sufficiently discussed in the preceding pages to require only the briefest summary here. The following points are its essential elements:

1. The industrial production of wealth, in which capital is responsible for the major portion of the wealth produced, and labor for only a small fraction of it.

2. The private ownership of capital, together with the widest possible diffusion of such ownership among the households of the economy.
3. The production of wealth by the voluntary association and co-operation of private owners of the factors of production (*i.e.,* private owners of labor power and private owners of capital) in which most of the persons involved will function as capitalists as well as workers.
4. The distribution of the wealth produced in accordance with the property rights of the persons engaged in its production, with the extent of the distributive shares accorded the various participants, determined by the extent of their contribution as that is evaluated through supply and demand under conditions of free competition.
5. The progressive reduction of the labor force (*i.e.,* the number engaged in mechanical labor) with the progressive automation of industrial production; and a steady increase in the employment of men in leisure work, or in subsistence work that is not mechanical in quality.
6. The maintenance of a generally high standard of living by means of earned incomes consisting of wages established under freely competitive conditions and the earnings of capital shares (the latter being especially important in those cases in which competitively set wages do not constitute a viable income).
7. The creation of widely diffused mass purchasing power as a means of supporting mass production, without an artificial expansion of production for the mere sake of providing employment, whether or not the wealth produced is desired.
8. The promotion and adoption of every technological advance that will result in a more efficient industrial production of wealth, accompanied by a progressive diminution in the amount of subsistence work needed for its production.

Certain widely prevalent errors have prevented, and may still prevent, those who are concerned with the economic problems of our society from understanding the theory of Capitalism as outlined above. It may be therapeutic to call attention to the most insidious of these fallacies in current economic thought, which are to be found not only in the writings of avowed socialists but also in the writings of the leading apologists for our present mixed capitalism. They can be briefly summarized as follows:

1. The failure to recognize capital instruments as active producers of wealth in the same sense that men doing subsistence work are active producers of wealth.

2. The consequent false distinction between being an active participant in the production of wealth through one's own labor and being a passive participant in its production through one's capital.

3. The further consequent notion that income derived from the productive use of capital is not earned in the same sense as is income derived from the productive use of labor power, together with the notion that property in capital, being passive, should not be accorded the same rights as property in labor.

4. The illusion that mechanical labor becomes increasingly productive in proportion as the whole industrial economy becomes increasingly productive through the introduction of more and more efficient capital instruments, together with a consequent blindness to the fact that mechanical labor in an advanced industrial economy such as ours produces a very small portion of our wealth (probably 10 percent or less).

5. The failure to realize that in our present economy property rights in capital have been substantially eroded, together with self-deception in the belief that our economy respects the rights of private property in capital.

6. The failure to recognize that diffusion of economic power is impossible without diffusion of private ownership of capital and without full respect for the rights of such ownership, together with the failure to see that effective private ownership of capital, widely diffused, is the only institution in a free society capable of containing and limiting the necessarily centralized political power of modern governments.

7. Recognition of the importance of effective and adequate capital formation, without recognition of the necessity of a progressively broader diffusion of its private ownership.

8. Blindness to the fact that a massive concentration of capital property in a minute proportion of the households in an industrial economy bars the way to an effective participation by all house-

holds in the production of wealth, together with consequent blindness to the fact that the economic security thus achieved by a few households is destructive of economic security for the rest.

9. The failure to recognize that it is the maldistribution of participation in production, through excessive concentration in the ownership of capital, that is the basic cause of the economic dislocations or periodic "depressions" in an industrial economy based on private property in capital and labor.

10. The mistaken belief that full employment and a laboristic distribution of wealth are indispensable to the creation of a widely diffused purchasing power adequate for the consumption of the wealth an industrial society is able to produce, and which is therefore necessary to prevent "depressions."

11. The false notion that labor-saving devices create employment; *i.e.,* the fallacy of supposing that technological advances are compatible with a policy of full employment in subsistence work, which often takes the form of concealing their incompatibility by an orgy of artificially stimulated overproduction.

12. Self-deception with regard to the fact that corporate managers or executives are subsistence workers in exactly the same sense as are all other employees of industrial corporations, differing from these others only in the degree of importance and creativeness of their work, together with the mistaken belief that the corporate managers or executives are the "real capitalists" in our society, in contradistinction to the "mere owners" of the capital that the corporation employs.

The correction or elimination of these errors and fallacies would open the door to a sound understanding of the economics of Capitalism. That, in fact, is almost impossible as long as these currently prevalent mistakes persist.

THE POLITICS OF CAPITALISM

As a political economy, Capitalism is not to be confused with the so-called *laissez-faire* system of an absolutely self-regulating market.

It does not rest on the utterly mistaken belief that if only government will keep its hands completely off the economy, the operation of natural economic laws will result in economic prosperity, general economic welfare, and justice, as well as freedom, for all.

As with regard to the economics of Capitalism, so with regard to the politics of Capitalism, a number of widely held beliefs prevent the truth from being seen. The most obfuscating of these beliefs relate to the economic function of competition. It is believed, for example, that free competition uninhibited by governmental regulation or interference will function as an automatic regulator of economic activity. It is also believed that free competition will provide full employment and that it will automatically sustain itself.

The repeated and widespread demonstrations that competition does not provide full employment, and that it normally and naturally tends to destroy itself, should by now have discredited these doctrinaire *laissez-faire* beliefs. But unfortunately they still persist in certain quarters. It is unfortunate also that so much of the virtue claimed in the past for free competition was based on the illusion that it would provide full employment and that it would perpetuate itself because, as a consequence, when these beliefs are discredited, the true functions of free competition are often discredited with them.[1]

As a political economy, Capitalism recognizes that free competition does not and cannot provide full employment, and further, that full employment itself is an undesirable objective and that the means of achieving it are equally undesirable. Insisting that, in the absence of

[1] A thorough analysis of the functions of free competition will be presented in *Capitalism*. In a brief summary of that analysis, we would like to emphasize the following points: that free competition in all the markets of the economy (other than those in the field of the technically unavoidable public utilities) will determine for the common good of the society (a) what items of wealth will be produced and in what quantities; (b) the technological manner of their production; (c) the identity of the producers, *i.e.*, the owners of labor and the owners of capital; (d) when items of wealth shall be produced and where; (e) the value of the contribution of each participant in production; and (f) the value of goods and services in all stages of production and at all times following the completion of their production.

freely competitive markets whereby economic values can be objectively and impartially determined, the whole conception of a just economy becomes hollow, Capitalism also recognizes that the most assiduous efforts of government to regulate the economy are required to preserve free competition in all markets against the inherent propensity of free competition to destroy itself. Under Capitalism, therefore, the government has the obligation to maintain free competition in all the markets of the economy.

Far from being a system of *laissez-faire,* Capitalism is a political economy in which the maximum freedom of the participants in economic activity is achieved by government regulation *consistent with the economic principles of Capitalism* and, especially, with its principles of justice. The absence of proper economic regulations can no more create a free economy than the absence of social regulations can create a free society.

It is the duty of government to promote Capitalism by giving the fullest protection to private property, not only property in consumer goods but also and principally property in the instruments of production, whether capital or labor power. In the case of property in capital instruments, the aim of government should be to make such property effective as a source of earned income. To do this, it must protect the rights of capitalists to receive the full return from the wealth produced by the shares of capital that they own. In addition, government should surround the economic status of the capitalist as stockholder with legal protections and privileges analogous to those it has conferred on the political status of the citizen, and for an analogous reason; namely, in order to make the capitalist, like the citizen, a man who can exert legal power in the control of his own affairs.

Where competition is the instrument of just evaluation, and hence of justice in the distribution of wealth, monopoly is an instrument of power whereby some men can impose their arbitrary will on others. Furthermore, a diffused ownership of capital property would thrive on a truly competitive system, whereas monopoly in all its forms facilitates every tendency toward concentrated ownership of capital. Our present antitrust laws are conceptually inadequate to foster free competition and to prevent all forms of monopoly.

In addition to giving full protection to the rights of private property and to safeguarding free competition against its own inherent tendencies toward monopoly, government should positively promote Capitalism by regulations designed to provide every household with the opportunity to contribute to production, either through the ownership of capital or through the ownership of labor, or through both, in ways that will justly enable each household to earn a viable distributive share of the wealth produced.

Government is under an obligation to make it possible at all times for each and every consumer unit or household to participate in the production of wealth to an extent sufficient for earning a viable income. If a capitalistic form of distribution is observed, this of necessity requires that, since the wealth is largely produced by capital, it must also be largely distributed in the form of returns to the owners of capital. As the burden of production shifts from labor to capital, an increasing number of the households in the economy must, therefore, become owners of capital.

There will always be millions of workers employed in an industrial economy. Nevertheless, if the contribution of an individual household toward the production of wealth is exclusively by labor; and if, when objectively and justly evaluated through free competition, what such labor earns is less than sufficient to provide a decent standard of living for that household, then the opportunity must be given it to enlarge its participation in production through becoming an owner of capital.

Under mixed capitalism, with its unjust laboristic form of distribution, our government pursues the objective of general economic welfare by a policy of full employment. Under Capitalism, with a just capitalistic form of distribution, the government would pursue the objective of securing everyone's natural right to earn a viable income by a policy of ensuring everyone's effective participation in production— by means of capital if labor alone does not suffice.

We have just indicated the positive duties of government in regulating the economy for the purpose of promoting and preserving Capitalism. In addition, government must, of course, regulate economic activities, as it must regulate all other activities in society, with an eye to preventing some men from inflicting injury on others. Such things as adulteration of products, unfair practices, or fraud in business transactions, should be no less subject to proscriptive regulation than embezzlement and highway robbery.

The role of government in relation to the economy has a negative as well as a positive side. To promote Capitalism, there are certain things government should not do, and these are as important as the things it should do. Government should not own and operate capital property except in those rare instances, such as public highways, in which private ownership is unworkable. With the exception just noted, government should not engage in the production of wealth; and, consequently, it should avoid engaging in the distribution or redistribution of wealth incidental to engaging in its production.

Finally, the theory of Capitalism as a political economy calls for a thorough re-examination and, probably, reformation of two quasi-political institutions—the stock corporation and the labor union. These two institutions are themselves the inevitable by-products of an industrial or capitalist mode of production.

In an industrial system of production the capital required for large-scale enterprises is of such magnitude as to require joint stock holdings and shared ownership; and with every stage of technological advance, it has become more and more necessary for the stock corporation, with a large number of nonoperating owners of the shares of its stock, to replace the solitary capitalist who both owned all the capital involved and managed the operation himself.

For a quite different reason the factory system of production, during the hundred years or more when primitive capitalism prevailed, necessitated the formation of labor unions in order to give those who could participate in production only by labor sufficient power to cope with the enormous power wielded by the few in whose hands the ownership of capital was concentrated.

Over a hundred years ago, de Tocqueville saw in the rise of these new forms of voluntary association the emergence of what he called "secondary agencies of government." These, he thought, might serve to prevent the concentration of all political and economic power in the hands of the State, as in a sense the feudal lords of the ancient regime, functioning as secondary agencies of government, prevented all political and economic power from being concentrated in the sovereignty of the king. The corporation and the union might thus prevent the mass society, which was just emerging and which he called "democracy," from degenerating into the tyranny of the totalitarian state.[2]

Soviet Russia, in which there are neither stock corporations nor labor unions, confirms de Tocqueville's brilliant insight into the conditions under which a mass society with an industrial economy would experience the tyranny of the totalitarian state. But de Tocqueville did not foresee the role that corporations and labor unions would play as opposing centers of power in the economic conflicts of mixed capitalism; nor did he foresee the difficulties that democratic governments would face in controlling these quasi-political institutions, some with more economic power at their disposal than most of the cities or states that constitute subordinate units of government in the federal organization of our political society.

In the American tradition, it has long been a maxim of government that it is not power as such, but irresponsible or uncontrollable power which endangers freedom. The giant corporations which now exist and the giant labor union which has just come into existence represent enormous concentrations of power which have not as yet been made fully responsible for the use they make of their power. The most difficult task that government faces, in effecting the transition from our

[2] See *Democracy in America,* Second Part, Book IV, especially Chs. 5–6.

present mixed capitalism, is to tame and harness the power of these creatures of capitalism and, by making them responsible in the discharge of the limited functions they should perform, make them serve Capitalism and democracy, or at least prevent them from despoiling either.[3]

The problem of the labor union under Capitalism is different from the problem of the corporation. Under Capitalism, the labor union will obviously not be needed as an instrument of power to effect a laboristic distribution of wealth. This was the function it performed in the transition from primitive to mixed capitalism, and is still performing. But to say that the labor union will not be needed to perform this function in a justly organized economy, with diffused ownership of capital and a capitalistic distribution of wealth, is not to say that there will then be no socially useful service for it to undertake. Voluntary associations of capitalist workers, operating through democratic processes of self-government, may serve their own members and the whole society by functioning as agencies for the economic education of the newly made capitalists, and as instruments for the protection of their property rights.

The problem of the corporation is largely one of restoring shareholders to their full powers and rights as the owners of capital and the employers of management. At present, the stockholder is almost disfranchised by the usurpation of economic power by management and boards of directors. This is aggravated by the prevailing shibboleth that the "passive" nonoperating shareholder should be quite content to abdicate the power and rights which go with his property, in favor of the "active" nonowning managers of the enterprise. This amounts to saying that it is to his own interest to relinquish his hold on his property for the sake of obtaining such returns as management, in its superior wisdom, thinks fit.

The theory of Capitalism calls for a radical reformation of the rela-

[3] On this subject, see the discussion of the corporation by Scott Buchanan in his *Essay on Politics*, New York, 1953: Ch. IV.

tion of the owners of capital to operating management. It envisages making corporations responsible, by making them compete for new capital in the open market instead of allowing them to withhold a large part of each year's capital earnings and to use that wealth, without the shareholders' consent, for further capitalization. It maintains that a full annual distribution of the wealth produced by the capital of mature corporations, *i.e.*, the distribution of the net income of such corporations to their stockholders, is indispensable to the restoration of the full rights of private property in the most important productive assets of our economy, as well as to the reduction of concentration of ownership and the elimination of a major source of market monopoly.

This proposition is absolutely essential to the practical program for creating Capitalism as the ideally just economy and the economic substructure for the justice and freedom of democracy. We will discuss its practical implications in Chapter Eleven, which treats of the modern corporation in the transition to Capitalism. For the present, no more need be said than that in the political economy of Capitalism the legal reconstitution of the corporation, as well as its effective regulation, is one of the primary positive tasks of government.

THE ETHICS OF CAPITALISM

Democracy and Capitalism are in themselves intrinsically desirable for the justice and freedom they establish as the essential conditions of a truly classless society. But establishing the conditions of such an ideal society will be a hollow triumph unless the human beings who live under such conditions put them to good use. Whether or not they will depends largely on whether our society, through the liberal education of all its members or through other means, can achieve a moral and intellectual revolution—one which leads human beings to put good institutions to good use.[4]

[4] The moral and intellectual virtues that are needed to make a man a sound and responsible capitalist are of no higher order than those required for intel-

That revolution is needed to reverse two tendencies that are almost universal in our society. Each expresses a wrong order of values. Each, therefore, springs from the same basic error in ethics—the error of mistaking a means for an end.

One is our tendency under a mixed economy to glorify toil or subsistence work for its own sake. We look upon economic activity as an end rather than as a means. We express this attitude by the way in which we subordinate to economic activity the much more important and difficult creative activities that lie outside the sphere of the production of wealth—the activities of politics, religion, the fine arts, pure science, philosophy, teaching, etc. We express this misguided tendency in our disdain for men who, with adequate income from capital property, do not continue to engage in one or another form of subsistence work. We express it when we speak of the cessation of subsistence work as "retirement," as though when the task of providing enough wealth for economic security is completed, the main purpose of human life has been accomplished.

The other tendency is found in our substitution of the pursuit of wealth for the pursuit of happiness. We regard wealth as if it were a good without qualification or without limit—the more of it the better, no matter how it is used. We forget that the acquisition of wealth by a household is only a means to an end, a means which is well-used only when it provides the members of a household with such physical comfort and security as is necessary to enable them to live good human lives. We, therefore, fail to recognize that the amount of wealth that any household needs is strictly limited, and that the amount in excess of reasonable needs which it can put to good use is relatively slight. In short, we give to wealth, which is at best a means of human development, the unlimited and unqualified goodness that belongs only

ligent and responsible citizenship. If liberal education ever becomes adequate to the task that confronts it in a society in which citizenship is conferred on all, and in which all need to be helped by education to become good citizens, it will also be able to help all who have become capitalists to acquire the virtues a good capitalist should have.

to the end we should pursue—the fullest perfection of ourselves as human beings.

These two tendencies run counter to the direction which the capitalist revolution must take.

The elevation of economic activity to a place it should not have in human life or, worse, the treatment of subsistence work as if it were intrinsically virtuous, instead of merely compulsory, blinds men to the moral significance of Capitalism's insistence that the ideal is not the full employment of men in the labor of producing wealth, but the full enjoyment by men of the liberal activities or leisure work that machine-produced wealth can make possible for all.

A revolution that seeks to make all men capitalists loses its moral point if men feel they can retain their self-respect only through earning their living by labor, instead of feeling that they are doing much more for themselves and their society by effectively and fully using its machine-slaves in order to devote a substantial portion of their time and energies to liberal pursuits and to the work of civilization. Unless an early release from the compulsion of subsistence work for all ranks of labor, managerial and technical as well as mechanical, is regarded, not as retirement, being shelved, or going off on a permanent vacation, but as a promotion or graduation to better employments, Capitalism offers a dreadful prospect instead of an inspiring challenge.

The attitude which looks upon the acquisition of wealth as a competitive game to be indulged in for the pleasure it affords,[5] or the attitude which looks upon the accumulation of wealth—without limit—as a morally acceptable measure of human achievement, must necessarily lead men to reject the proposition that the individual acquisition and accumulation of wealth should serve the things that wealth itself is needed to support.

Rejecting this proposition, they are also likely to reject the proposal that individual accumulations of capital should not be permitted to

[5] On this point, see Frank Knight's essay, "The Ethics of Competition," in a volume of essays which bears that title (New York, 1935).

grow beyond the point at which they necessarily exclude other households from adequately participating in the production of wealth. The feeling that their individual liberty would be infringed by such limitation will make them deaf to the clearest proof that justice requires it. Since the principles of economic justice are essential to Capitalism, and since it regards nothing that justice demands as an encroachment on freedom, the program of Capitalism cannot avoid meeting strong emotional resistance in some quarters of contemporary society.

It is our hope that such resistance can be overcome by enlightened self-interest, if by nothing else. Beyond that, it is our deeper hope that liberal education can alter the attitudes and even reverse the tendencies which turn men away from or against the goals of the capitalist revolution.

If that revolution were to take place through the pressure of circumstances and without moral commitment to its aims and principles, the result would be a society whose economic and political institutions were morally better than its human beings. An industrial economy which persists in the maldistribution of capital, its most productive factor, or which cannot find a way of checking inflation, may contain the seeds of its own destruction; but that is as nothing compared with the human havoc and corruption engendered in a society which is ideally suited to the best in human nature but for which men have not made themselves fit.

Even the best institutions do not operate automatically for the benefit of mankind. Their ultimate result is no better than the ethical goals or ideals men set themselves and discipline themselves to seek. Freedom gives men the opportunity to live well, and justice makes that opportunity equal for all. But neither guarantees that men will avail themselves of it for the highest development of which each is capable.

PART TWO

THE PROGRAM OF THE CAPITALIST REVOLUTION

9 SUMMARY OF THE PRACTICAL PROGRAM

THE NATURE OF THE PROPOSALS

The argument that the capitalist revolution is our only choice, no matter how sound, would be an academic exercise if a feasible program of bringing it about could not be devised. The conception of Capitalism as the only just organization of an industrial economy, and as the economic counterpart of democracy, deserves sustained public attention only if it has practical as well as theoretical truth.

We think that the theory of Capitalism can be put into practice. We think that those who are convinced by the argument that carrying out the capitalist revolution is our only way of avoiding complete socialism are right now in a position to begin acting on that conviction. The main propositions that constitute the theory of Capitalism and the argument for it lead to a whole series of practical proposals for accomplishing the necessary reforms of our present, only partly capitalistic, economy. The chapters which follow set forth the practical steps we recommend as worthy of the most serious consideration.

It is one thing to state the propositions of a theory and quite another to advance practical proposals for the reform of existing institutions. In the one case, we are engaged in the kind of thinking that stands or falls by the ordinary tests of truth—the evidence of facts and the soundness of principles. But in the other, we are trying to plot a course of change in human affairs, beset by future contingencies that are not foreseeable, or only dimly so, and complicated by the habits and prejudices of all the human beings involved. Any thinking one can do about such matters stands or falls by a different sort of test—the agreement, on the part of all who are asked to undertake the changes proposed, that the proposals advanced are, or are not, worthy of practical deliberation and public debate.

At one time, we felt that we had discharged our responsibilities to the future by stating the theory of Capitalism and arguing for the truth of its propositions, including the proposition that the future of our democratic society requires the capitalist revolution to provide it with the economic substructure it needs. We felt that any practical program for carrying out that revolution must be developed by the joint efforts of everyone involved, especially by the practical deliberations of the leaders in our political and economic life—our statesmen, legislators, administrators, business executives, labor leaders, bankers, lawyers, engineers, economists, scientists, philosophers, and educators. We felt that any attempt on our part to lay down a detailed blueprint for a course of action that it may take fifty years or more to carry out would be presumptuous, not only because of all the unforeseeable future contingencies involved but also because of all the sources of wise opinion that should be consulted before practical deliberation can come up with a sound program of action.

Our reluctance to risk the presumption involved in advancing practical proposals, no matter how tentatively they are presented, has been overcome by the experience we have had again and again in discussing with others the idea of the capitalist revolution and the theory of Capitalism. We were repeatedly asked to give some reasons for thinking that our mixed capitalism could be transformed into a completely capitalistic economy. We were repeatedly told that, regardless of the truth of the theory and regardless of the consequences for mankind of failing to put it into practice, it is now too late to do anything about it. It might have been possible to create Capitalism out of whole cloth, had its principles been recognized and accepted at the outset of the industrial revolution; but the path we have already taken from primitive capitalism to mixed capitalism no longer permits us to turn the other way.

It is in response to these queries, doubts, and misgivings that we have decided to outline what we hold to be a feasible practical program. We think that its proposals show that it is not too late to change the direction our society has been following. We think that the proposals are sufficiently practicable as outlined to warrant the best efforts of everyone concerned to make them more practicable.

We have no doubt that they can be improved in every way, that they can be supplemented by additional recommendations as unforeseeable developments must be taken into account, and that they can be implemented in detailed ways that no one at present may be able to devise. These proposals are necessarily dated. Were we or anyone else to reconsider them a quarter of a century from now, the proposals would most certainly be modified to fit circumstances beyond anyone's present imagination. What has always been true of the task of plotting for the future is especially true in a century of constantly accelerated technological progress.

In submitting these proposals to our fellow citizens, we are acutely aware that the detailed legislative and business reforms which are necessary to bring about the transition to a completely just and also a completely capitalistic society call for the most intense study that can be given them by the best economic, political, legal and scientific minds in our society. With such study, we have no doubt that an entirely workable program can be devised for guiding our economy away from its trend toward socialism and in the direction of Capitalism. We also have no doubt that that program can be put into effect through due process of law and under the auspices of public as well as legislative debate. Both the program itself and the ways of working it out are perfectly consonant with the genius of our established institutions.

We know that any set of practical proposals for a radical change will elicit ill-considered criticism as well as careful study and constructive effort to improve them. We are willing to risk the one for the sake of the other. But in facing both of these alternatives, we hope the following things will be borne in mind: that we do not believe these proposals are the final or the best proposals which can be devised; that we do not believe they can be acted on without sustained study and deliberation; and that we do not believe that all their shortcomings can be foreseen by anyone whose vision of the future is limited.

Nevertheless, we do believe that the measures proposed are workable, and that they demonstrate the feasibility of the capitalist revolution. In fact, we would argue that they are more workable than any measures we would have to take to postpone or prevent the complete socialization of our mixed economy without at the same time trying to direct it toward Capitalism. If that is so, then our proposal of these measures does not relieve others of their own obligation to consider the problem that confronts all of us. Everyone is called upon to think practically about how that problem can be solved.

With these cautionary remarks, we turn at once to an outline of the practical program, stating first its general policies and then its specific recommendations. The chapters to follow will discuss the practical implications of the specific measures proposed.

GENERAL POLICIES

The following general policies should guide the course of action to be undertaken. Our concerted effort should be:

1. To broaden the ownership of existing enterprises.
2. To encourage the formation of new capital and the organization of new enterprises owned by new capitalists.
3. To discourage the concentration of the ownership of capital by households where such concentration has passed beyond the point determined to be the maximum consistent with a just organization of a completely capitalistic economy.

SPECIFIC RECOMMENDATIONS

Pursuant to the general policies stated above, we recommend the following specific measures:

1. Increasing the use of equity-sharing plans in industry.
2. Modification of death and gift tax laws to encourage the creation and the inheritance from generation to generation of a vastly increased number of viable capital estates.
3. As the transition to Capitalism progresses, elimination of the corporate income tax, together with adjustment of the personal income tax for the purpose of raising the necessary revenues of government from all the households of the economy in an equitable manner.
4. Elimination of governmental practices which directly aggravate the concentration of the ownership of capital.
5. Effective regulation of the economy by government to assure that free and workable competition is maintained in all markets except those rare instances in which, for technical physical reasons, monopolies must be permitted.
6. Recognition by the government of its obligation to assure all households in the economy a reasonable opportunity to partici-

pate in the production of wealth to an extent sufficient to earn a viable income.

7. Adoption of legislation designed to require mature corporations to pay out 100 percent of their net earnings to their stockholders.

8. Development of a system of investment preferences for those households which have subviable capital estates, in order to promote their acquisition of viable capital estates.

9. Encouragement of the acquisition of viable capital holdings by all households in the economy by tax and credit devices, accompanied by restrictions on the use of these devices calculated to prevent their being misused to develop concentrated or monopolistic holdings, or their being used for speculative purposes.

10. Primary use of our credit system to promote new capital formation under the ownership of new capitalists in holdings of submonopolistic size, together with a diminishing use of credit to support consumption as balanced participation in production is progressively achieved.

10 THE POINT OF DEPARTURE
FOR THE REFORMS PROPOSED

THE SITUATION FROM WHICH WE START

The present high standard of living in the United States is attributable primarily to the high productiveness of capital. The weakness of our mixed capitalist economy lies in the fact that, on the one hand, the ownership of most of the capital producing about 90 percent of the wealth of the economy is concentrated in about 5 percent of the households of the economy; while, on the other hand, more than 70 percent of the stream of income representing wealth produced is distributed through labor. In our society a high standard of living for all households has become a morally approved objective. In fact, it is an economic necessity if mass consumption is to support mass production.

The capitalistic resolution of these conflicting elements in our mixed economy lies in bringing about a balanced participation in production through diffusing the ownership of capital. As the burden of production shifts from labor to capital, so must the means of participating in production shift from ownership of labor to ownership of capital.[1] As the wealth of the economy is increasingly produced by capital, the distribution of the wealth of the economy must be increasingly achieved through the ownership of capital. The alternative to this is the erosion—to the vanishing point—of the private ownership of capital itself.

As we consider the means of accomplishing the capitalist revolution, we must recognize that our task today is different from what it would have been one hundred fifty years ago if, standing on the threshhold of the industrial revolution, we had then a clear idea of how a capitalist economy should be organized. In that case, our primary obstacle would have been the scarcity of capital instruments. Our attention would have focused on the problem of diverting sufficient current production from consumer goods to capital goods, in order to shift significantly the burden of production from labor to capital. Under such circumstances, little effort on the part of government would have been required to promote Capitalism through bringing about a progressive diffusion in the ownership of capital as its productive power progressively increased.

Surprising as it may seem, our task today in bringing about the transition to a fully capitalistic society is perhaps easier than it would have been at any time in the past. We are possessed of capital equipment capable of producing nine-tenths of our goods and services. We have adjusted ourselves to the erosion of private property in capital as the inevitable consequence of distributing income laboristically in

[1] The shift from participation in production as worker to participation as owner of capital carries with it no certainty of a decline in aggregate employment. It is true that as progressively more of the total wealth is produced by capital, and less by labor, employment in terms of man-hours will decline unless increases in total wealth produced offset the decreasing demand for labor. But it will also be true in a completely capitalistic society that the economy need not produce surpluses in order that the technologically displaced be enabled to participate in production. When the effect of technological displacement falls upon men who are capitalists as well as workers, they will still continue to participate in production as owners of capital. Their contribution to production may even be enlarged.

our mixed economy. We have learned to bear artificially high and inflationary wages, unnecessary toil (*e.g.,* featherbedding), and dozens of varieties of artificial stimulants to industry for the sake of producing employment. We have come to endure painfully high graduated personal and corporate income taxes.

In short, while preserving the superficial appearances of private property in capital, we are submitting to measures already more severe (and they must become even more severe as technology advances) than those necessary to effect the capitalist revolution over a reasonable period of time.

We shall see that the capitalist revolution can be in part accomplished by the use of currently tolerated and familiar income taxes, estate taxes, and credit mechanisms. We shall also see that as the distribution of income becomes less laboristic and more capitalistic (with a wider diffusion of ownership of capital), a progressive reduction in the use of these measures will become both possible and necessary. At the same time, as the diffusion of economic power becomes more complete, the danger of abuse of the taxing and credit-control powers of government will diminish.

THE ROLE OF PRIMARY DISTRIBUTION IN A CAPITALISTIC ECONOMY

Primary distribution is the distribution of purchasing power that automatically results from participation in production. The contribution of the worker to production results in his receipt of wages, salaries, fees, bonuses, or other compensation. The contribution of the owner of capital results in his receipt of rent, dividends, interest, or payments for raw materials.

In a free economy, each participant receives in purchasing power the value, competitively determined, of his contribution to the wealth produced. It is the fact that the contribution has been made by the use of his productive property which entitles each participant to receive in some form, usually in money, the value of his contribution toward the production of wealth.

The market value of the wealth produced sets a limit to what producers and suppliers receive in the aggregate as their distributive shares of purchasing power. While the use of credit may smooth out the operation of this system, it does not alter it in principle, since sums borrowed must be repaid. The equality between the wealth created and the purchasing power received can be expressed in the following manner:

Value of capital used in production in the form of land, raw materials, plants, machinery, office buildings, working capital, etc.	= Aggregate purchasing power received by the individual owners of capital in the form of rents, payments for raw materials, interest, dividends, royalties, etc.
Value of labor expended in production	= Aggregate purchasing power received by the individual owners of labor in the form of wages, salaries, bonuses, interest in goods, fringe benefits, etc.
Value of wealth produced [2]	= Total purchasing power created by production, *i.e.*, the cost of the total product to consumers.

The ownership of the capital and labor engaged in any productive enterprise determines *who* shall receive the purchasing power resulting from each contribution to the final product. The competitively determined value of each contribution determines *how much* of the total wealth produced shall be distributed to each owner participating in

[2] As Harold G. Moulton has tersely stated it, "the truth is that there is an identity between the market price of a commodity and the sums received by those who have engaged in its production" (*Income and Economic Progress,* Brookings Institution, Washington, 1935: p. 39).

its production. This is the automatic distribution of wealth—the *primary distribution*—which would result from participation in the production of wealth in a completely capitalistic economy.

Under Capitalism, primary distribution would, therefore, be responsible for the general distributive pattern of the economy. Secondary distribution, which includes transfers of wealth taking place outside of the production-distribution process, is made up of such transactions as gifts, inheritance, transfers of wealth through marriage, losing and finding, thefts, exchanges of property after it has been acquired by its original ultimate consumer, and various other forms of distribution not occasioned by the return upon productive effort. While the distributive pattern which results from secondary distribution may accord with, exaggerate, or tend to counteract the pattern of primary distribution, primary distribution determines the general distributive pattern of a capitalistic economy.

It is evident from the nature of primary distribution that the purchasing power which arises from participation in production must be fully applied, either to the purchase of consumer goods or to the purchase of capital goods, if the prevailing level of production is to be maintained or expanded. If purchasing power is sterilized in idle savings (*i.e.,* savings which are not or cannot be invested in capital goods), output must be adjusted downward until the wealth produced and the income used to purchase consumer goods and capital goods are again in balance.

We have observed the fact that the ownership of capital may be concentrated to any degree, while the ownership of labor in a non-slave society is always completely diffused—each man being the proprietor of his own labor power. The chief cause of the present highly concentrated ownership of capital is the discrepancy between the increasing productiveness of capital and the nearly constant productiveness of nonmanagerial and nontechnical labor. This differential productiveness began with the industrial revolution and has been increasing relentlessly ever since.

There are two subordinate causes of concentration in the ownership of capital. One is itself a direct result of the greater productiveness of capital: among the higher incomes of the economy, it is generally true that the higher the income, the higher the proportion that is derived from capital. The other cause is simply a well-known pattern of economic behavior: excluding the great number of persons in the low and lower middle income groups who account for no capital formation, the higher the income, the smaller the proportion that is spent upon consumer goods and services; or, what is the same thing, the higher the income, the larger the proportion that is normally invested in further capital formation.

Thus we see why the ownership of capital by individuals or households tends in general to increase in a geometric progression. In the absence of governmental regulations designed to counteract it, the natural functioning of an industrial economy with private property in capital results in a progressively greater concentration rather than in a progressively greater diffusion of capital ownership. So amazingly productive has capital become under the relentless advance of technology that this phenomenon has continued in spite of the graduated corporate income tax (which falls entirely upon the wealth produced by capital), and the steeply progressive personal income tax (which generally confiscates a much greater proportion of the income of the capital owner than of the worker).

INDIVIDUAL SECURITY VS. SECURITY FOR ALL INDIVIDUALS

One of the motives of the owner of capital in seeking to "plough back" his income and thereby to expand his ownership of capital is to provide himself and his household with ever more massive economic security. The same process takes place, under much the same influences, at the corporate level.

This phenomenon—the concentration of the ownership of capital—

is, on the other hand, the basic cause of depressions in a capitalist economy. That insulation against the effects of a depression is one of the motives for concentration is not in itself startling. But that it is itself a cause of depressions indicates why the widely diffused ownership of capital is a necessity for the healthy functioning of an advanced industrial economy.

The possession of massive economic security by a small proportion of the households of the economy is destructive of the economic security of all. The concentration of the production of wealth in the hands of the few is inconsistent with participation in its production by all. This is but another way of saying that the production of most of the wealth by a small proportion of the households is inconsistent with a just distribution of income to all households. To the extent that all the households of an economy derive an income under conditions of concentrated capital ownership, the principles of charity or expediency (or both) must be operative.

There is necessarily a limit to how concentrated the ownership of capital can become without disrupting the stability of the economy. The advancing productiveness of capital may be viewed as the comparatively declining productiveness of submanagerial and subtechnical labor. With these changes, an opportunity to participate in the production of wealth to an extent sufficient to provide a viable distributive share comes increasingly to mean an opportunity to participate as a capitalist. The degree of concentration compatible with the right of every household to participate in production is thus progressively lowered as technology advances. Similarly, the degree of concentration compatible with the right of every consumer unit to participate in production is progressively lowered as the lowest income groups in the economy demand the opportunity to produce more wealth in order that they may enjoy a higher standard of living.

In a completely capitalistic economy, the balancing of participation in the production of wealth with the gradual shift from participation through the employment of one's own labor to participation through the employment of the capital one owns will be effected at a rate commensurate with that of technological progress. This can only come about, in an economy that retains the institution of private property, through an ever greater diffusion of the private ownership of capital. And when this comes about under Capitalism, it will, by eliminating the cause of economic instability, provide all with the sense of personal security that only some have enjoyed in the past through their highly concentrated ownership of capital.

The principles of Capitalism make it apparent that the achievement by the few of massive insulation against poverty causes poverty for the millions. Under Capitalism, such security cannot exist for the few alone, but only for the many. In addition, the balanced relationship which Capitalism will establish between (a) participation by all households in production and (b) the distribution of the proceeds of production to such households in proportion to their productive contributions will eliminate the primary hazard of equity ownership itself—the cyclical depression.

THE DEGREE OF CONCENTRATION IN THE OWNERSHIP OF CAPITAL

It is necessary to examine more closely the extent and character of the concentration that constitutes the central problem to be solved in order to effect the transition from mixed capitalism to Capitalism.

We must first distinguish between the concentrated ownership of capital and the concentrated ownership of consumer goods. The regulatory problem of a capitalistic economy centers on unbalanced participation in production. This can only come about through concentration in the ownership of capital, or through some combination, within a household, of concentrated capital ownership with participation in production by one or more of its members as workers. No degree of concentration in the ultimate ownership of consumer goods is significant for the problem of the production and distribution of wealth in a capitalistic society. The number of houses a man owns does not affect his participation in production so long as he does not rent them to others. It makes no difference how many yachts a family owns, so long as it does not go into the transportation business. Similarly, it makes no difference how many books or suits a man owns, so long as he does not open a bookstore or a clothing business.

With regard to the concentrated ownership of productive capital, common knowledge renders wholly unnecessary an extended review of the many studies that have been made during the past twenty-five years. We will content ourselves with two brief references.

The great bulk of the productive capital in our economy consists in the assets of corporations. In a study sponsored by the Merrill Foundation for the Advancement of Financial Knowledge and made by J. Keith Butters, Lawrence E. Thompson and Lynn L. Bollinger in 1949, it was found that between 65 percent and 70 percent of all the marketable stock held by private individuals was owned by families with estates in excess of $250,000. Such families constitute a minute fraction of 1 percent of the households in the economy. This study also disclosed that 75 percent of all such marketable stock was held by the 2 percent of the population with the largest incomes— $15,000 per year and over.

Nonmarketable stocks of corporations (*i.e.,* the stocks of closely held corporations) are even more concentrated in ownership, while the highest concentration, of course, is to be found in proprietorships and partnerships.[3] In the July, 1956, issue of *Labor's Economic Review,* published by the CIO-AFL, it was reported that 92 percent of American families own no stocks of any kind. Studies show that the ownership of corporate debt is even more highly concentrated than

---

[3] The results of this study are summarized in "Effects of Taxation on the Investment Policies and Capacities of Individuals," by Lawrence E. Thompson and J. Keith Butters, and published in the *Journal of Finance,* May, 1953, pp. 137–151

the ownership of equities.[4] A comparable concentration in ownership exists for individually owned real estate used in business. Even in the case of farms, a strong tendency toward large holdings is stimulated by technological advances which give a great productive advantage to the large farm.

The real test of the concentration of ownership of capital in the United States lies in the number of households owning a sufficient amount of capital in any form to provide them either with a viable income at present levels, or any significant portion of such income. The available evidence confirms what anyone would suspect—that the number of such households is minute. It is not, in any event, over 5 percent of all households.

THE FORMS OF CONCENTRATED OWNERSHIP OF CAPITAL

To consider the forms which the concentrated ownership of capital takes, we must remember that the essence of private property is to give its individual owners control over the use and disposition of their property.

In the case of property in capital, the forms which such ownership

---

[4] In its publication *Who Owns American Business, 1956 Census of Share-owners,* the New York Stock Exchange, which has long urged a broadening of the ownership of capital, reported that between 1952 and the end of 1955, the number of people owning shares in publicly held corporations (corporations with securities listed on a Registered Stock Exchange and having 300 or more stockholders) increased from 6,490,000 to 8,630,000—an increase of 33 percent. The inconsistency of this fact with the concentration of ownership as shown by all major studies is apparent rather than real. The Exchange's study does not even purport to reflect concentration of ownership. The ownership of ten shares, or even one share in a public corporation, is all that is necessary to be counted as a shareholder in this study. Two-thirds of the share-owners counted were in the $7,500 per year income level or below—a group shown by all other studies to be insignificant in the formation of the equity capital of American business. What the Exchange's study does show is that an increasing number of people are interested in becoming owners of capital or of securities representative of capital.

can take are various. Capital privately owned by individuals may be held in corporate form. In this case, the owner of the capital is a fictitious person—the corporation. In legal theory, the ownership of the corporation lies in its stockholder or stockholders. The stockholders may at any time eliminate the intermediate entity, by dissolving the corporation and assuming direct ownership of its assets and business. The corporation is, however, a most effective method of uniting the productive power of capital with the talents of managers, technicians, and other workers; and it is ordinarily not convenient (even aside from tax considerations) to dissolve a corporation in order to enforce the property rights of a stockholder.

Most of the productive capital in the United States is held in the corporate form. Nevertheless, substantial amounts of capital are subject to direct individual ownership (proprietorships), or held by partnerships, trusts, and other forms of association. Whatever form ownership takes, it is vitally important, if a capital asset is to be private property, that its control be vested in its owners as such. When, for example, corporate management is more influenced in the making of decisions, by the state (or by those to whom the state has loaned its countervailing power) than by its own stockholders, then the corporate capital is no longer predominantly private property. It has become predominantly state controlled and, correspondingly, state owned.

We regard the household as the basic unit of ownership because the household is the basic unit for spending income and because it is family or household income that generally determines the standard of living of the individuals in the family unit.

We have already called attention to the distinction between an actual concentration of private ownership of capital and what is merely an apparent concentration of privately owned capital. The real measure of concentration where ownership is partly nominal and partly effective is the extent to which the wealth produced by capital actually flows into the hands of its owner or owners. The real measure of concentration where ownership is fully effective would be the magnitude of the income received within a given period by the owners of the capital in question.

For example, let us consider the case of a household owning capital invested in an incorporated business (or in diversified investments in a number of such businesses) which produces, after taxes, $200,000 a year. If the ownership of this capital were fully effective and the household received the entire $200,000 annually, it is clear that this household would have the earning power or wealth-producing power of 40 worker households in which the earning power of the worker or workers averaged $5,000 a year per household. On the other hand, if this capital-owning household received only $50,000 a year, the rest being drained off through artificially high wages and the uncontrollable decisions of management to withhold the disbursement of a portion of corporate income to stockholders, and if this condition continued year after year, it is clear that the ownership of the capital in question would be 25 percent effective and 75 percent illusory or nominal. Where income taxes levied upon the corporation provide funds for expenditures outside the proper sphere of government (e.g., for redistribution of wealth to submarginal farmers, or to support economically unnecessary toil), the ownership of the capital may be even further attenuated.

The ownership of capital may be partly or wholly nominal, i.e., it may in varying degrees lack effectiveness, regardless of the form of ownership. If it is owned in corporate form, such ownership may become ineffective through the short-circuiting of the flow of wealth produced by the capital so that none, or only a part of it, reaches the capital owner. This may come about through income taxes, excise taxes, or property taxes levied to provide funds for purposes outside the proper sphere of government, i.e., for the redistribution of income. It may come about through diversion of the wealth produced by capital to workers, as it does wherever wages are raised by legislation or union pressure above the level at which they would be set by free competition. It may come about through the ineffectiveness of the laws of property as applied to stockholders' rights in corporations, as it happens whenever these laws leave stockholders without any means of enforcing their right to receive the income or wealth produced by their equity capital. Corporate management can then, without consulting the stockholders, "plough in" earnings for the purpose of indefinitely expanding the enterprise, instead of being forced to persuade and justify further investment by stockholders who have been fully paid their shares of the corporation's earnings.[5]

One other form of concentration of productive power remains to be mentioned before we consider ways of solving the problem that concentration raises. As we have seen, productive power may be concentrated by combining within a household the ownership of productive capital with the participation in production by one or more members of the household as workers. Such concentration reaches its peak when ownership of a large amount of capital is combined with holding a very highly paid position as a managerial or technical worker in one or more businesses, or with a lucrative professional practice in law, medicine, engineering, accountancy, etc. Where there is a surplus of workers (*i.e.,* of persons whose only means of participating in production is through labor), this becomes a most important form of concentration.

HOW MIXED CAPITALISM DEALS WITH THE EFFECTS OF CONCENTRATED OWNERSHIP

Before we discuss the transition from our mixed economy to Capitalism, let us ask how our present form of mixed capitalism handles the natural tendency of capital to increase in the hands of its owners at a geometric rate. To reduce the question to figures, if capital, the great bulk of which is owned by about 5 percent of the households, pro-

---

[5] These causes of the ineffectiveness of private property held in corporate form, except for the withholding of dividends by corporate directors, also operate in other forms of ownership.

duces 90 percent of the wealth, what prevents this 5 percent of the households from receiving 90 percent of the income?

Were the property rights of the owners of capital fully respected, that is precisely what would happen. A completely capitalistic society would be so regulated by its government that if 90 percent of the wealth were produced by capital, the diffusion of private ownership would be sufficiently broad so that 90 percent of the income could be distributed as a return to capital and still maintain widely diffused purchasing power.[6]

How does mixed capitalism meet this problem? The answer in general is obvious. Our mixed economy does not attempt to diffuse the private ownership of capital throughout the households of the society. Instead, it diffuses the wealth produced by capital; that is, it distributes to labor a large part of the income which would go to the owners of capital if their property in capital were fully respected.

The following are the more important of the entirely familiar devices by which our mixed economy transfers at least two-thirds of the wealth produced by capital to the noncapital-owning households of our society:

(1) First and foremost is the method urged by the *Communist Manifesto* in 1848: "A heavy progressive or graduated income tax." Because most of the high incomes are largely capital incomes, the graduated personal income tax relieves the owners of capital of a far greater share of their income than it does in the case of the owners of labor. The graduated corporate income tax has a different effect. It is not heavier on capital-income than upon worker-income. It falls totally and exclusively on the wealth produced by capital. This is true

[6] This would be true whether or not the labor force were "fully employed." Thus if, as a matter of competitive evaluation of all contributions to production, labor produced only 10 percent of the national wealth, then the total wage share of the national income would be 10 percent. There might still be full employment if, despite the low labor content in the goods and services produced, consumer demand raised production to a level at which all available employment was absorbed. This condition would probably exist in an advanced industrial economy only when it was in the throes of war.

of manufacturing excise taxes and property taxes on capital instruments.

(2) The graduated personal income tax itself discourages the distribution to stockholders of corporate earnings. Few corporations pay out more than half their net earnings. Many go on for years retaining much more than half. The tax laws are designed to prevent "withholding" payment of dividends where the purpose is to avoid taxes. But intent to plough earnings into further capital investment is an effective and recognized excuse for the indefinite accumulation of earnings.

The laws of property, as applied to stockholders, are almost attenuated to nonexistence in this instance. The decision whether stockholders shall receive the wealth that their capital produces lies not with stockholders, say the courts, but with management—the top echelon of workers. Generations of stockholders come and go without ever possessing or controlling more than a small fraction of the wealth their nominally owned capital produces.

The weakness of the property rights of stockholders and the overpowering strength of the graduated personal income tax conspire to corral within corporations vast quantities of the wealth produced by capital. From this collective reservoir, by arrangements between government and unions, it is used richly to supplement actual wages. It may with little resistance be appropriated by the government to pay for agricultural surpluses, subsidize foreign distributions of wealth, pay for excessive quantities of arms, and promote all manner of artificially stimulated toil.

(3) One of the largest employers of labor is the construction industry. Governmental policies of easy mortgage credit enable a home buyer, for example, to create employment today by spending wealth that he will produce over the next twenty or thirty years. Here is an instance of a policy to credit-finance a consumer item of the magnitude of a small capital holding. The shortage of homes of a desired quality is sometimes incidentally mentioned in connection with this program.

For the most part, however, the proponents of these programs and the political leaders who echo their proposals are more frank. The objective is full employment.

(4) Another large employer of labor is manufacturing. Our mixed economy stimulates employment through governmentally supported easy consumer credit to encourage the purchase of durable goods. Among these durable goods are some of the most important consumer items in our high standard of living: automobiles, washing machines, dish washers, vacuum cleaners, furnaces, refrigerators, freezers, televisions, bathroom fixtures. Our mixed economy provides the households of the economy with credit to enjoy these consumer goods—just as a completely capitalistic economy would make it possible for its households to acquire them largely through their capital incomes.

(5) Farm employment is stimulated through the governmental purchase of agricultural surpluses, the "soil bank" program, and the direct fixing of prices above their competitive level as in the case of the dairy industry. Both of these types of program result in the elevation of the cost of living for all households. These programs to a large extent redistribute income to farmers as part of the general program of redistributing income to non-capital-owning households.

(6) Employment is "spread" through a multiplicity of restrictions upon worker output. Limitations are placed on the number of bricks that may be laid, the number of pieces of work that may be handled, the number of minutes of work between intermissions. Employers are forced to hire more drivers than they need, more helpers than can effectively work, orchestras that merely sit in the wings, linotype operators who unnecessarily duplicate the type already set up, etc. With government protection and encouragement, rules of work-jurisdiction have been established by labor unions so that construction jobs require maximum employment rather than maximum efficiency, skill, ability, or effort.[7]

[7] There is another type of concealed unemployment which, though less well known than featherbedding, may be just as prevalent and just as effective in

(7) Through a device called "collective bargaining" (which originally and wholesomely meant giving employees as much "weight" as the employers with whom they must discuss wages, hours and working conditions), government and unions collaborate to raise wages far above their competitive level. This is the most direct method of awarding to workers the income produced by capital. It introduces into the economy a governmental enfranchisement of unions to levy taxes upon employers, stockholders, and upon the economy as a whole. It sanctions a form of monopoly and conspiracy made effective by organized force which dwarfs any industrial monopoly ever contrived. It eliminates from a major area of the economy the use of objective, impartial, and free competition as a just determinant of economic values. Its only "justification" is that without a redistribution of income effected in this manner, there would not be sufficient mass purchasing power in our present economy to support mass production.

(8) Our mixed capitalist economy frequently increases employment by the regularization of war expenditures. War goods require the employment of labor to produce, but they do not satisfy consumer demand. They create purchasing power in a manner which requires further employment to satisfy that purchasing power. However critically important war goods are in meeting the actual needs of defense, *beyond defense* they are ideal for creating "full employment" in a mixed economy. That would not be the case in a completely capitalistic society where defense would be defense, not a device for increasing employment.

(9) As in the case of the production of war goods in excess of defense needs, our mixed economy can promote the laboristic distribu-

---

promoting laboristic distribution. It has been examined satirically by Professor C. Northcote Parkinson, who shows that because "work expands so as to fill the time available for its completion," there is no limit to the growth in size of the clerical or administrative staff of a corporation or a government office, whether its work increases, stands still, or decreases. This tendency, called "Parkinson's Law," undoubtedly accounts for incalculable clerical and managerial "featherbedding" within corporate and government offices. See *Parkinson's Law,* by C. Northcote Parkinson, Boston, 1957.

tion of wealth through foreign aid programs which are beyond the needs of, or are entirely outside of, the requirements of defense. Our mixed economy makes some foreign aid grants which are inspired neither by international charity nor by sound defense needs, but by the advantages to full employment of disposing abroad of our surplus machine tools, agricultural commodities, etc.

(10) Our mixed economy periodically interrupts the process of concentration of ownership of capital by imposing progressive death and gift taxes. Not only do these taxes result in transfers of large amounts of accumulated capital wealth to the government, but they frequently impair market competition and promote the further concentration of ownership of the physical assets involved. In the case of many closely held corporations, taxes can be paid only by sale of control of the business, and the buyer is often the company's most powerful competitor.

(11) Our mixed economy may by its tax laws promote a form of socialization not ordinarily recognized as such. It is a form of redistribution known as the charitable foundation. Charitable foundations are, in legal contemplation, public entities. The wealth within them is under the control of the state, and the foundations themselves are so designed that the wealth can never revert to or benefit those who transfer their wealth to such semigovernmental agencies. From these foundations, wealth is distributed, under rules laid down by government, for all sorts of purposes recognized as charitable. From time to time, government may and does change its views on how such income must be distributed.

Many of these expedients, resorted to by mixed capitalism, to promote the laboristic distribution of the wealth produced by capital in order to supplement the wealth actually produced by labor, tend further to concentrate the nominal ownership of capital within the economy. This is sometimes referred to as the "trickle down" principle. Purchasing power is artificially introduced into an economy which, to whatever extent the concentrated ownership of capital is still effective, tends further to concentrate the ownership of capital. This in turn requires imposing even stiffer graduated income taxes to convert whatever effective ownership remains into nominal ownership and diffused purchasing power.

11 MEASURES AIMED AT BROADENING THE OWNERSHIP OF EXISTING ENTERPRISES

EQUITY-SHARING PLANS

Profit-sharing, including the variety of pension plans most commonly used today, is fairly widespread. It is promoted by corporate income tax deductions for contributions paid into these plans.

Until the transition to Capitalism has reached the point where a predominantly capitalistic distribution has supplanted a predominantly laboristic distribution of our nation's wealth, it will be necessary to retain the steeply progressive income tax in order to prevent the sterilization of dangerous amounts of purchasing power that would take the form of savings in excess of capital formation.

Of itself, the income tax does not tend in the slightest degree to broaden the diffusion of the ownership of capital. It relieves existing capitalists of a large portion of the wealth their capital produces, but it does not make new capitalists. But where deductions against such heavy income taxation are permitted for contributions to plans resembling our present profit-sharing—particularly stock-bonus—plans, the income tax can be made to have a significant effect in bringing about the transition to a completely capitalistic economy. This can be done within existing tax rates.

To recognize the importance of these devices, it is necessary to distinguish between *profit-sharing* or pension plans, which are merely designed to supplement income to be spent by households on consumption, and *equity-sharing* plans designed to make new capitalists. Only the latter can be significant in broadening the capital-owning group within the economy. Equity-sharing plans reach their maximum usefulness where they are of such magnitude that the income from the equities accumulated for an employee can make a significant addition to his worker income. So far as the creation of new capitalists is concerned, the usefulness of an equity-sharing plan is severely impaired if the arrangements are such that, when the employee obtains his portion of the trust, the equities are sold and the proceeds spent on consumer goods.

Where equity-sharing plans are so designed that a man who begins as a worker becomes, at the end of some years, an owner of a substantial capital interest, such plans can make a positive contribution toward transforming mixed capitalism into Capitalism. They can do this without subjecting businesses to more severe tax surgery than they are at present accustomed to.

Requiring mature corporations to pay out to their stockholders the entire earnings of corporate capital (a subject we will discuss later) would greatly improve the effectiveness of equity-sharing plans where funds are invested in the equities of mature corporations.

Equity-sharing plans should not be built around the concept of retirement, as that is currently understood in our "full employment" economy. The objective should be to build permanent, diversified capital estates—estates that will enable the new capitalists to shift their participation in production from the employment of their labor to the employment of their capital.

There is a profound difference in principle between laboristic profit-sharing and capitalistic equity-sharing. The former provides only an income or supplement to income for the worker to live on when he ceases to earn wages. The latter enables the worker gradually to shift, over the period of his employment, from absolute dependence on toil as the source of his income to dependence, in a substantial degree, on his ownership of a capital interest. Such a capital interest, if not impaired by estate or inheritance taxes (except where its size, as a matter of public policy, is monopolistic), would also provide income for the individual's heirs upon his death.

MODIFICATION OF DEATH TAX LAWS
AND GIFT TAX LAWS

For reasons which we have already discussed—primarily the tendency of the ownership, or at least nominal ownership, of capital to increase in a geometric progression—an industrial economy finds it necessary, from time to time, to counteract excessive concentrations of economic power in certain households. It does this through steeply graduated death taxes and gift taxes. Little, if any, thought seems to have been given to the fact that while this eliminates one type of concentration, it promotes others. At most, the effect of these taxes upon the concentration of ownership of capital in particular families from generation to generation is to limit personal ownership without promoting a diffused ownership of capital.

Let us explain. Very large personal fortunes are, of course, eventually reduced by gift and estate taxes, although the assistance of competent tax counsel can postpone and greatly minimize the impact of such levies. Franklin Roosevelt answered criticism of the socializing effect of the federal estate tax by saying (in 1939) that while the government collects its tax in cash, the business organizations established and nurtured by deceased capitalists still remain. What President

Roosevelt neglected to observe was that the necessity of raising cash to pay such taxes frequently results in the sale of a closely held business to a former competitor.

The present form of our death and gift taxes aggravates the concentration of capital ownership in another way. Where it is otherwise impossible by long-term trusts and other astute devices to avoid the decimating effect of death and gift taxes, large capital holdings today are transferred to tax-exempt foundations. In most cases, such bequests are a kind of compulsory charity. The establishment of charitable trusts is more often traceable to the tax laws than to genuinely charitable motives. As contrasted to the quiet martyrdom of paying federal estate taxes in the 77 percent bracket (in addition to state inheritance taxes), the establishment of a "personal foundation" permits some use of one's imagination in disposing of a fortune.

Today there are over 7,300 charitable foundations in the United States with assets of over five billion dollars. The number is increasing at a rapid rate. When they are viewed in the light of the objective of the capitalist revolution (*i.e.,* the diffused private ownership of capital), these foundations are subject to the following criticisms.

They in effect convert concentrated *private* ownership into concentrated *public* ownership. In legal theory, as well as in legislative contemplation, the holdings of charitable foundations are public property. It should, therefore, be acknowledged that the transfer of productive wealth to charitable foundations gives a huge impetus to state control over capital. The establishment of tax-exempt foundations therefore promotes socialism and works against Capitalism.

As great fortunes further accumulate in these tax-exempt sanctuaries, their use has become increasingly subject to legislative scrutiny. The funds of foundations do not perform the function of private property. They do not provide a means by which individual households in the economy can, through ownership of capital, participate .n the production of wealth to a degree beyond the capacity of mere labor.

Before proposing changes in the death tax and gift tax laws of the federal government to make them serve the cause of Capitalism, we must consider the importance of these laws to federal revenue. The present rates of the federal estate tax progress from 3 percent on the first $5,000 of the tax base (after various exclusions) to 77 percent on estates over ten million dollars. Federal gift tax rates are about 25 percent less, and state inheritance tax and gift tax rates are in general substantially less. Nevertheless, in 1956, the federal estate and gift tax collections together accounted for only about 1.5 percent of the revenue of the federal government. Hence the contribution these taxes make to the support of government is not sufficient to deter modifying them if doing so would significantly promote the transition to Capitalism. The same holds for state gift and inheritance taxes.

Several points emerge when we examine the use of gift and estate taxes in terms of the theory of Capitalism. As we will show presently, there is no question that these laws can be modified to promote the transition to Capitalism. Let us keep in mind, however, that while it is of vital importance to reduce unworkable concentrations of capital ownership, it is of equal importance to promote the inheritance of viable capital interests by families and dependents.

John Stuart Mill once expressed the view that estate tax laws should, as a matter of public policy, fix a limitation upon the amount an individual may inherit, leaving him in a position where if "he desires any further accession of fortune, he shall work for it." This would not be entirely applicable under Capitalism. The usefulness of Mill's formula diminishes as the gulf between the capacity of capital and that of labor to produce wealth widens. Under Capitalism, if a man should desire "further accession of fortune," it would only be through the ownership and husbanding of highly productive capital that he could have a significant chance of success.

To promote the transition to Capitalism, estate and gift tax laws should be modified in the light of the following considerations. The end to be encouraged is the acquisition of viable capital interests, lying within reasonable limits fixed by public policy. *Hence the tax incidence should be tailored to the size of the recipient's capital holding, not to the size of the donor's estate.* The tax deterrent should be nonexistent or light upon gifts or bequests that help to broaden the private ownership of viable capital holdings. Estate and gift taxes should be heavy upon gifts or bequests which either fail to promote this fundamental policy or which work against it by promoting excessively concentrated ownership of capital.

Many considerations would enter into the legislative deliberations necessary to fix the lower limit of capital holdings to be recognized by law as *viable* capital holdings. Within limits, this minimum might vary with the number of persons in a household. It might be measured by market value appraisal, or it might be measured by yield, or by both.

Many considerations will also enter into the legislative deliberations required for drawing the line between capital holdings that are viable (and so are to be legislatively encouraged) and holdings that are monopolistic (and so are to be discouraged).

Some comment is needed on the significance of such limitations. The specification of the minimum size of a *viable* capital holding would be in effect a legislative determination that a capital holding of at least this size (assuming wise diversification and reasonable husbanding) is sufficient to support a household of a given size in comfort. The specification of the level at which a capital estate is to be regarded as *monopolistic* would be a legislative determination of the point beyond which concentration of the ownership of capital by a single consumer unit operates to exclude others from participating in the production of wealth to an extent capable of providing a viable income. These laws should be framed to encourage the accumulation of capital by households in submonopolistic amounts.

We have used the word "monopolistic" to characterize capital estates which, in the determination of Congress or state legislatures, are so large that they tend to exclude some households in the economy from participating in production to an extent that results in their having a viable income or decent standard of living.[1] This, to be sure, is a use of the word "monopolistic" that is somewhat different from the sense in which it is customarily employed. However, in the theory of Capitalism the concept of *monopolization of participation in production* is just as critical as that of *market monopolization*.

Market monopolization is destructive of free competition, without which there can be no just, objective, and impartial evaluation of the contributions to production. Monopolization of participation in production is destructive of the right of every household to participate in production in order that it may participate in distribution. Precisely because excessively large capital holdings represent monopolization of participation in production, the form of distribution in our mixed economy must be predominantly laboristic and be governed by principles of charity and expediency rather than of justice.[2]

In addition, such monopolization is largely responsible for making

[1] For legislative purposes, some determination of a decent minimum standard of living would have to be used in arriving at a determination of the limit at which a capital holding of a consumer unit of given size shall be regarded as monopolistic. The national median income, for example, might be used for this purpose in estimating how large capital holdings could become before menacing the right of those participating in production only as workers to supplement their insufficient incomes by capital earnings.

[2] The principle of just distribution operates to establish a direct relationship between contribution to production and receipt of income out of production. Those who do not participate in production cannot justly receive any part of the primary distribution of the wealth produced. Monopoly enters the picture when the participation in production by some, through their excessive ownership of capital, excludes others from the opportunity to participate in production or to participate adequately. But we should also bear in mind that the greater the diffusion of capital ownership, the higher will be the tolerable limit of concentration of capital ownership in particular households. We can best see this by considering the extremes. Where the productive capital of an economy is owned by only a handful of the total number of households, a very severe limit on concentrated capital ownership will be required to prevent the almost monolithic growth of capital in the hands of a few families. At the other extreme, we can at least imagine a society in which the ownership of capital by all households is substantially equal and increases at a uniform rate. In such a society no limit whatsoever would be required to enable all households to participate in the production of wealth *at any level of national income, however high*. The significant point of this imaginary case is that, as the transition to Capitalism progresses, progressively greater individual holdings may accord with public policy.

the private ownership of capital increasingly illusory or nominal. If we were at present to give monopolistic private ownership its full rights, the immediate result would be so violent a maldistribution of income that we would be on the verge of complete economic collapse. Hence, from sheer economic expediency, if for no other reason, we must in our mixed economy deny such monopolistic private ownership its full rights. In doing so, we simultaneously dilute the property rights of all owners of capital. In fact, we must attenuate those rights to an extent that almost constitutes an alienation of the property, and certainly leaves it private property in a nominal sense only.

So much for the fundamental concepts to be used in modifying our present gift and estate tax laws in order to promote Capitalism. What is the essence of the modifications proposed? It is that gifts and bequests which facilitate the creation of viable capital holdings *should be wholly free of tax.* The revenue loss, as we have noted, would be small. The benefits to the economy would be great. On the other hand, gifts and bequests which facilitate the creation of monopolistic capital holdings should be steeply taxed—sufficiently so as to render them nonexistent in our economy. The effect of gifts and bequests would be measured *after the gift or bequest.* If the recipient household owned less than a monopolistic capital holding *after* the gift or bequest, it would be free of tax. If its capital holding exceeded the monopolistic limit after the gift or bequest, that part in excess of the limit would be progressively and steeply taxed.

This would place transfers of capital holdings by gift or bequest to households without viable capital interests or having holdings below the level of monopolistic size, on a parity with gifts to charity. There would be no occasion to discourage gifts or bequests of noncapital property because of the size of the recipient's holdings of either capital or noncapital property, *except insofar as gifts of noncapital property might be used as a disguise for creating monopolistic capital holdings through gifts or bequests of noncapital property.* There can be little doubt that wise and reasonable donors or testators would prefer this means of disposing of capital estates to the kind of empty, shotgun charity that is encouraged by the existing tax laws.

One further modification of the gift and estate tax laws remains to be considered. It would have special applicability to large, closely held businesses. Provisions similar to the income tax provisions of the equity-sharing type already discussed could be designed for the gift and estate tax laws to enable equity interests in closely held businesses to be distributed to employees through nondiscriminatory equity-sharing plans. Such dispositions would be given tax exemption under the gift and estate tax laws similar to the exemptions now available for contributions to charitable corporations.

Owners of large, closely held businesses are now faced with the alternatives of the 77 percent bracket or an elegantly contrived charitable foundation. Is there any doubt that many of these, given the choice, would prefer to make capitalists of their employees, if gift and estate tax exemptions enabled them to do so? For a relatively slight loss in federal revenue, since *no* tax is collected on the vast tax-inspired gifts to charity that are prevalent today, a great acceleration in the broadening of the capital base could be achieved, and in a manner that would promote the diffused private ownership of capital instead of a socialized control of it.

What we have just said should not be construed either as impugning the motives of those who establish charitable foundations, or as questioning the traditional forms of charitable donation to religious and educational institutions, or the giving of alms to the needy. These traditional charities have never been a serious problem in the United States, and it is generally felt that they function best when they are supported by widespread small contributions. These legitimate charities can serve their purpose without causing the erosion and alienation of private property in capital, as the vast general-purpose foundations cannot.

The need for charity in an economy is largely a measure of the failure of the economic system to achieve a balanced participation in production and thereby to avoid a maldistribution of wealth. Thus, for example, if every household in the economy could afford to pay in full for the education of its members, the full expense of which is conceivably a part of a decent standard of living, then charitable contributions to educational institutions for the support of their teaching functions would be unnecessary and out of place. On the other hand, the traditional charities which take care of the destitute and incompetent will always remain indispensable, though even here success in eliminating destitution will minimize their task.

It is quite a different matter with the vast general-purpose foundations. Allowing for all the good they do, we cannot overlook the fact that they contribute substantially to preventing the number of capital-owning households from increasing at a rate that keeps pace with that of technological advances in the production of wealth. These foundations represent the best use their donors could make of their vast capital interests in the light of corporation laws, tax laws, and economic policies which are incompatible with the principles of Capitalism. Under such conditions, as we have observed, these foundations constitute a menace to the institution of private property. That fact, together with the necessity that the equity capital concentrated in them should be widely diffused among private owners, requires a reappraisal of the gift and estate tax laws that now encourage the formation of such foundations or charitable trusts.

MODIFICATION OF PERSONAL INCOME TAX LAWS

Since about half of the revenue of the federal government is provided by the payment of personal income taxes, a far more cautious study of this proposal is required than in the case of the estate tax and gift tax proposals outlined above. We should try to discover the extent to which personal income tax deductions might be safely permitted to allow for transfers of wealth that facilitate the broadening of our economy's capital base. Within certain limits, it might thus be possible and advisable to place such transfers on a parity with contributions to charity, so far as the personal income tax laws are concerned.

The laboristic distribution of wealth in our mixed economy has necessitated a shockingly heavy progressive income tax. This tax can unquestionably be used to help establish the balanced participation in production that Capitalism envisages as ultimately achievable through diffused individual ownership of capital. Until the capitalist revolution is well advanced, the adoption of permissive deductions, within reasonable limits, for transfers of wealth that aid in broadening capital ownership might be far wiser than rate reductions.

TERMINATING DELIBERATE GOVERNMENTAL PROMOTION OF CONCENTRATION OF OWNERSHIP AND OF MARKET MONOPOLY

As we have seen, most of the efforts to "make capitalism work" are in fact devices for combining a predominantly laboristic distribution of wealth with a predominantly capitalist production of it. Many of these "expedient practices" are not merely un-Capitalistic in their failure to bring about a widely diffused private ownership of capital, but in fact are anti-Capitalistic in directly contributing to the concentrated ownership of capital. One example of this is the "five-year amortization of emergency facilities" program used extensively during the Second World War, again during the emergency following the Korean outbreak, and in the period since the termination of the Korean hostilities.

The theory of this program is that, while the government may in time of emergency need quick additions to plant capacity, loss may result to the investor if the emergency period is short and does not enable him to derive the benefit he would normally expect from the new capital equipment or facilities. To compensate for this risk, the government extends to selected businesses the privilege of deducting the "certified" cost of the new facilities against income taxes over a five-year period. The ordinary economic life of capital instruments as recognized for income tax purposes is frequently much longer than five years. It varies for periods up to twenty-five years for certain types of plant facilities and even for some types of manufacturing equipment. The effect, therefore, of the special statutory privilege is that of "an interest-free loan by the Government to the taxpayer claiming amortization allowances." [3]

The theory is that a taxpayer corporation which receives a "certificate of necessity" from the Office of Defense Mobilization for accelerated amortization of new capital equipment would not be willing to construct the additional facility in question without this added stimulus. The fact of the matter is that the all-out effort to promote "full employment" has eliminated the slumps in recent years, and the industries to which such certificates have been granted have generally been the most basic, highly productive industries in the peacetime economy as well as in the wartime economy. By June 10, 1957, 38.3 billion dollars of accelerated amortization certificates had been granted under the Revenue Act of 1950. On the 38.3 billion dollars of new capital formation thus inspired, 23.1 billion dollars of rapid depreciation was authorized.

There can be no question of the propriety of granting an interest-free government loan for new capital facilities to General Motors, for example, if the nation's immediate safety depends upon it. If the same physical or military result could not be achieved by means which at the same time created new businesses owned by new capitalists, or if this extraordinary advantage *could not* be made contingent on fulfilling the requirement that the newly formed capital be accompanied by a concurrent increase in new private owners of capital, then the program might be justified in its present form. But the only consideration

[3] See the memorandum prepared by the Staff of the Joint Economic Committee, dated May 28, 1956, on *Implications of Recent Expansion of Special Amortization Program*, p. 10.

taken into account by this program is *new capital formation* resulting in new productive capacity. No thought has been given to the possibility of using this program to create new owners of capital in the process of increasing productive capacity by stimulating the formation of new capital.

Since 1950, such stimulation has increased the concentrated ownership of the capacity to produce wealth, principally in industries in which the ownership is already highly concentrated, to the extent of 38.3 billion dollars. This massive quantity of capital formation has resulted from a government policy that is exactly the opposite of what the policy should be in order to broaden the base of capital ownership and maintain freely competitive markets. Instead of using the power of government to increase the number of owners of highly productive capital investments, we have used it to increase the present concentration of ownership.

Other examples can be cited to show how government and industry work together to boom up the expansion of capital, which is good, while concentrating its ownership, which is bad. Our great corporations, General Motors, General Electric, United States Steel, Ford Motor Company, and many others, are showered with praise for their boldness in announcing that over the "next *x* years, we will spend *y* billions in capital expansion." In each case, the import of the announcement is that a corporation is going to place in operation an enormous additional quantity of the most potent wealth-producing factor in history. Almost none of these announcements contemplates any increase in equity capital by any method other than the investment of earnings withheld from the existing owners. Even where new equity capital is involved, almost none of it comes from households that are not already large owners of capital.

There are still other ways in which government policies encourage further concentration of ownership in our mixed capitalistic economy. The policy of legislative and administrative support for jurisdictional rules, excessive job classification, work limitation rules, and infinite varieties of "paid unemployment" in industry, all in the interest of "full employment" and a laboristic distribution of wealth, tends to encourage and promote the concentration of ownership rather than its diffusion. These practices increase operating costs to a point at which they can be absorbed only by the most heavily capitalized businesses, since they divert a large portion of the wealth produced by capital from the owners of capital to workers. The ultimate effect is to discourage new business enterprises, and thereby to impede potential new owners of capital from becoming capitalists.

12 THE MODERN CORPORATION AND
THE CAPITALIST REVOLUTION

CORPORATIONS IN THE PRESENT MIXED ECONOMY

The modern corporation has proved a matchless form for associating together the productive powers of workers (including technicians and managers) and the productive power of capital. This cannot be better evidenced than by the fact that the largest, most complex, and most productive businesses are, for the most part, conducted in the corporate form.

From the point of view of the theory of Capitalism, the corporation is an ideal instrument for assembling the capital owned by many households in aggregations of such size as to permit production to be carried on in the most efficient and least toil-consuming manner. Within a single corporation, any amount of capital owned by any number of shareholders may be combined with the managerial, technical, and mechanical skills needed to carry on production in the technologically most advanced manner.

Mixed capitalism, however, misuses the corporation. Instead of using it to diffuse the private ownership of capital among the households of the society, it diffuses the wealth produced by capital to those who should, but *do not,* own capital. Its method of doing this is governed by principles of charity and expediency.

The laboristic distribution of capitalistically produced wealth is, to be sure, not confined to corporate business. For example, collective bargaining agreements, which raise wages far above their competitive level, are becoming as common with unincorporated businesses as they are with corporations. Nevertheless, the use that is made of corporations to carry out a laboristic distribution of wealth gives the corporation first place among the redistributive agencies of our mixed economy.

The corporation facilitates a laboristic distribution of wealth in the following three ways.

(1) It is subject to a graduated income tax that is levied only upon the wealth produced by capital. The federal government and most states levy such taxes on corporations doing business within their respective borders. These taxes provide about half of the revenue of the federal government. They constitute a smaller, but still important, source of state revenue. They are, therefore, a basic source of income for the redistributive programs which are operated directly by the state, such as the subsidization of submarginal agricultural enterprises, and the numerous programs that are designed to promote full employment.

(2) Corporations are the largest employers of organized labor. By a web of federal and state laws that have largely eliminated the free play of competitive forces in the fixing of wages, wages have been raised to a height far above the economic value of the work for which they are paid. This is probably the most direct method of diverting the income due to owners of capital to the owners of labor.

(3) Corporations are not merely permitted indefinitely to plough back the wealth produced by their capital. They are constrained to do so by the effect of the steeply graduated personal income tax on the

dividends received by their larger stockholders. Though the benefits of this involuntary investment by stockholders are to some degree vaguely reflected in the increased market value of the stockholder's shares, this is a fragmentary and frequently elusive substitute for receipt by the stockholder of the full return on his capital. These withheld dividends, to which stockholders would be entitled if their property rights in equity capital were fully respected, are the primary source for the formation of business capital. The instruments which are brought into production by such newly formed capital in turn become sources of new income to be disposed of under government supervision in accordance with the redistribution policies of mixed capitalism. So entirely distorted have our views become that we admire the restraint of a labor union which demands no more than *all* the increased wealth produced by improved or additional capital instruments. It is becoming common for collectively bargained wage increases to outrun the "productivity increase."

In our partly capitalistic and partly laboristic economy, the modern corporation has thus become an instrument for a distribution of wealth that is predominantly laboristic. It has served as a device for attenuating the property rights in capital, and for almost alienating that property from its owners. In the early years of its existence, it was an ideal vehicle for the concentration of effective ownership in stockholders. But as the concentration grew and brought on depression after depression, it became impossible to permit a full return to the owners of capital of the wealth produced by their capital. Failing to recognize that private property in capital in an industrial society eventually becomes untenable unless its ownership is broadly diffused, our mixed economy settled upon the other alternative. It brought about the erosion of private property in concentrated holdings of capital through the diversion of the wealth such capital produces, from the stockholders who own it to the mass of workers who need it and whose use of it provides a mass market.

CORPORATIONS IN THE TRANSITION TO CAPITALISM

In the operation of our great corporations today, the wealth produced by capital is divided by reference to considerations of expediency. Some goes to supplement the wages labor really earns; some, to pay the double tax on wealth produced by capital; some to provide a major portion of new capital formation. A trickle is returned to the nominal owners—the stockholders.

In a completely capitalistic economy, the division would be made on the basis of the relative contributions made to production by the owners of capital and the owners of labor. Effective property in capital would replace the present merely nominal property in capital. The truth that capital is the major producer of wealth would correct the illusion that labor is the major producer of wealth. The fact that the productiveness of capital constantly increases (relative to that of labor) with advancing technology would eliminate the pretense that the productivity of mechanical labor is increasing. The major contribution made by capital to the output of wealth would be reflected in the return to capital of a major portion of the wealth produced. The conflict between the concentrated ownership of capital and the right of all households to participate effectively in production would be resolved by a widely diffused private ownership of capital.

A business corporation is an association of workers of various talents and capacities with capital instruments and working capital *for the purpose of producing wealth*. In a completely capitalistic society, business corporations would be the basic vehicle of Capitalism itself, whereas under mixed capitalism, they are the basic vehicle for the expedient or charitable distribution of income and the alienation of property in capital.

To effect the transition from mixed capitalism to Capitalism, business corporations should, therefore, be reformed and reconstituted with the following objectives in mind.

(1) *The revitalization of the property of stockholders in the capital*

immediately owned by their corporation. As we will point out later, the essence of this lies in the return to stockholders of *all* the wealth produced by their corporate capital.

(2) *The greatly expanded use of present corporate income taxes as instruments for diffusing private ownership of capital.* The increased use of equity-sharing plans, already discussed, would be a prime application of this principle.

(3) *The reduction and eventual elimination of corporate income taxes as the transition advances and the economy approaches "capitalistic balance."* [1] The corporate income tax is justifiable in a mixed economy where the wealth produced by capital must be largely distributed to labor in order to prevent the collapse of the economy. It would not be justifiable where 90 percent, or more, of the national income can be distributed to the owners of capital property where its ownership is widely diffused and where the national policy is to encourage the shift of the burden of production from labor to capital. At the end of the transition, only personal income taxes would be levied, for only in this manner can all households be treated for tax purposes with proportionate equality.

(4) *The regulation of business corporations by government in accordance with the principles of Capitalism.* This envisages the extirpation of the capitalistic heresy of *laissez-faire.* As long as government regulation is designed to encourage the broadest diffusion of private ownership of capital, to restrict government itself from owning capital,[2] and to give full effectiveness to private property in capital, the

[1] The economy approaches "capitalistic balance" as it approaches the point at which the diffusion of private ownership of capital is so broad that the wealth produced by capital can be fully distributed to the owners of capital.

[2] Under Capitalism, the only justification for government ownership of capital is the sheer technical physical impossibility of private ownership. The public roads are an example. Freedom in an industrial society is dependent upon the widely diffused private ownership of economic power (the power to produce wealth) as a check to inevitably concentrated political power. Every attempt by government to unite in itself political and economic power should be subjected to this test. The frequent attempt to justify government's engaging in the production of wealth on the grounds that particular projects are "too large" for private industry is absurd, as we will show.

regulation of business by government *diminishes* rather than increases the power of political office holders. The use of political power to regulate the economic system, so that economic power remains widely diffused, vested in private property, and protected in its property rights, can never endanger individual freedom.

(5) *Government regulation of business corporations so that, on the one hand, they may grow to such size as to enable them to employ fully the most advanced techniques of production; and so that, on the other hand, they will not become so large as to impair free competition in the markets affected by them.* As we will point out later, there is no reason to assume today that such middle ground of corporate size does not exist in every case except that of public utilities, *i.e.*, industries in which free competition is not feasible for technological reasons. If and when an instance is found in which efficient techniques of production cannot be employed unless a business is of such size as to impair free competition, such an industry has by this very fact become a public utility. The number of such instances are few today, and there is every reason to believe that the advance of technology will reduce the number rather than increase it. In all cases, however, the government regulation of corporations should try to see that growth in the size of a corporation is accompanied by the broadening of its ownership.

(6) *The employment by government of all reasonable and proper powers to carry out the transition to Capitalism.* When the transition has been effected, government should employ its regulatory powers to maintain balance between the diffusion of private ownership of capital and the perpetual increase in the proportion of the total wealth produced by capital. The principles which should underlie all such regulations are (a) the protection of property; (b) the maintenance of free competition in all markets; and (c) the discharge of the obligation of government to assure all households of the opportunity to participate in production to an extent sufficient to provide them with a viable income.

RESTORING EFFECTIVE OWNERSHIP OF CAPITAL
TO THE STOCKHOLDERS OF BUSINESS CORPORATIONS

The essence of property in productive wealth is the right to receive its product. Legal recognition of this right would consist in the legal requirement that the entire net income of a mature corporation during or immediately after the close of each financial period be paid out in dividends to its stockholders. Some allowances would have to be made for the need of relatively undeveloped new corporations to plough in capital in order to survive, as well as for the needs of any business for working capital and contingent reserves. Failure to apply the laws of private property to the capital owned by stockholders permits corporate managers in effect to hire capital at a price dictated by themselves.[3]

The voice of the stockholder is ineffective unless he receives the entire product of his capital and then determines, by his own affirmative action, whether he will return any part of such earnings to the corporation as a further investment of capital. No other conceivable arrangement can force corporate management to justify its performance from time to time before stockholders, just as holders of political office must justify theirs from time to time before the electorate.

---

[3] That the right to receive the income of capital is the essence of property in capital is an undisputed legal proposition. It has never been more tersely stated than by Chief Justice Fuller of the United States Supreme Court in the case which held unconstitutional an income tax of 2 percent, thus making necessary the 16th Amendment to the Constitution. The Chief Justice, delivering the opinion of the court, said: "But is there any distinction between the real estate itself or its owners in respect of it and the rents or income of the real estate coming to the owners as the natural and ordinary incident of their ownership? . . . As, according to the feudal law, the whole beneficial interest in the land consisted in the right to take the rents and profits, the general rule has always been, in the language of Coke, that 'if a man seized of land in fee by his deed granteth to another the profits of those lands, to have and to hold to him and his heirs . . . the whole land itself doth pass. For what is the land but the profits thereof?' . . . A devise of the rents and profits or of the income of lands passes the land itself both at law and in equity." *Pollock v. Farmers' Loan & Trust Co.,* United States Supreme Court Reports, 1895, Vol. 157, p. 429 ff.

Government without the consent of the governed is despotism. Benevolent or paternalistic care of the interests of the governed does not lessen the despotism. If the governed are men, not children, they are entitled to take care of themselves through processes of self-government in which they express their consent by exercising a voice in their own affairs. Nothing could be more a man's own affairs than the disposal of his own property. For the management of a corporate enterprise to dispose of what rightfully belongs to its stockholders without their free, present, and affirmatively expressed consent is despotism, and it remains despotism no matter how benevolent or wise management is in acting for what it thinks to be the "best interests" of its stockholders.

In the political sphere, those elected to public office are expected to exercise the powers of government, and should be allowed to do so without the interference of the electorate. In a representative democracy, the citizens do not exercise these powers directly. They delegate them to the men of their choice. But while the citizens do not themselves perform the technical tasks of government, they do retain the ultimate power of government through the choice of their representatives and through the constitutional acts by which they give or withhold their approval of the policies and conduct of the officials who hold office at their pleasure.

Analogously, those who hold the offices of management in large corporate enterprises have, in theory at least, been selected because of their technical competence for the tasks of management. They should, therefore, be expected and allowed to perform these tasks without interference from the stockholders. Corporate management must be responsible not only for the day-to-day operation of the corporation's business, but also for long-term policies and planning which involve the future capital needs of the corporation. But the ultimate control of the corporation should rest with those who own it, not with those who merely run it.

That ultimate control, which belongs to the stockholders by their right of property, cannot be exercised by them if they have no power beyond saying who shall sit on the corporation's Board of Directors. For the stockholders to exercise ultimate control over their property, they must also be able to say how *all* the wealth produced by that property shall be disposed of. To give them such control, which by right should be theirs, would not invade the professional or technical sphere of management. It would simply make management responsible to their principals, the owners, as the officers of government are responsible to their masters, the citizens. It would reconstitute the corporation by creating it in the image of constitutional government. Just as government with the consent of the governed made popular sovereignty effective and barred the way to all dictatorial usurpations of power, so management with the consent of the owners would make private property effective in corporations and would bar the way to all usurping alienations of property.

Once the laws of private property are applied to the property rights of stockholders, the power and effectiveness of the stockholder's voice in corporate affairs will give him the control he should have. The burden of explaining long-range plans and of making a convincing case for them before stockholders will be thrown upon management. The task of educating stockholders in the affairs of corporations—an indispensable requirement in a society of capitalists—will be placed upon management. Stockholders will have the incentive to become knowledgeable about the activities of their corporations. The stockholder's present apathy to corporate communications cannot be overcome as long as he feels that the economic effect upon him will be the same whether he scrutinizes them meticulously or wholly disregards them. But if the stockholder's hand is restored to the economic throttle of the corporation, his decisions will then affect the return upon his capital, and he will be attentive.

It is hardly necessary to point out that a modification in personal income tax laws would be required if corporations are compelled by law to pay to stockholders the income which their capital produces. One guiding principle of such statutory amendments in the early phase of the transition should be that the revenue of government ought not be increased as a result. With that kept constant, the tax burden on a stockholder, after he has been made to assume his proportionate share of the corporation's income tax, should not be increased.

The proposed reconstitution of the corporation is indispensable to the restoration of the rights of private property held in corporate form. The restoration of such rights would go a long way toward effecting the transition from our present mixed capitalism to a completely capitalistic economy. Even during the transition, it would cauterize the dangerous concentrations of irresponsible power that are now uncontrollable growths in our economy. But in the economy that will emerge when the transition to Capitalism is completed, it is of the utmost importance that the corporation should be an instrument of private property and completely responsive to the rights of property. A society of capitalists without an effective franchise vested in the rights of property would be as much a hollow mockery as a society in which all men are citizens but without the rights of suffrage.

FINANCIAL EFFICIENCY IN BUSINESS CORPORATIONS VS. TECHNICAL EFFICIENCY

The application of the laws of private property to such property in its corporate form has other implications. At present corporations are permitted to withhold the income due stockholders *ad infinitum,* so long as it is employed in new capital formation for the corporation. In many of our greatest corporations, it is this illegitimate power, rather than their superiority of production techniques or management, which has catapulted them to the magnitude of competition-destroying monopolies.

It is a tenet of Capitalism that technological progress must never be impeded or slowed down. The goal of Capitalism is the most efficient production of all the wealth that is needed—with the least human toil. Such *technical efficiency* is desirable without qualification or limit. *Financial efficiency,* however, is another matter. From the point of view of Capitalism, the fact that the techniques and capital of a particular corporation are superior in productiveness does not justify management in forcing stockholders to remain quiescent with a minute share of the income to which they are entitled, while the residue is used by management to give the corporation market dominance. Financial efficiency, according to the theory of Capitalism, should always be subordinated to the primary objectives of the economy.

In acting to bring about the capitalist revolution, as well as in regulating a completely capitalistic economy, government should not hesitate, therefore, to prohibit corporate conduct which thwarts the diffusion of capital ownership or which impairs market competition, merely because the financial efficiency of the corporation would thereby be impaired. Increased financial efficiency is generally a gain made at the expense of other participants in production. Increased technological efficiency is a gain which reduces toil.

Admittedly, these principles would not be as easy to administer as they are to state. This does not, however, lessen their soundness as principles. Practical instances of their application will be discussed later as we examine other proposals for accomplishing the transition to Capitalism, such as the credit financing of the formation of new capital under the ownership of new capitalists.

OTHER CHANGES AFFECTING BUSINESS CORPORATIONS

In an economy in which most new capital formation has its source in income withheld by corporations from their stockholders, corporate giantism and the disappearance of free competition is a matter of course.[4] Where it is recognized, however, that the same financial means that are now used to finance consumption can be used to finance new capital formation, the link between adequate formation of new capital and the continued concentration of ownership of capital is broken.

We will discuss the underlying principles of this proposal in Chapter Thirteen. But in the present connection it should be pointed out that our mixed economy has gone so far in fostering corporate monopolies that in the early phases of the transition to Capitalism the program of financing new capitalists should direct a predominant share of new capital formation into new enterprises owned by new capitalists. The restoration of free competition requires an increase in the number of competitors in hundreds of markets.

We have called attention to the fact that the accelerated amortization provisions of the federal revenue laws have been deliberately used to increase the concentrated ownership of capital. Such use impedes the transition to Capitalism. To effect that transition accelerated amortization might be used in exactly the opposite way— to promote directly the diffused ownership of capital and to restore competition to markets which have fallen under the control of oligopolies. The same differential treatment, guided by the same economic principles, might be employed in fixing the depletion rates in extractive industries.

At all times, regulatory procedures designed to broaden ownership of capital and to promote freely competitive markets would have to be employed in such a manner as to give free play to the competitive forces that weed out technologically inefficient, mismanaged, or otherwise submarginal businesses. Such weeding out is essential to technological advance and the reduction of toil. It is indispensable to a healthy capitalistic economy.

---

[4] See "Profit Margins at General Motors," a background study by the American Institute of Management, published in *The Corporate Director*, July, 1956, Vol. VI, No. 3.

In disposing of war plants, in the development of atomic energy as a source of industrial power, in making military expenditures, in breaking up monopolistic combinations under the antitrust laws, in making expenditures in those few instances where it is proper for government to own and operate capital instruments (such as the public roads), and in purchasing military equipment, buildings to house public offices, supplies, etc., government should act to promote Capitalism, not to prevent it. War plants should not be disposed of in a manner calculated to foster increased concentration of ownership or decrease market competition. Where such plants now belong to the government, their transfer to private ownership presents an opportunity to bring into existence new, privately owned businesses under the ownership of new capitalists.

It seems certain that atomic energy will be the basic source of industrial power for the production of wealth in the future. Atomic energy can be harnessed to produce wealth with only minute contributions from subtechnical and submanagerial labor. Large amounts of capital formation will be needed to realize the potential benefits that atomic energy holds in store for mankind.

Here is a case in which the officers of government, under our mixed economy, are in a position to fuse their political power with the vast economic power that is inherent in government ownership of atomic energy plants. But under Capitalism government would have here a magnificent opportunity to guide the development of great wealth-producing capital instruments into widely diffused private ownership. Any atomic plant that can be directly built and financed by government is *per se* capable of being built by private corporations owned by new capitalists, *on condition that the credit facilities of government are used to assist them if private credit facilities are not available or adequate.*

In each of these instances, the policy of government, in seeking to diffuse and broaden the ownership base and to establish free competition, should be cautious to go no further in diverting new capital formation away from the giant corporations than is necessary to restore competitive markets and to bring about a workable diffusion of ownership. Although only a minute number of stockholders are at the present time dependent upon the capital of these corporations for their participation in production, the number will grow as the transition to Capitalism is effected. An expanding number of households will look to their ownership of equity interests in these corporations as their primary means of participating in production and in the resultant distribution of income. Our largest corporations have gone far beyond the size dictated by mere technological efficiency. They have long since passed the point where their continued growth would promote *technological efficiency*. On the other hand, regulation should not impair their service to their stockholders as an effective means of participating in production.

13 MEASURES AIMED AT DETERRING AN EXCESSIVE OWNERSHIP OF CAPITAL BY INDIVIDUAL HOUSEHOLDS

INVESTMENT PREFERENCE FOR SMALL OR NEW CAPITALISTS

We have asserted the necessity of requiring a full periodic distribution to stockholders of the net earnings (*i.e.,* the wealth produced) by corporations. This might be accomplished through tax deterrents that do not differ in principle from those provisions of the present Revenue Code that restrict accumulations in excess of the reasonable needs of a business.

Any such enforced payment of corporate net earnings would have to be accompanied by great improvement in the efficiency of investment banking practices for the marketing of new equity issues. The costs of marketing security issues would have to be materially reduced, and regulations to insure fair dealing and full disclosure of relevant information would have to be made more effective.

No government efforts are of greater importance to the rights and interests of its citizens than regulations aimed at molding the base of private ownership to fit the state of technology and the needs of the people for a high standard of living. There do not appear to be any insurmountable obstacles to the development of security flotation procedures which would help to broaden the capital base and to discourage concentration of ownership of capital.

Effective security flotation procedures during the transition period may require the establishment of preferential opportunities for investment by households whose aggregate capital interests are subviable. Any study of present and past financing practices quickly discloses that the choice investment opportunities are available to those whose capital ownership is already concentrated. To date, political leaders, economists, and businessmen focus their attention on the amount of capital formation needed to furnish desirable growth for the economy. They pay almost no attention to the sources of the capital and the diffusion of its ownership. An outstanding but by no means solitary example of this is the money, amounting to billions, which the government has granted in tax-free loans (*i.e.,* the accelerated five-year amortization privileges) to the largest corporations. As a result, highly concentrated ownership is further intensified and freely competitive markets are impaired. The establishment of effective investment preferences for new and small capital owners would be one means of accomplishing the dual responsibility of all concerned to see not only that adequate capital formation takes place, but also that the growth in the number of households owning viable capital interests occurs at a satisfactory rate.

We cannot explore here all of the possibilities of making reasonable use of a system of investor preferences which would tend to advance the capitalist revolution. In general, such controls should operate through (1) preferential credit financing of the acquisition of viable capital interests by noncapital-owning households or households with subviable capital holdings; and (2) giving households with very large holdings of capital low investment preferences which might limit them to investment in fixed income bonds (*e.g.,* the bonds of financing institutions designed to provide the credit necessary to carry on the program of financing new capitalists).

To illustrate the type of investor preference we have in mind, investments in public utility enterprises, including new atomic energy plants, would undoubtedly be rated for investment priority by new capitalists with subviable holdings, and should be favorites for capital-acquisition loans of types we will discuss later. The enormous power needs of the future will provide the opportunity for a vast number of new viable capital holdings. One well-informed estimate places the amount of capital investment in power resources to be required in the United States over the next twenty years at nearly 100 billion dollars.

INCOME TAX DETERRENTS TO PERSONAL CONCENTRATION

The ownership of a large amount of productive capital is not the only manner in which the excessive concentration of participation in production may come about. It may also come about in a particular household through combining a very large holding of capital with the performance of highly paid work. The combination of ownership of a large capital estate with the performance of highly paid managerial or professional work gives a single household the possession of great productive power. Whether this form of concentration presents problems different from those of concentrated capital ownership by itself depends upon certain factors which we will now consider.

The economic goal of Capitalism is to shift the burden of producing subsistence from human labor to capital instruments as far as it is possible to do so. The state of technological advancement and the standard of living which an economy sets for itself will determine at any particular time the amount of subsistence work for which there is a real demand in the economy. The more successful an economy is in substituting the production of subsistence by capital for its production by labor, the smaller the actual demand for labor, *whatever the given standard of living.*

In terms of these relationships, we can see several things. At the beginning of the transition to Capitalism, the proportion of households whose only opportunity to participate in production is through toil will be at a maximum. At the conclusion, when a balanced capitalistic economy is achieved, there will certainly always be some portion of the population who, for reasons of mental incompetence or moral delinquency, will fail to husband their property in capital and otherwise fail to adapt themselves to the exigencies of a completely capitalistic economy. Hence there will always be some whose only possibility of participating in production is through the performance of toil. Aside from this, the production of wealth will always require millions of workers, although it seems absolutely certain that the amount of necessary toil will progressively diminish in relation to the amount of wealth produced.

The government of a completely capitalistic society should do the very opposite of promoting "full employment," for to promote the employment of all employables under a nonlaboristic distribution of wealth would be to make an end out of toil itself or to encourage individuals to make the same slavish mistake. A capitalistic economy could countenance full employment only at a time when methods of production are technologically so primitive that the employment of all employables is necessary to enable it to achieve the standard of living it desires. Even then it would seek to promote technological advance in order to correct this deplorable condition. But if, in an advanced industrial economy, there are households whose only opportunity to engage in production is through the performance of toil, *at a time when the demand for labor is less than the supply of persons seeking employment,* the government of a completely capitalistic society cannot fulfill its obligation to provide an opportunity to all to participate in production *unless it inhibits the particular kind of*

*concentration that is involved in combining participation in produc-
tion as a worker with participation as the owner of a monopolistic
capital estate.* This kind of concentration does more than diminish
the opportunities of others to participate in production. It destroys
them.

Whatever may be determined to be a monopolistic capital holding
at a particular time, if the need for jobs is less than the supply, the
government of a completely capitalistic society should prohibit the
pre-empting of employment opportunities by those who do not need
them, to the harm and detriment of those who do. The performance
of toil for subsistence is a means to the enjoyment of wealth. But the
nature of production and distribution in a completely capitalistic
society is such that if some hoard more of the opportunity to produce
than is consistent with the participation in production by all, whether
it be through avarice, ignorance or foolishness, then the obligation
falls upon government to deter them from doing so.

As we continue to make technological progress, the importance
of preventing this type of concentration of participation in production
will increase. As more men become holders of viable capital estates,
and as the capital formation that is concurrently taking place represents an ever greater shift of the burden of production from labor
to capital, the greater will be the danger that those whose only opportunity to participate in production is through labor will become
wards of charity as a result of the combination by others of large
capital ownership with highly paid employments.

The policy of government in this respect should be more than
regulatory. It should be educative. It is the greatest of all slanders
on humanity to think that only through the production of wealth can
men find outlets for their creative energies and impulses. This is a
falsehood that civilized society should make every effort to refute.
Through preventing men from adding an increment to their income
which they do not need, *by doing subsistence work where their doing
so would deprive others of their only opportunity to participate in the*

production of wealth, government can drive home a truth that all men in industrial societies must learn.

How can government most effectively prevent the combining of very large holdings of capital with compensation for subsistence work, where well-paid employment opportunities are less than the number of those whose only possibility of participation in production is through work? Our answer to this question is no more than a tentative suggestion. The problem is a matter of the deepest importance, and the study given it should be commensurate.

It appears to us that the problem can be dealt with through a deterrent use of taxation. Income from capital sources and income from labor sources might be separately classified for income tax purposes. After a household's capital income reaches the magnitude of a monopolistic capital holding, any additional income it derives from *subsistence work* (as distinguished from such income as may be derived from liberal pursuits) might be subjected to a separate progressive tax, rising—perhaps precipitously—to the level determined necessary to discourage this type of concentration. This might eliminate any economic incentive for those who try to combine such incomes with incomes resulting from subsistence work.

One other possible form of income tax deterrent to personal concentration should be mentioned. It should be the policy of a completely capitalistic society to encourage the acquisition of viable capital holdings by a maximum number of households, but at the same time to discourage capital holdings from growing to monopolistic size. Consequently, it would seem essential that this policy be reflected in the establishment of personal income tax rates. Graduated rates might be designed to rise steeply at the point where any increase in income would represent a monopolistic capital holding.

14 MEASURES AIMED AT DIRECTLY STIMULATING AN INCREASE IN THE NUMBER OF NEW CAPITALISTS

THE PRIMARY FUNCTION OF CREDIT IN A CAPITALISTIC SOCIETY

We have already discussed the possibility of greatly increasing the number of new owners of capital through the indirect device of equity-sharing. We pointed out that this could take place painlessly, *i.e.*, that it could be accomplished within the severe progressive corporate income tax rates to which we are accustomed. While there is some prospect that such corporate income taxes can be reduced to what is required for the basic costs of government as we approach our goal of a balance between production by capital and diffusion of capital ownership, there is little chance of tax reductions in our present mixed economy. The chances are all the other way.

Let us now consider the possibility of creating millions of new "financed capitalists"—men who have become acquainted with the principles of a capitalistic economy and whose acquisition of viable capital holdings has been financed with something approaching the effectiveness of our present financing of the acquisition of consumer goods. The latter has facilitated the acquisition by consumers of 142 billion dollars of durable goods, nearly 250 billion dollars of residential housing, 54 billion dollars in farm lands, and 35 billion dollars in farm improvements.[1]

The view that an orgy of production is needed to keep our mixed capitalist economy functioning effectively is frequently stated in terms of an economic pie. We are told that the problem is not one of dividing up the economic pie, but rather one of making an ever larger pie. Neither is a correct statement of the problem. The task of a truly capitalistic society is to broaden the ownership of the pie-making machinery and to build a vast number of new pie-making machines that will be owned by people who do not now own such machines.

HISTORICAL PRECEDENTS

The explanations of "how capitalists got to be capitalists," advanced during the last two hundred years, have of necessity been conflicting, implausible, absurd, and frequently even whimsical. Without an explicit formulation of the theory of Capitalism, and especially without the basic insight that capital is the major producer of wealth in an industrial society, any account of the distributive dynamics of Capitalism tended to be fragmentary and distorted.

One of the most widely accepted of the traditional explanations of how men become capitalists is that individuals by thrifty and sacrificial savings of sums earned by toil, combined with courageous, imaginative and shrewd investment, are able to build up capital

[1] Estimates of wealth for 1952 by R. W. Goldsmith, *A Study of Saving in the United States* (Princeton, N. J.: Princeton University Press, 1956), Vol. III, Table W–1.

holdings.[2] This is certainly a correct explanation of how many viable capital fortunes were *started*. But the explanation is valid only for the early beginnings of such fortunes; for with the tendency of capital to accumulate in a geometric progression, the period of sacrificial frugality is soon over. Furthermore, this traditional explanation has no application to the great number and frequently vast size of the capital fortunes built upon inheritances, family gifts, transfers through marriage, and other ways of acquiring an initial equity holding without any frugality or postponement of consumer satisfactions.

There are other explanations of how men become owners of substantial capital holdings. They range from one extreme of claiming that the successful capitalist is always a man of superior intelligence, if not a genius or wizard, to the opposite extreme of saying, as Julius Rosenwald did, that 95 percent of all large fortunes were the result of luck.[3]

One thing is certain: not only has capital always been a producer of wealth, but its productiveness has evolved so far and risen so high in relation to that of labor that it is now the primary producer of wealth in an industrial society. Where private property in capital was fully respected as under the system of primitive capitalism, and even where it is respected only to some degree as in our present mixed capitalism, substantially all capital formation out of savings has taken place under the ownership of the existing proprietors of capital. The reasoning behind this statement can be simply stated.

[2] For example, the Invest-In-America Committee, sponsored by the investment banking fraternity, whose motto is "Invest in American *for more and better jobs*," states in its 1957 campaign propaganda: "A million new jobs a year call for at least $14,000 new capital investment per job—fourteen billion dollars per year! And at least another twenty billion dollars a year will be needed to maintain the plants and machinery providing the sixty-six million present jobs. Where is the money coming from? *From the same sources of capital that have provided it in the past* . . . savings in the form of retained earnings of corporations *and the savings of the American people . . . your savings, we hope. . . .*" (Italics added.)

[3] See Gustave Myers, *The Ending of Hereditary American Fortunes*, New York, 1939: p. 236, Note 8.

If economic values, including the values of the respective contributions of capital and labor to production, are competitively determined, then the large incomes and the substantial savings will be those of the owners of capital.

So completely accurate is this statement of the relationship between the high wealth-producing power of capital and the ownership of new capital formation arising out of savings, that it has held in spite of the enormously discriminatory effect of the double graduated income taxes. In spite of the corporate income tax, which falls only upon the wealth produced by capital, and the graduated personal income tax, which falls much more severely upon capital incomes (because they are the largest incomes) than upon labor incomes, the bulk of new capital currently formed out of personal and business savings is acquired by the present owners of capital.

In a competitive economy, the acquisition of capital through savings from wages and salaries is wholly inadequate to maintain the balance between the growth in the number of capital owners and the growth in the productive power of capital. The power of labor to produce wealth is small. In the absence of monopolistically controlled wage levels, the productive power of labor is wholly inadequate to support a standard of living anywhere approaching that which prevails in the United States today. Even with artificially high wage levels, unless they were to rise to a point where they resulted in the total extinction of private property in capital, the withholding of sufficient labor income from consumption to diffuse the ownership of capital and to create a significant number of new capitalists would immediately precipitate a depression.

Even with the present wage levels of our mixed capitalist economy, designed as they are to shift some 70 percent of our national income to labor in spite of the fact that labor produces less than 10 percent of our national wealth, our savings institutions currently operate to separate the wage saver from effective ownership of the productive capital in which his savings are invested. Savings made through life insurance policies illustrate this. The buyer of a life insurance policy or his selected beneficiary gets back, on the average, the fixed dollar amount representing the savings portion of his policy, plus a small fixed interest rate. The vast wealth produced by the factories and other capital instruments which are built on life insurance company loans accrues to the borrowers, to the insurance companies, to the self-perpetuating highly paid officialdom of insurance companies, and to the general recipients of laboristically distributed wealth. The life insurance buyer, instead of becoming a capitalist in the proprietary sense of the word, receives—in our inflationary mixed economy—the number of dollars he saved plus a small interest return, all duly devalued by the intervening inflation.

The same may be said for savings bank deposits and other forms of savings which do not result in direct equity ownership of capital.

The fact of the matter is that our entire attention has been concerned with providing a sufficient flow of funds into the formation of capital to insure the growth of industry, without regard to how the ownership of capital is diffused. At the same time, we strive to provide employment for all those who wish or need employment in order to support the mass consumption of goods and services. We have shown great imagination in the invention and refinement of credit mechanisms to diffuse the ownership of consumer goods because we have found that the broad distribution of consumer goods is a prerequisite to the effective functioning of a mass production economy and to satisfying the popular demand for a high standard of living. We have shown great poverty of imagination in the invention of credit mechanisms to diffuse the ownership of capital, for the following reasons.

(1) We have not yet become fully persuaded of the truth that widely diffused capital ownership is *an absolute necessity* in a completely capitalistic economy.

(2) We are still prone to the superstition that some people are destined to be owners of capital and some are not.

(3) In the few instances where something like credit financing of new owners of capital has been resorted to (*e.g.,* the 10 percent margin requirements for the purchase of equity securities prior to the 1929 market crash), the nature of the arrangement was conceptually inadequate to foster the growth of viable capital holdings and at the same time it failed severely to punish the use of this credit system to promote concentration or mere speculation.

The fascinating history of the laws dealing with the transfer of our public lands to private ownership provides something of an exception. As early as 1785, Congress considered an ordinance directing the Secretary of War to draw by lot certain townships in the surveyed portion of the public lands for bounties to the soldiers of the Continental Army. Under the Homestead Act of 1862, under various acts granting land bounties to railroads for pushing their systems into the wilderness, and under other acts for reducing the public domain to private ownership, nearly a billion acres of public land passed into private hands. It is to the results of the Homestead Act and of the federal and state laws relating to the patenting of mineral deposits that we may turn for one of the few examples our history affords of the art of creating, on a large scale, millions of private owners of capital.

Two basic conclusions may be drawn from the experience gained under these laws. (1) They were effective in creating millions of private owners of farms, ranches, mines and timber tracts. Had these same individuals been dependent on frugality and on sacrificial savings from the earnings of toil, few of them could ever have achieved such ownership. (2) These laws were conceptually inadequate to serve the objectives of Capitalism to the extent that they failed to prevent men from taking advantage of their provisions to create great concentrated proprietorships and to carry on wild and unscrupulous speculation.[4]

---

[4] "Millions of acres of valuable timber, mineral, and grazing lands were literally stolen under the eyes of dishonest or negligent officials in the federal land office; and other millions were wrested from the government by chicanery of one kind

The lesson which can be learned from the history of the laws relating to the transfer of land from public to private ownership must be read in the light of the pre-industrial, *i.e.,* agricultural, system of producing wealth during the period when most of the transfers took place. But the credit significance of these laws, which enabled the new private owners of land to "pay back" to the federal and state governments billions of dollars in taxes over the years, cannot be overestimated.

Those new individual owners of farms, ranches, timber tracts and mines may be looked upon as the pre-industrial models of tomorrow's "financed capitalists."

The lesson to be learned is that families who have no proprietorship of productive property but who understand the advantages of it can quickly shift from an environment in which they are wholly dependent upon wages from toil to one in which their income is in substantial part derived from their ownership of productive property. In spite of many failures through misfortune, mismanagement or profligacy, the Homestead Acts demonstrated that millions of households could learn to husband productive property, improve it, depend upon it and pass it on to succeeding generations of their families to do likewise.

Our experience with the transfer of public domains to private ownership refutes the claim that men who have not always been capitalists cannot be taught to become capitalists in modern society.

---

or another. In the history of political corruption, seldom, if ever, had there been transactions on a scale so prodigious or conducted with more brazen effrontery. Thousands of great fortunes in the East as well as in the West were built out of resources wrung from the government for a pittance or for a bribe to its officials, if not actually stolen. Nevertheless, in the process of dividing the national domain, millions of new farms were staked out. . . . Between 1865 and 1900 billions of new wealth were added annually to the national output" (Charles and Mary Beard, *A Basic History of the United States.* New York, 1944: p. 295). See also Frederick Turner's "The Significance of the Frontier in American History," reprinted in *The People Shall Judge,* Chicago, 1953: Vol. II, pp. 129–141.

Nor can it be said that the lesson of the Homestead Act and the Mineral Patent Act is limited to the kinds of capital represented by farms, mines, and timber lands. Any household that could learn to exploit the productive value of a farm yesterday can learn to exploit the productive value of an anhydrous ammonia fertilizer plant, a cotton ginning factory, a frozen food processing plant, a lumber mill, a synthetic rubber plant, or of any other capital instrument today. There is nothing esoteric about the fact that a one hundred thousandth interest in a steel mill may produce far more wealth than full ownership of a farm.

Socialist writers and some American economists who are not aware of the socialistic implications of their views frequently try to distinguish between (a) private property in farms or in small craft industries (in which the owner must, or at least traditionally did, add his personal toil to his proprietorship of capital in order to produce wealth) and (b) the holding of an equity in a modern industrial enterprise (in which the owner need only add his voice as a stockholder). To equate this distinction with one between (a) "active proprietorship" and (b) "passive ownership," or with one between (a) being an actual possessor of property and (b) being only a passive recipient of some of its earnings, is to misunderstand the nature of property rights and to ignore the *productive activity* of capital.

In a pre-industrial society, toil constitutes more than 90 percent of all productive activity. But in our advanced industrial economy, toil furnishes almost none of the energy and but a minute fraction of the control that enters into production. By approving the wholesomeness of private property only where it is of such a nature as to require the personal toil of the owner, socialists have tried to make modern industrial economies conform to the productive and proprietary pattern of pre-industrial societies. The financed capitalist of tomorrow cannot be expected to match the productive power of his capital with toil, for the productive power of labor cannot match that of capital. The very essence of industrialization is the elimination of human toil wherever possible.

There is one other, fairly recent, exception to our general failure to develop methods of financing the acquisition of viable capital interests. It is the farm finance system provided by the Federal Farm Credit System and by the Farmers Home Administration of the Department of Agriculture.[5]

Here is a case in which the power of government is used to assist the acquisition or increase of capital holdings by households engaged

[5] The Farm Credit Administration, successor to numerous federal agencies designed to aid in farm finance, is an independent agency of the executive branch of the government. The system consists of 1,100 national farm loan associations, the stock of each of which is owned on a temporary basis by member borrowers, who purchase stock equal to 5 percent of their loans. The farm loan association then in turn purchases a like amount of stock in the federal land bank located in its farm credit district. The nation is divided into twelve farm credit districts. Farmers and ranchers may obtain land bank loans through their local farm loan association in amounts varying from $100 to $200,000. Loans are on the basis of 65 percent of the appraised "normal agricultural value" of the farm offered as security. Funds of the federal land banks are obtained primarily from the sale of consolidated federal farm loan bonds to the investing public. These bonds are not guaranteed by the federal loan programs. Rates of interest on the loans are established by the Farm Credit Administration in each district.

The Farmers Home Administration was established in 1937 as an agency of the Department of Agriculture for the purpose of providing credit for farmers who are unable—usually because of the marginal nature of their holdings—to obtain credit through normal banking channels. The Farmers Home Administration makes production and subsistence loans to farmers or stockmen to buy equipment, livestock, seed, fertilizer, supplies, and for other things which are in effect working capital. It also makes loans on a joint basis to two or more farmers to enable them to purchase heavy equipment, high-grade breeding stock, and like capital advantages which they could not afford on an individual basis. Loans are made on the basis of applications which are screened by a "county committee." These committees determine the character, ability, industry, and farm experience of the applicant. This Administration also makes farm ownership loans to enable the purchase of family-type farms and to improve and equip them. Loans are amortizable over a forty-year period, with a variable payment plan under which advance payments may be made in good years. The value of farms so financed may not exceed the average value of efficient family-type farms in the particular county.

The program of the Bureau of Reclamation in the construction of irrigation dams and distribution systems is only partially a credit program for the promotion of the formation of farm capital, since only about half of its costs are repaid by the farmers benefited.

in farming. The system developed in response to the needs of small farmers whose operations have been rendered submarginal by the advance of farm technology, and to give relief to many small farmers who were impoverished during the depression.

The credit procedures of these farm finance programs are valuable sources for the studies that must precede the establishment of the financed capitalist program as a major step in the capitalist revolution. Unfortunately, however, the economic lessons to be drawn from our experience in providing credit to farm owners are mainly negative.

The federal farm credit system has operated to preserve and perpetuate productive enterprises that are highly inefficient when compared with well-capitalized large farms. Like handcraft factories, horse-drawn harvesters and sailing vessels, small farms have been technologically superseded by more productive agricultural enterprises with more efficient methods of production. Governmental efforts to preserve them, both through direct credit assistance and through buying the surplus commodities they produce, does not constitute a policy to be imitated in carrying out the capitalist revolution.

Not only has the farm credit program preserved the existence of the submarginal farm, but it has pegged the price of agricultural commodities consumed by the entire population at well above competitive prices, raising the costs of living for all and "jamming" the value-determining communication processes of competition in a large and important area of economic activity.

CREDIT AND THE DIFFUSION OF CAPITAL OWNERSHIP

Our mixed capitalist economy has developed highly efficient credit facilities by which a family may purchase a home costing $20,000 with a small down payment, and in some cases without any down payment at all. The loan, bearing a low interest rate, may be repaid in installments over a period of twenty-five years. Equally liberal credit is available to consumers who desire to purchase an automobile, or household equipment, or indeed any consumer item. These highly efficient consumer credit facilities have no counterpart which can now be used for the purpose of financing the acquisition of capital interests by households.[6]

The flourishing financing systems for the purchase of homes and other durable consumer goods, as contrasted with the negligible facilities for financing the acquisition of capital interests, cannot be explained by the greater inherent practicability of credit financing in the case of homes and other durable consumer goods. On the contrary, the differences between the credit financing of consumer goods and the credit financing of capital goods are conspicuously favorable to the latter.

The ownership of an interest in actively productive capital entitles the owner to the wealth produced by the interest, and under a completely capitalistic form of distribution, he would receive all the wealth his capital property produced. By its own earnings, the ownership of a capital interest can contribute to the ability of the owner to discharge the debt incurred in its acquisition. The ownership of consumer goods provides a household with enjoyment, not with income.[7] Thus houses

[6] The New York Stock Exchange has sponsored a system for the purchase of equity securities through monthly payments. However, the purchaser through this plan merely organizes his purchasing of shares in small quantities as odd lots. It is not a system of credit or installment financing for the acquisition of substantial holdings of equities. Indeed, the Federal Reserve System rigidly limits the "margin," or difference, between the full market value of a security listed on a registered exchange and the maximum loan value. These margin requirements have varied from 50 percent to 100 percent since 1934, and at the present writing are 70 percent. Margin loans are useless as a financing device for acquiring equities as investments, since the loan can be "called" at any time by the bank, and if the stock drops in market value, the owner is of necessity forced to put up enough additional cash to make up his margin. Margin loans are usable only by speculators, and the restrictions on them are intended only to restrain speculation.

[7] Whether a particular item is a consumer item or a capital item depends, of course, upon the purpose for which it is held. A residence held by a household as a place in which to live is a consumer item, while a residence owned for purposes of rental to others is, from the standpoint of the owner, a capital item.

and other durable goods, as well as many other consumer items, if purchased through credit, must be paid for wholly out of earnings derived from other sources. The financing of the purchase of capital interests, or equity stockholdings representative of productive capital, is therefore a far simpler transaction, for the buyer's ownership of the capital is itself some insurance of his ability to pay.

To put it another way, in an economy in which seasoned corporations would be required to pay out their earnings to stockholders, the yield of securities could be expected to be materially higher than they have been in the past. Any system of credit which enabled an individual to acquire a viable capital interest through being able to borrow the purchase price (normally secured by a pledge of the securities) at an interest rate lower than the average net yield of the securities, would therefore enable the equity holding to "pay for itself." [8] This is never true of the purchase of consumer goods on credit.

One further fact is worth mentioning. The easiest equities to finance through long-term installment purchase plans or long-term loans, where the earnings of the securities can be expected to amortize their purchase price, would of course be those of the largest, best-established, and most stable corporations, *e.g.,* the equities of public utility corporations. Thus, an overall program for facilitating the development of a great number of new financed capitalists might well require that securities meeting particular investment tests be given a preferential rating. This, in turn, would give those seeking to assemble viable equity holdings a priority on original issue over those whose capital interests have reached monopolistic magnitude. From everything which has been said, it should be clear that a credit system intended to bring into existence millions of new financed capitalists should be

[8] The prices, in a freely competitive market, for equity securities which return to their owners the full economic yield of the capital they represent might or might not, on the average, be higher than under our present mixed economy. It must be remembered that a continuous—a deliberately continuous—dilution of the concentration of ownership would take place through the constant seeking by corporations of new funds in the market, rather than from internal sources and loan sources as at the present time.

designed to create viable equity holdings and be absolutely unavailable to those whose ownership of capital is already monopolistic.

FINANCED CAPITALISTS

When we realized in the nineteen-thirties that a mass-production economy cannot survive—and certainly cannot provide a high general standard of living—without mass consumption, we jumped to the obvious conclusion: *stimulate mass consumption directly*. This maxim was central in the economic theory behind our highly effective credit facilities for consumer goods.

It is almost a truism to say that if the rapid broadening of the ownership of capital had been recognized to be as vital to the prosperity of an industrial economy as technological progress itself, we should long ago have developed methods of "merchandising" capital interests comparable in effectiveness to those we now use to sell consumer goods. We would long since have learned that the effective broadening of the capital base would render the use of extensive consumer financing unnecessary and perhaps even unwise. We would understand that the central aim of all government efforts to promote Capitalism is to broaden participation in the production of wealth *as a means of broadening the just distribution of income*. From the point of view of Capitalism, a need for consumer financing might therefore be construed as indicating the inadequate stimulation then currently being given to the broadening of the ownership of capital.[9]

[9] John Maynard Keynes popularized the "multiplier theory" of the relationship between the amount spent upon capital formation and the resulting increase in employment. See his *The General Theory of Employment, Interest and Money,* New York, 1935: Chapter 10. This, in economic slang, is the theory of "pump priming." It should be noted that the theory of Capitalism contemplates no use of pump priming. The distribution system of a completely capitalistic economy may be likened to a system of developing permanent new connections between the production pump (predominantly capital) and consuming households. Thus, the efforts in a capitalistic society to broaden ownership do not provide a mere temporary multiplier to create employment but a permanent source of income for new capital-owning households.

Let us assume that an understanding of industrial production and of a completely capitalistic distribution of wealth becomes a matter of common knowledge, and also that we as a people begin to think economically in terms of the principles of Capitalism. What more can be done, aside from the various steps already discussed, to change households wholly dependent upon toil for their subsistence into households partially or wholly dependent upon their ownership of capital for their participation in production and their resulting distributive share of the wealth produced?

The problem of financing the broadening of the capital base in a completely capitalistic economy, like that of financing consumer purchasing in our present mixed capitalism, is to a large extent a matter of the skillful use of credit. But we must also determine what emphasis should be given to broadening the ownership of existing capital and what to financing new capital formation to be owned by new capitalists. This in itself is a major subject for study. However, it is possible within limited space to show the feasibility of using modern credit and merchandising methods to create millions of new capital-owning households. In the process of doing so, we can also take note of some of the problems to be solved.

Forms of credit financing familiar in the consumer field today can be readily adapted to financing capital acquisitions by new capitalists.[10] Among these are straight loans for the acquisition of equity capital holdings. These would normally be secured by a pledge of the equities purchased. The pledge arrangement, as in the case of conventional banking practice today, would involve an installment repayment plan. The right to receive dividends, the right to exercise voting privileges, and other rights of equity holders would be vested in the buying household as long as the loan was not in default. The simple pledge

[10] Given adequate statutory safeguards against abuse of the system for financing acquisition of capital interests by persons other than those acquiring viable capital estates, the commercial loan department of any bank could produce dozens of workable financing plans for financing the acquisition of viable capital interests by new capitalists.

arrangement could be used to purchase either outstanding equities or new equities upon original issue by corporations, although the credit features might differ in each of these cases.[11] For example, excessively easy acquisition credit for outstanding equities would tend to inflate the prices of outstanding securities, while the easing of credit terms for the acquisition of new equities on original issue would readily expand the rate of formation of new capital.

Another familiar consumer credit financing device could be readily adapted to the program of financing new capitalists. This is the installment payment plan. Corporations with certain types of capital needs might well find it possible to issue equities to purchasers who would assume the obligation to pay for them over a period of months or years. While a corporation might, during the installment payment period, be required to pay out earnings on stock representing capital not fully paid in, it might be compensated for this by being able to raise capital on terms more favorable than those otherwise available.

In the case of loan and pledge financing of the purchase of already outstanding securities, these arrangements would be made an exception to the margin requirements that apply to the purchase of securities. Margin requirements, perhaps of 100 percent, might well continue to apply in the financing of equity purchases by persons whose equity holdings are already of monopolistic size or by persons purchasing for speculation rather than for investment. Absolutely effective regulatory measures should be adopted to prevent use of capital financing plans by speculators (those not buying for investment, regardless of the size of their capital estates) and those with very large capital holdings.

As the capitalist revolution progresses, the difficulties of appraising corporate equities for loan purposes would diminish as the result of

11 The laws of most states prohibit a corporation from extending credit on the security of its own stock. State corporation laws are generally not designed to facilitate the broadening of the ownership base.

measures requiring the full payment of earnings by mature corporations. It is the present discretionary right of management to withhold or pay out earnings that contributes substantially to the erratic fluctuation of security values today. The discretionary right of management to withhold or pay out earnings to stockholders at present vitiates the tests used for appraisal purposes in determining loanable values as well as the everyday composite appraisals which underlie market values. As the capitalist revolution progresses, the danger of cyclical economic disruption would diminish, so that the danger of depression which always hangs over the stock market today would also diminish and should eventually disappear.

Pledge arrangements in connection with loans to finance the acquisition of capital interests could be conventional, except that it would be desirable to provide terms of repayment that would generally leave some margin between the return on the financed capital interest and the amount of the repayment installments. If the purpose of broadening the capital base is to enable new individuals to participate in production as owners of capital and thereby to participate in the distribution of capital earnings, it is essential during the transition that there be no excessive suspension of the income available for consumption purposes—only a diminution to whatever extent is required to amortize the installments of purchase price.

The principle of investment diversification is an essential and sound principle of capital husbanding, and should be a condition of the availability to households of capital financing arrangements. This, combined with a plan for investor preference for the benefit of those in the process of acquiring viable capital holdings, would make such financing plans highly effective in broadening the capital base.

Interest upon capital-acquisition loans should be made deductible for income tax purposes as is the case with most interest payments at the present time. All reasonable steps should be taken to channel the investible funds of those who do not have capital-acquisition investment preferences (because of the already monopolistic size of their capital holdings) into the program of financing the broadening of the capital ownership base.

In the case of capital-acquisition loans to purchase newly issued securities, certain additional problems would have to be met. Intelligent diversification, as a requirement of the availability of such financing, would itself suggest a balance between securities of well-seasoned corporations and those of still somewhat speculative businesses.[12] The securities of brand-new and completely unseasoned enterprises should undoubtedly be given an investment rating which would exclude them from capital acquisition financing eligibility until they became seasoned. They should also be excluded from investor preference for small investors. This would leave unseasoned and speculative securities available for investment by those with already large capital holdings, who are therefore better able to afford the risks involved.[13]

The program of financing new capitalists would recognize the vast needs of our economy for capital formation and would provide the

[12] Investments in public utility enterprises, for example, should undoubtedly be rated for investment priority for new capitalists with subviable holdings, and should be favorites for capital-acquisition loans. It would appear that the enormous power needs of the future will provide an opportunity for a vast number of new capital holdings. The Joint Committee Report in 1954 estimated that, by 1965, annual capital expenditures of 35 billion dollars for new capital formation would be required (*Potential Economic Growth of the United States During the Next Decade,* Joint Committee Print, p. 11). These enormous capital requirements, which might well be substantially higher even in early stages of the transition to a completely capitalistic economy, indicate the opportunity in the years ahead to promote that transition more rapidly than it could ever have been carried out in the past.

[13] Some indication of the massive future needs of our economy for capital formation may be gleaned from the work of three scientists of the California Institute of Technology who foresee that if the underdeveloped regions of the world become fully industrialized during the coming century, we will have exhausted all high grade mineral deposits, all petroleum and other fossil fuels, and will require water in quantities exceeding the fresh water supply of the world. "By that time the mining industry as such will long since have disappeared and will have been replaced by vast, integrated, multipurpose chemical plants supplied by rock, air, and sea water, from which will flow a multiplicity of products, ranging from fresh water to electric power, liquid fuels, and metals" (Harrison Brown, James Bonner, John Weir, *The Next Hundred Years,* New York, 1957: p. 151).

sources for capital formation. It would at the same time begin to do something about the presently neglected task of diffusing the ownership of capital.

Since the government, in encouraging or directly providing for such capital acquisition financing, would be acting in discharge of its obligation to afford an opportunity for all households to participate effectively in production, there would be adequate justification for the establishment of a loan insurance program covering such capital-acquisition loans. The general principles of the loan insurance program of the Federal Housing Administration, now applicable to housing mortgage loans, could be adapted for this purpose.

One of the common explanations for the dearth of capital raised by issuance of equity securities today is the high cost of underwriting. The existence of an insurance fund for capital acquisition financing should help to reduce underwriting costs, since the risk of failing to sell qualified stock issues within a reasonable time might either be greatly diminished or entirely eliminated. This, with a revision of the corporate income tax laws designed to discourage long-term debt financing, would not only dry up a major source of concentration but would also facilitate equity diffusion. It is important to note that such an insurance arrangement—let us call it the "Capital Diffusion Insurance Corporation"—would not directly underwrite any of the risks of business enterprise. That is the function of the stockholder. It would only be insuring or guaranteeing the stock subscriber's or stock purchaser's obligation to pay for the stock that he purchases.

When the necessity has arisen in the past, we have, largely through the skillful use of private and public credit, *simultaneously* produced unprecedented quantities of war goods (to be destroyed in the process of destroying wealth and life), unprecedented quantities of consumer goods and unprecedented new capital formation. Who, then, can seriously doubt our ability in the years ahead to finance, through public and private means, the formation of the vast quantities of capital *largely under the ownership of new capitalists?* Such newly formed capital, so financed that it will be owned by new capitalists, will be self-liquidating. The wealth that such new capital creates will reimburse those who have extended credit to bring about new capital formation under the ownership of new capitalists.

In the transition to Capitalism, and in the preservation of a balanced capitalistic economy once Capitalism is achieved, the purpose of the program we have been considering would be to make certain that suitable credit mechanisms are developed to assure the expansion of our economy and simultaneously to assure the rapid and efficient broadening of the capital-owning base. In the task of providing credit facilities, commercial banks, investment banks, and other private financial organizations should be given primary responsibility and priority of opportunity. Government should not hesitate, however, to make up for any deficiencies in private credit facilities, either by the insuring of credit or by directly providing it.

There is no need to fear that government, by using its powers to promote this program, will aggrandize the power of the state or threaten individual freedom. Our Founding Fathers accurately observed that the freedom of citizens lies in their individual possession of sufficient economic power to check the inevitably centralized political power of government. The application of their principles of free government in our modern industrial society compels the conclusion that the diffusion of privately held economic power—and this now means the broadly diffused private ownership of capital—is the only means of counteracting centralized political power. Hence the performance by government of its obligation to broaden the private ownership of capital is at the same time a guarantee of the separation of political from economic power and a guarantee of individual freedom.[14]

14 The false and historically refuted doctrine of *laissez-faire* has made such a deep impression upon some minds that the idea of deliberate creation of the conditions of economic and political freedom by government regulation immediately raises for them the specter of totalitarian government. To maintain that the dif-

THE NEED FOR NEW TYPES OF INSURANCE

One problem remains to be discussed in connection with all efforts to diffuse capital ownership as widely as possible.

As the transition toward Capitalism progresses, the risk of major economic dislocations or depressions will diminish until, with the establishment of a balanced capitalistic economy, it will disappear altogether. This will eliminate one of the major risks of our present mixed capitalism. But one type of risk will remain. It is the natural risk inherent in an industrial and competitive economy—the risk of loss of investment through competitive superiority and through technological supersession. In proportion as more households become more dependent upon their ownership of capital as a source of earned income, more households will incur this risk or incur it to a higher degree.

The problem suggests its own solution. The theory upon which most disability and life insurance is purchased is that the head of the family (usually the one insured) through his or her ability to work constitutes the source of economic support for the household.[15] Sickness or disabling accident and death usually involve loss of income for the household. It is against such risks that insurance protection is sought. But when a household owns a viable capital estate, its participation in production is to that extent vicarious, and the disability or death of a member of the household no longer has the same economic significance that it has when the family income is earned mainly by toil.

Where a household is primarily dependent for support upon its ownership of capital, the primary risk to be guarded against is simply

---

fusion of economic power cannot be purposely promoted by governmental action is to subscribe to economic anarchy in precisely the same sense that those who maintain that the only politically free society is one without civil government subscribe to political anarchy.

[15] The intricacies of our tax laws, both income tax and estate tax, frequently provide an artificial motive for the purchase of life insurance. Such purchases are exceptions to the normal economic motive.

the business risk inherent in a competitive and technologically evolving economy. In large measure this risk can be minimized through investment diversification, but beyond this it should be possible to devise casualty insurance designed to protect the family income against a coincidence of business failures that would materially impair the support derived from capital holdings. This would be a logical application of the theory of life insurance to a completely capitalistic economy.

Furthermore, while a completely capitalistic economy would be exempt from the causes of major economic breakdowns, it is unlikely that it would be wholly exempt from cyclical variations of more and less intense economic activity. It may well be that at the governmental level an insurance plan protecting the owners of capital against the troughs of even these mild cycles could be devised. If so, such insurance arrangements in a fully capitalistic economy would be the complete substitute for the patchwork quilt of pump-priming schemes now constituting the devices used by government to deal with the cyclical variations in our mixed economy. This plan for insuring capital income against certain kinds of risks might be integrated with the income taxes levied by the federal government in such manner that its operation would be largely one of absorbing the dips of the cycle against the income tax and collecting the premiums against the peaks.

THE NEW CAPITALISTS

In the period of the transition to Capitalism, as efforts to create employment for the purpose of distributing wealth are withdrawn, the number of persons seeking employment in the production of subsistence may exceed the number of jobs. The educational task of elevating human interest and effort from subsistence work to leisure work cannot be accomplished overnight. Members of households whose participation in production is already of monopolistic extent through their ownership of large capital estates may still erroneously persist in looking upon the performance of subsistence work as the only outlet for their creative energies. Only when the nature and objectives of the capitalist revolution are so fully understood that those with monopolistic capital estates look to the liberal tasks of leisure work as the socially useful occupations in which they should be engaged, will their clamor for full employment in the production of subsistence die away. It is a function of government to exercise its regulatory powers to facilitate this change.

Where the demand for labor is less than the "full employment" of all potentially employable persons, the incidence of "unemployment" —so far as subsistence work is concerned—should fall first upon the owners of monopolistic capital estates.[16]

In the sphere of subsistence work a large number of mechanical tasks will always have to be performed in order to produce the wealth that will provide a generally high standard of living for all. Millions of mechanical workers will always be needed. For its educational effect, however, if for no other, every member of society should have the opportunity to engage in such work. In applying this general policy, nevertheless, two things should be borne in mind. Where the employment demand for mechanical workers is smaller than the number of employable persons seeking such employment, widespread participation in mechanical work is not possible for all except on a limited basis. Furthermore, where the aggregate demand for subsistence work is less than the "full employment" of those who either desire to engage in such work or who have no other means of participating in production, the proper regulation of a capitalistic economy would prevent members of households having capital estates of monopolistic size

---

[16] It should be remembered that a principal consideration in the legislative determination from time to time of what constitutes a monopolistic capital holding is the excess of the number of persons seeking subsistence employment over those for whom viable employment opportunities exist.

from further monopolizing participation in production by engaging in subsistence work for compensation.

During the period of the transition to Capitalism, the healthy growth of the economy as well as the enhancement of its stability would be best promoted by a steady upward movement of men from exclusively wage incomes to incomes more and more largely derived from capital property. This should, of course, begin with workers who, through experience and education, show themselves best qualified to become financed capitalists. There should be a steady movement from the ranks of the most important and responsible workers (including technical and managerial workers) into the group whose participation in production is largely or exclusively through the ownership of viable capital estates.

The extent to which households might combine the ownership of viable capital estates with the participation in production of one or more of their members as workers would be entirely dependent on the needs of the economy for subsistence workers. The point at which regulatory limitations would discourage such combined participation would have to be determined legislatively as a matter of public policy from time to time and in relation to the prevailing state of technology and the desired standard of living.

Throughout the transitional stage, the objective of regulatory efforts should be to reduce the number of households dependent on the wages earned by one or more of their members to a figure commensurate with the number of actual, not "made," opportunities for subsistence work in the economy. This would mean squeezing out all forms of "made work," the featherbedding, the paid unemployment, and the technologically superseded jobs which are now artificially created and maintained by our policy of full employment. It would mean eliminating the jobs resulting from the subsidization of farm surpluses, from the making of unnecessary "defense" purchases, from "stock-piling" in excess of actual defense and normal production needs, and from all other programs that derive their real support today from the desire to multiply subsistence jobs as a means of promoting a laboristic distribution of wealth.

This, as we have already indicated, would be accomplished by a general upward movement within the economy, shifting the incidence of "unemployment" (so far as subsistence work is concerned) to the members of households having monopolistic capital holdings or viable capital estates approaching that magnitude. The maintenance of viable wage levels for those whose incomes are largely or exclusively obtained from subsistence work would be accomplished, not by the fixing of wages at higher than the competitively determined value of such work, but by eliminating from the labor market a number of workers equivalent to the number of those who have been technologically superseded under then current conditions.

One of the guiding aims of the capitalist revolution is that all men should become capitalists, *i.e.,* owners of viable capital estates, as early in their lives as possible. The more advanced the technology of our economy becomes, the earlier this should become possible for all men or, more exactly, for all households. Hence, during the transition period, the guiding policy should be to eliminate as rapidly as possible all deterrents to technological advance, for these directly frustrate the promise which Capitalism holds out—the promise of an early release from wage earning by toil.

The small farms, thousands of which are technologically obsolete, must not be preserved as a drag on the economy. Many of these have long ceased to be capable of supporting a household in a freely competitive market. They can be preserved only at the cost of utter waste of human toil. The hundreds of thousands, perhaps millions, of workers who, through infinite varieties of featherbedding, are forced to maintain the pretense of producing wealth when they in fact do not should be given the opportunity to rise in their economic position. They should come to fill the places of others who have also moved upwards in the real economic importance of their work; and these, in turn, should move to the top of the ladder of subsistence jobs, filling the places of those whose capital holdings are viable and sufficient to enable them to transfer their energies to the liberal tasks of leisure work. Members of households who hold viable capital estates should increasingly, and members of households who hold monopolistic capital estates should exclusively, come to engage in such activities for the sheer satisfaction of doing so and not for the purpose of acquiring additional wealth.

As men shift from the ranks of labor into the ranks of capitalists, they would be followed by others who are moving toward such a change in their economic condition and, even more important, in the occupation or employment of their time, energies, and talents. The general upward tendency envisaged by the capitalist revolution is not only a shift from direct participation in production through toil to vicarious participation through ownership of capital, but also an elevation of human life itself from the unrewarding, extrinsically compensated tasks of subsistence work to the intrinsically rewarding tasks of leisure work, which men can gladly engage in without thought of financial compensation.

In all the pre-industrial societies of the past, the fortunate few who belonged to the leisure class and had the moral and intellectual virtue to profit from their good fortune, engaged in the pursuits of civilization—in the liberal arts and sciences, in political and religious activities—for their own sake, not for financial returns. Virtue is not the prerogative of the few, certainly not of those whom good fortune, in the form of income-bearing property, emancipates from toil. When, in the transition to Capitalism, a larger and larger number of men are thus emancipated, the central task of liberal education, in school and out, must be to cultivate the virtues that prepare men for the work of leisure—work that is both harder and better than the drudgery of toil.[17]

17 There may always be persons who, through mental or moral incompetence, fall below the level of life which, according to its own ideal, Capitalism strives to make possible for all. We may now greatly overestimate the probable number of such persons because we have not yet begun the process of educating men for life under Capitalism. Nevertheless, it remains highly probable that

Once the first stage of the transition to Capitalism has been completed and a balanced capitalistic economy has been established, the objective of the various transitional programs, including that of creating new financed capitalists, should be to maintain a steady decrease in the proportion of households that are entirely dependent on wages and a steady increase in the number that are able to live on capital earnings. The rate at which these changes can be effected must, of course, correspond to the rate of technological advance.

In the first stage of the transition to Capitalism, the shift from participation in production through toil to participation in production through ownership of capital must be achieved as rapidly as possible. Thereafter, the shift from being a worker to being a capitalist should be a more gradual one for most men and their households. This shift may occur for some men at a relatively early period in their lives and for others somewhat later, especially those who are not aided by inheritance, family gifts, or other transfers of capital.

Where a particular creative activity is receiving less attention and support than it warrants for the common good of our society, such activity may be encouraged directly through making income derived from performing it tax-exempt or through lowering the rate at which such income is taxed. Thus what may be by its nature purely liberal work, such as teaching, may earn a decent income, even though such work is intrinsically rewarding and should be done without extrinsic compensation by those who can afford to do so.

It is hoped that, with the advance toward Capitalism, the opportunity to engage in such work would be highly prized and sought for its own sake by more and more persons who do not need extrinsic

---

there always will be some. Such persons will necessarily have to earn their living in the performance of subsistence work; or, if they are unsuited for this, either by natural endowment or educational failure, then they will have to be the wards of a social security program designed to provide humane subsistence for them simply because they are human beings. But except for the unfit, which no society can hope to eliminate entirely, a capitalistic society will use every means to discourage dependence on the state for subsistence.

compensation or need less and less of it. Where we have a great short-age of teachers today, we should, in a fully capitalistic society, have many who, engaging in the production of wealth vicariously through their ownership of capital, would delight in teaching—without com-pensation or even where they might be put to some expense in order to do so.

What is here said of teaching applies to other forms of leisure work performed as vocations, not avocations. In an advanced indus-trial society with a fully capitalistic economy, it should be normal for ministers, research scientists, philosophers, musicians, poets, painters, lawyers, physicians, statesmen, and those engaged in mass communica-tion, to carry on such purely leisure work for the inherent satisfaction and creative pleasure it gives them. The measure of their merit would not be the amount of income they derive from such vocations, but rather the excellence they achieve in their art and the significance of the contribution they make to the advancement of civilization.

In a balanced capitalistic economy, we should in general expect to see those young people who desire to do so enter into the field of sub-sistence work after the completion of their schooling. As they grow older, they would gradually become the owners of viable capital estates through equity-sharing plans, through inheritance, gifts and other transfers of capital equities within families, and through the program of creating new financed capitalists. Consequent thereon, their eco-nomic need to engage in subsistence work for compensation would gradually diminish.

Their recognition of their obligation to participate in the hard, but intrinsically rewarding, work of civilization would be increasingly reflected in the forms of activity in which they engaged as they gradu-ated from employment in subsistence work to employment in leisure work. At no point would they regard themselves as "unemployed" or as "socially useless" because they were not working to produce wealth. At no point would they "retire" or look forward to "retirement"; for in that conception of human life which Capitalism holds forth, retirement from socially useful activity is a refuge only for the mentally unfit or physically disabled.

Instead of looking forward to the nightmare and emptiness of "retirement" when they cease to be employed in subsistence work, men will from the very beginning of their lives prepare themselves for eventually turning to humanly better forms of employment; and as they gradually acquire capital estates, they will also gradually shift their interests from one form of employment to another. When at last their capital estates become large enough to provide a viable family income, it is to be hoped that they will hasten the day when they turn all their energies and talents to the performance of the liberal tasks of leisure. The number that do so will be the most critical measure of the effectiveness of education under Capitalism, as well as the best indication that a capitalistic economy is serving its ultimate human purpose.

15 CONCLUDING SUMMARY

We have considered some of the practical problems involved in a transition from our present partly capitalistic and partly laboristic economy to a well-balanced and completely capitalistic economy. Our attention has been divided throughout between the disadvantages of the one and the advantages of the other. It has been important to keep reminding ourselves of the economic pains we have suffered as a result of trying to fit, after the fashion of Procrustes, a capitalist system of production, which retains the vestiges of private property in capital, into the bed of a predominantly laboristic distribution of wealth.

True, we have almost become inured to pains that once seemed less bearable when we first experienced the steeply graduated income tax, the subsidization of some producers at the expense of others, the empowering of organized workers to levy private taxes upon the rest of the economy or some part of it, and the direct intrusion of government into the business of producing wealth and redistributing it. But this should not lead us to suppose that things cannot get worse or that our endurance is without limit.

Our whole analysis of the ways in which a laboristic distribution of wealth retards the advance of technology, causes the alienation of private property in capital and the erosion of its basic rights, tends to create an overwhelming consolidation of economic and political power in the already highly centralized government of our country, and threatens the existence of individual freedom leads us to one inescapable conclusion: *there is no way of preventing all these things from becoming unendurable except by dissolving our mixed economy in favor of Capitalism.*

However formidable the central task of the capitalist revolution may have appeared to us at the outset, *i.e.,* the task of broadening capital ownership to include millions on millions of new capitalists, we should be strengthened in our resolution to undertake it and surmount all its difficulties when we consider the risks we incur and the problems we face if we try instead to perpetuate our present mixed capitalism.

To focus our full attention on the critical choice that we are called upon to make by the best use of our intelligence and our power of free decision, it may be helpful in these closing pages to summarize the alternatives that confront us.

(1) Capitalism recognizes that capital is the principal producer of wealth in an advanced industrial economy. Mixed capitalism must continue to pretend that human labor is the principal producer of wealth.

(2) Capitalism acknowledges that subsistence work, which is mechanical in quality, is an evil that men are compelled to endure to a certain extent but which, since it is humanly unrewarding, should be reduced to the minimum in human life. Mixed capitalism cannot afford to acknowledge the clear distinction between doing necessary labor for extrinsic compensation and the free engagement of men in liberal and creative pursuits; nor can it accept the superior human worth of work that produces the goods of civilization over work that produces the goods of subsistence.

(3) Capitalism makes possible an eventual reduction of the tax burden to the point at which the revenue government procures by taxation does no more than pay the operating costs of its services. Mixed capitalism must contemplate a constantly growing tax burden the revenues from which, in excess of the costs of government, must be used by government to redistribute wealth in ways that prevent the economy from collapsing.

(4) Capitalism gives maximum encouragement to technological improvements that progressively make the production of wealth more efficient and at the same time transfer more and more of the burden of it from men to machines. As one of the main consequences of its laboristic distribution of wealth, mixed capitalism tends to retard technological progress.

(5) The broadening of the ownership of existing capital and the creation of new capitalists with the formation of new capital can be carried out by self-liquidating means. The laboristic redistribution of the wealth produced by capital is never self-liquidating. Instead it liquidates private property in the capital instruments which produce the bulk of an industrial economy's wealth.

(6) Under mixed capitalism, the laboristic redistribution of wealth is a never ending process. It must continue, driven by the force of technological progress, until all the wealth of the economy is distributed under the control or mandate of central government. Under Capitalism, and even in the transition to Capitalism, the ever increasing number of proprietors of capital permits an automatic and direct distribution of wealth through participation in production.

(7) Under mixed capitalism, the alienation of private property in capital and the attenuation of its rights, together with the assumption by government of the powers needed to redistribute wealth and thus maintain the economy, lead to the concentration of economic and political power in the hands of central government. Under Capitalism, the restoration of private property in capital and full respect for its rights, together with the elimination of the need for government to

engage in the redistribution of wealth, keeps political and economic power in separate hands and gives the individual proprietor of capital the economic power and independence he needs as a leverage against improper encroachments by government. As capitalists and *only* as capitalists can the citizens of an industrial democracy preserve and strengthen their free political institutions.

(8) Capitalism alone is perfectly compatible with democracy, alone provides it with the economic substructure it needs, and alone creates the justly organized industrial economy that is the counterpart of democracy as the justly organized polity of a mass society. Under the unalterable conditions of a mass society, mixed capitalism necessarily tends away from democracy and toward socialism, *i.e.,* State capitalism with its inevitable concomitant, the totalitarian state.

(9) Capitalism achieves general economic welfare through economic justice in the distribution of wealth and thereby achieves it with no loss of human dignity or freedom. Mixed capitalism achieves general economic welfare through a mixture of charity and expediency in the distribution of wealth, and consequently degrades men either to the condition of children benevolently provided for or to the condition of puppets used as means to economic ends.

(10) Capitalism and democracy together create an approximation of the ideal classless society in which all men are citizens and all are capitalists, and in which the good life that was possible only for the few in the pre-industrial plutocracies and slave economies of the past becomes equally possible for all. Mixed capitalism must always remain an economically class-divided society, in which the perpetuation of the class war involves a continuing conflict of interests and struggle for power. Unless the ultimate resolution of the class war is found in Capitalism through justice for all and with freedom for all, it will be found in socialism and the totalitarian state—that caricature of the classless society in which all men are equally enslaved, for none has the political freedom of a citizen or the economic freedom of a capitalist.

APPENDIX: THE CONCEALMENT OF THE DECLINING PRODUCTIVITY OF LABOR IN OUR PRESENT ECONOMY

We have asserted that, with negligible exceptions, increases in the output of wealth per man-hour have been achieved in our industrial economy with a steadily *diminishing* contribution of both power and skill on the part of mechanical workers, and a steadily *increasing* contribution of skill on the part of technical and managerial workers. A major portion of the efforts of technical and managerial workers has been devoted to increasing the inherent productiveness of capital instruments. While their inherent productiveness has increased at every stage of technological advance, the inherent productiveness of mechanical labor has at best remained constant, and so, relative to the increasing productive power of capital, the productive power of mechanical labor has progressively declined.

If these things are true, as we claim they are, then it is also true that mechanical workers, who constitute the great bulk of our labor force and of our population, make a relatively small contribution to the production of our society's wealth as compared with the contribution made by the owners of capital. From this truth, one further consequence should follow. Since a factor of production is presumably valued primarily for its ability to produce wealth, the inherent productiveness of labor should bear about the same relationship to its economic productivity as the inherent productiveness of capital bears to its economic productivity, *on condition, of course, that the value of their relative contributions is objectively determined through the mechanism of free competition.*[1] Hence, to whatever extent free competition is operative among the factors of production, we should expect to find that the economic productivity of mechanical workers has progressively declined.

In the light of statistics on the distributive shares of the national income going to labor and to capital, the objection may be raised that even though the physical contribution of mechanical workers to the production of wealth has long been declining, their distributive share, and consequently their economic productivity, has long been rising.

Let us consider first the central question of fact. Labor's share of the national income, *i.e.,* the share of the wealth produced in a particular year, rose from 50 percent in the decade beginning in 1870 to

[1] Although it would seem that the economic productivity of labor should rise or fall, relative to that of capital, with a rise or fall in its physical capacity to produce wealth (*i.e.,* a rise or fall in its inherent productiveness), the truth of this relationship depends upon circumstances other than the one that a factor of production *is* valued primarily for its ability to produce wealth. Among these other circumstances are the following: (a) the fact that capital formation (at least where not directly overstimulated to produce "full employment") takes place only in response to growth in consumer demand for the products or services requiring the newly formed capital, whereas an increase in the labor supply takes place through population increase and not in response to such consumer demand stimulus; (b) technological advance increases the *demand* for capital, but increases the *supply* of labor; an increase in employment resulting from increased demand for wealth—now directly stimulated to achieve full employment—is frequently mistaken for evidence that labor-saving devices of themselves increase the demand for labor; (c) population increase, in an advanced industrial society, increases the supply of labor more than it increases the demand for labor through increased consumption. Throughout, it is assumed that population tends to increase and that technological advance continues.

58 percent in 1929, 68.5 percent in 1953, and 70 percent in 1956.[2] From these figures, it would seem that the economic productivity of mechanical workers, who comprise some three-fourths of the labor force, has risen; that is, *if* their distributive share of the national income can be taken as an accurate and objective index of the value of their contribution to production.[3]

How shall we explain the discrepancy between (1) our assertion that the relative economic productivity of mechanical labor has declined along with its relative inherent productiveness and (2) the figures which show that the distributive share received by such labor has increased for many decades and that it is largest in the most important sector of our economy, *i.e.,* the corporate sector?

Were we to admit that the distributive share of the national income received by labor is an accurate and objective index of the value of labor's contribution to production, then we would have to concede that the relative economic productivity of labor has increased in spite of the fact that its relative inherent productiveness has declined; or we would be compelled to question that fact itself and, perhaps, to dismiss it as illusory even though it appears to be so amply and clearly evidenced.

We think that the relatively declining inherent productiveness of mechanical labor cannot be questioned, and that the apparent discrepancy between the declining economic productivity of labor and its increasing distributive share of the national income can be explained.

[2] See *Historical Statistics of the United States,* 1789–1945, Bureau of Census, 1949, p. 15; *National Income,* 1954 edition, U.S. Department of Commerce, p. 9; *Economic Report of the President,* 1957, p. 132. Statistics for the earlier period are, of course, subject to question; *e.g.,* how much labor was performed at home for which no money compensation was paid? In the corporate sector of the economy, which accounts for more than half the national income, the employees' share of total income was stable at about 74 percent from 1929 to 1951. It rose to 76 percent in 1952, 77.5 percent in 1953, and to 79 percent in 1956. See *National Income,* 1954 edition, p. 9, and *Survey of Current Business,* U. S. Department of Commerce, July, 1957, p. 15, Table 12.

[3] See *Statistical Abstract of the United States,* 1956, pp. 208–214. It appears that the real wages of mechanical workers have risen at least as fast as the real incomes of managerial and technical workers, if not faster.

Before we set forth that explanation in detail, we should say at once that we challenge the assumption made by those who think that labor's increasing share of the national income represents an accurate and objective evaluation of its contribution to the production of wealth. We hold a view exactly the opposite of those who maintain that the action of labor unions, supported by legislation and other applications of governmental power, has made it possible for the contribution of labor to be fairly and objectively evaluated. On the contrary, we hold that this, among other things, has prevented a freely competitive evaluation of labor's contribution, with the consequence that labor's share of the national income is by no means a true index of its economic productivity.

The wage levels of organized workers, who constitute about 35 percent of the nonagricultural labor force, do not represent freely competitive determinations, but result from the unified efforts of organized labor to increase hourly earnings against the background of a large number of federal and state laws designed to prevent employers from resisting wage demands made by employees.[4] While coercion and duress are recognized by our legal system as vitiating all other types of contractual obligation, we have established a system of collective bargaining to determine wages and other economic benefits of organized labor, under which something very close to duress is the decisive factor in the "bargaining."

Before we argue in support of this basic point, two other considerations should be mentioned. One is the corporate income tax, which now takes 52 percent of corporate income at the federal level and an additional small percentage at the state level in most states. This large percentage represents wealth produced by capital, but in national income statistics it is not attributed to either capital or labor. Thus over one-half of the wealth produced by the capital of corporations (and

---

[4] For a brief review of these laws, see Roscoe Pound, *Legal Immunities of Labor Unions,* published last year by the American Enterprise Association, Washington, D. C.

corporations produce well over half the wealth of our society) is wholly omitted from the statistical picture. In reckoning the distributive shares of the wealth produced, it should be attributed to the owners of capital. If it were, it would greatly change the picture of the relative economic productivity of capital and labor.[5]

The second consideration is the fact that corporations distribute to their stockholders only a part of the wealth produced by their capital —generally not more than one-half of corporate earnings after taxes. As the Bureau of Census has noted, "some parts of income earned, such as corporate savings, have definitely not been received by the individuals concerned and indeed may never be received by them." [6] The vast sums withheld by corporations from stockholders and invested to form additional corporate capital must also be included in the computation of the distributive share of the wealth produced that belongs to the owners of capital. Not to include these sums in the computation further distorts the picture of the relative economic productivity of capital and labor, for it measures the economic productivity of capital by the distributive share awarded the private owners of capital in an economy in which private property in capital has been greatly attenuated.

If we combine these two points, which show that the actual distributive share received by the private owners of capital is far from being a true index of the economic productivity of capital, with the point that labor's share is not a true index of its economic productivity because it is not determined by free competition, there is no longer

[5] Such levies as the employers' share of social security contributions, taxes on real and personal property, manufacturers' excise taxes and other indirect taxes represent wealth produced by capital to the extent that the impact of such levies is not passed on to consumers. Except in rare instances, they do not fall upon the distributive share that workers draw from production. The extent to which such levies are passed on to consumers varies with the circumstances. It seems likely that many billions of dollars of such taxes do represent wealth produced by capital and would have to be included in the distributive share of the owners of capital before the relative economic productivity of capital and labor could be appraised.

[6] *Historical Statistics of the United States,* 1789–1945, p. 6.

any basis for believing that the available statistics give us an accurate picture of the relative economic productivity of capital and labor.

However, it may be still objected that the wages of nonunion workers—approximately 65 percent of the nonagricultural labor force —have risen almost as rapidly as the wages of union workers. This, it may be argued, indicates that where the wage determinations are in fact competitive, the distributive share of labor has been rising for three decades; and so we are once again confronted with the fact that the economic productivity of labor has been increasing. Such a view overlooks many factors of critical importance. The effect of administered wage levels in the unionized sector of the economy has been to produce similar, and sometimes even higher, wage levels in the nonunionized sector. The following considerations explain why this is so.

(1) Unionization is concentrated in the leading industries of the economy: manufacturing, trucking, railroads, shipping, warehousing, construction, air transport, electric power, communications, petroleum, chemicals, rubber, etc. By pre-empting these basic and critical industries, the competitive field for unorganized workers is narrowed. Many of the companies in these key industries are of oligopolistic size and are able to raise their prices in order to pave the way for further wage demands.

(2) The power of organized labor to raise the level of wages and to increase other economic benefits is frequently as effective in benefitting nonunionized labor as it is in the case of unionized labor. The employers of nonunionized labor often raise wages in order to prevent unionization. Who is not familiar with the automatic extension of "collectively bargained" wage increases for operating employees to clerical employees and other employee groups, in order to discourage the organization of the latter into unions? Who is not familiar with the employer who is determined to pay more than the union wage scale or to give greater benefits than those secured by unions, regardless of costs, in order to spare himself and his employees the "unpleasantness" of being organized? Who has not heard the complaint of union leaders

that, because of the duress that unions exert on the employers of non-union labor, the efforts of labor unions tend to confer equal benefits on unionized and nonunionized workers, in spite of the fact that the latter make no contribution to the support of the union?

(3) In the 35 percent of nonagricultural labor that is organized, the excess of collectively bargained wages over their competitively determined levels has a distributive effect favorable to labor that goes far beyond the industries in which workers are organized. In laying the foundation for the use of pump-priming public expenditures to create employment, J. M. Keynes pointed out that such expenditures in capital goods industries create demand for several times the employment they directly stimulate.[7] This occurs through the successive spending of the additional income of the workers in the capital goods industries to purchase consumable goods, thus creating further employment and further income, etc., until the "propensity to save" on the part of successive income recipients dissipates the original stimulus.

An analogous "multiplier effect" results from diverting substantial quantities of the wealth produced by capital to organized labor through noncompetitive wage determinations. The additional income of the workers is spent over and over again, causing an increase in employment and an enlargement of the distributive share that labor receives, which is out of all proportion to the initial wage increase. Were it not for the two considerations mentioned on pp. 259–260, this "multiplier effect" might impartially benefit capital and labor, but under present conditions that is not the case.

(4) The tendency of the high-wage unionized industries to draw the best qualified labor and to give them first claim on the labor supply has the effect of eliciting wage increases from the employers of non-unionized labor, quite apart from the point made in (2) above.

(5) To the extent that union practices retard technological advances, unions further diminish the distributive share received by

[7] *The General Theory of Employment, Interest, and Money,* Ch. 10.

owners of capital and so increase the relative size of the share received by owners of labor power. Such retardation is far from negligible where unions impose heavy additional costs as a condition for allowing the technological displacement of workers by more efficient machinery.

(6) The effect of union pressure to raise wages and increase other benefits is one thing during a period of substantial unemployment, but it is quite another when superimposed on an effective governmental policy of full employment. The consensus of the testimony of labor leaders before the Temporary National Economic Committee in 1940 was that the best that unions had been able to do up to that time— and they had organized an average of about one million new members a year from 1934 to 1941—was to offset, by collectively bargained wage increases, the loss of income to labor that resulted from the displacement of workers by machines. This testimony related to a period during which unemployment ranged between ten and fourteen million.[8]

Since the Employment Act of 1946 and the effective implementation of its policies,[9] labor unions, even though they represent only 35 percent of the nonagricultural labor force, have been able to do much more than offset the losses resulting from technological displacement. The superimposition of collective bargaining by a third of the industrial labor force upon a full employment economy has approximately the same effect as a corner on 35 percent of the steel

---

[8] Hearings, Part 30: *Technology and Concentration of Economic Power.*
[9] The implementation referred to includes, in addition to the determination of wages through collective bargaining, the following: (a) easy credit subsidization of the construction industry and hard goods manufacturing industries; (b) the subsidization of farm employment through the purchase of agricultural surpluses and the fixing of agricultural prices; (c) the massive expenditures on war materials through which we have, in the economic sense, normalized war; (d) the employment-supporting foreign aid program; (e) interest-free government loans to industry for the construction of plant and equipment through the accelerated tax amortization program; and (f) the statutory or administrative fixing of prices in thousands of instances in such a manner as to promote increased employment. These efforts have succeeded in providing full employment in the sense that everyone seeking employment can be satisfied, including those who seek two or more employments in areas where shortened hours permit this to occur. Only temporary or frictional unemployment remains.

or wheat market would have on the price of steel or wheat in a year in which demand at current prices, without the effect of the monopolistic corner, would fully take the supply off the market. There is, in fact, no way to estimate how much the distributive share of the national wealth received by labor, unorganized as well as organized, is distorted by these practices and conditions.

Yet one thing is sufficiently clear. The effect of all these practices and conditions has been to raise wages far above what they would be if the economic productivity of labor were evaluated by free competition in an economy not controlled by a government policy of full employment.

There are good reasons for believing that, even under freely competitive conditions and in an economy not governed by a policy of full employment, the economic productivity of labor would be represented by wage levels higher than those labor would receive if its relatively declining economic productivity were strictly proportionate to its relatively declining inherent productiveness in an advanced industrial economy. For one thing, there is an absolute point beyond which wages cannot fall without being totally inadequate for subsistence. Another reason is the fact that a considerable amount of mechanical labor remains indispensable at any stage of technological advance, no matter how far that amount may fall below the level of full employment. Still another reason is the general belief, shared by labor and capital alike, that the existence of widespread poverty in a society which is able to produce enough wealth for a generally high standard of living indicates social mismanagement and calls for drastic political remedies.

All these reasons may operate to keep the economic productivity of labor, as reflected in labor's share of the wealth produced, from declining, relative to the economic productivity of capital, as far as its inherent productiveness has relatively declined. But they do not alter the fact that the inherent productiveness of labor, relative to that ot capital, has now reached the point where it produces less than 10 percent of our economy's total wealth. Nor can they do more than conceal the fact that the economic productivity of labor is but a fraction of what it appears to be.

ABOUT THE AUTHORS

LOUIS O. KELSO. Born in Denver, Colorado, in 1913, Louis Kelso was educated in the public and parochial schools of that city and its suburbs. He graduated from the University of Colorado in 1937, where he received his LL.B. in 1938.

Mr. Kelso is a corporate and financial lawyer. He is a partner in a large San Francisco firm where he has practiced since 1947. From 1938 to 1942 he practiced law in Denver, Colorado, specializing in public finance. He served as a Naval Intelligence officer during the war and held the position of Associate Professor of Law at the University of Colorado during 1946.

Mr. Kelso's study of the political-economics of capitalism began with the Great Depression and has continued down to date as a strenuous avocation. At the date of this publication, he is completing the manuscript of a comprehensive treatise on the theory of capitalism, to be published in the near future under the title *Capitalism*.

MORTIMER J. ADLER. Born in New York City in 1902, a graduate of its public schools and of Columbia, where he also received his Ph.D., Mortimer Adler taught at Columbia University from 1923 to 1929, and then at the University of Chicago from 1930 to 1952, where he was for many years

Professor of the Philosophy of Law. In 1952 he left Chicago to establish the Institute for Philosophical Research in San Francisco, of which he is now President and Director.

Dr. Adler is one of the original instigators of the great-books program in liberal arts colleges and in adult education. He is a director of the Great Books Foundation; and was Associate Editor of *Great Books of the Western World* and Editor of *The Great Ideas,* a Syntopicon, published by Encyclopaedia Britannica.

Author of the popular best seller, *How to Read a Book,* Dr. Adler has written books about a wide variety of subjects, among which are *Art and Prudence, What Man Has Made of Man, A Dialectic of Morals, How to Think about War and Peace.* With Father Walter Farrell, O.P., he published in *The Thomist,* between 1941 and 1944, a series of articles on the Theory of Democracy which are directly relevant to the thesis of *The Capitalist Manifesto.*